The Man Who Fell From the Sky

D1268111

Bill Fletcher Jr.

HARDBALL

PRESS

The Reviewers Agree,
The Man Who Fell From the Sky is a great read!

"...hit me right on the head... I wasn't expecting a novel so tight-knit, subtle and historically compelling. Fletcher takes the deep, arbitrary racism of the US military in World War II and traces it out to its almost inevitable conclusion, which is murder. Please, Bill, a sequel!" **~Barbara Ehrenreich, author of** *Nickel and Dimed*

"Set amidst the rich cultural mix of Cape Verdean and Portuguese fishermen who came to the country as free men and consequentially fought being seen as the descendants of slaves, Fletcher lets a son of those men tell the story, a journalist. Bent on relieving the suffering of one family, he ends up finding the truth is more complicated, the villain a victim too of a bigger cruelty and devastation that stretched through the generations." **~Walter Mosley, author of the** *Easy Rollins Mysteries*

"Bill Fletcher pulls together history and mystery to create an exciting and compelling story of race and revenge. It is truly an unexpected page turner." **~Danny Glover**

"The characters are complex -- some compassionate, others absolutely violent. For readers who love a progressive mystery, this one will keep you up way past bedtime. Progressive mystery? Oh, yeah." **~Bruce Hobson, Health educator and translator,**

"Fletcher's first effort as a novelist...shows him to be not just a sage storyteller but no less than literature's prized canary, warning of dangers past and present... Fletcher's latest is a keeper. Enjoy this well-crafted, politically engaging thriller." **~Michael Hirsch,** *New Politics*

"Fletcher is able to expertly handle the historical (WWII) and "contemporary" (Vietnam-era) story lines and use them to elaborate the conflicted consciousness of Cape Verdean African immigrants seeking assimilation in the US..." ~**Michael Novice, De-Colonize LA**

"Bill Fletcher succeeds in combining history and mystery, in a well-written page-turner. A brutal murder grabbed my attention in the first pages, and then kept me riveted with a tangled story of racism and identity, based in a New England Cape Verdean community." ~**Ruth Needleman, *Portside***

"It's too late in the year to read this novel on the beach, but you can safely read it with the sense that you will have a good read...[and] you will return to any struggle that you may fancy it worthwhile to partake in with a little bit more vigour because of it." ~**John S. Saul, *Canadian Dimension***

"Fletcher has woven an engrossing story that harkens back to the forties while he connects the seventies and sprints forward into the 21st Century. I feel this is just the beginning of a trove of fiction waiting to spring from this author's deeply creative imagination." ~**Herb Boyd, *Neworld Review***

"This is a very human story, a good mystery and a great read. It moves very quickly - once started I couldn't put it down." ~**David Bacon, Saludos, author of *In the Fields of the North/ En los Campos del Norte***

"Fasten your seatbelt. This story of Cape Verdean intrigue steadily accelerates, folding family, community, race and identity into a thoughtful whodunnit." ~**King Downing**

Copyright © 2018 by Bill Fletcher, Jr.
Library of Congress Cataloging-in-Publication Data:
Fletcher, Bill Jr.
The Man Who Fell From the Sky
1. Cape Verde —Fiction 2. Immigration 3. Mystery story 4.
Investigative journalism 5. World War II 6. United States Air
Corps 7. Bill Fletcher, Jr.
Cover photo courtesy of John Eddyart
Cover design by T. Sheard, D. Bass and K. Thompson
Book design by D. Bass
Set in Palatino Lino.
Published by Hard Ball Press, Brooklyn, New York
ISBN: 978-0-9991358-4-6
www.hardballpress.com

Dedication

To Candice Cason and Yasmin Fletcher, who convinced me that I had a story to tell…and maybe a few more.

On that warm June morning in 1970, Margie Smith had no idea that after giving him his morning kiss good-bye she would never again see her husband alive. She would later ask herself whether she would have done anything differently. Would she have held onto him a bit longer? Would she have whispered something to him that she wanted him to have always known, even if she had told him the same thing a thousand times? Would she have looked at him differently?

That early morning was not especially different than any other morning in the Smith household. Thomas Julius Smith, "TJ" to his friends and business associates, was the owner of a construction firm in Osterville, Mass, on Cape Cod. As with every other work day morning, TJ and Margie were up by 5 AM preparing for the day. His wife moved quickly, washing up and putting on a simple house dress, then headed into the kitchen to prepare breakfast. TJ joined her, taking his seat at the kitchen table.

With a kiss on the top of her husband's head, Margie placed a steaming cup of coffee in front of him prepared just the way he liked it. TJ patted her hand and turned back to his plans for the day.

Their oldest child, Antoinette, had just graduated from American University in Washington, DC and was preparing to enter Northeastern University Law School that fall in Boston. Their son Frank, a high school graduate, was preparing to enter the US Coast Guard. While it was true that Frank loved the water, his main preoccupation was staying as far away from the Vietnam War as possible.

TJ and Margie never spoke much in the morning, they both needed time to sort out their tasks for the day and for shaking loose the cobwebs in their heads. This particular morning was no different.

Margie was a multi-tasker. In her late 40s, like her husband she was always busy with her projects. She sold Avon products. On occasion she would work as a cashier in a local grocery store. But most importantly, she did the books for TJ's construction company, All-Cape Construction. She was very much TJ's partner in thinking through business decisions and watching the firm's finances, despite the many men associated with the company who resented a woman playing such a role.

On this particular morning, while their son was asleep in his room TJ and Margie sat drinking coffee and eating a light breakfast of cold cereal and toast. In the background the television announced the early morning news from Providence, Rhode Island, a story playing about US troops in Cambodia and another speech by President Nixon.

TJ looked at his watch and sighed. "Well, Margie, it's that hour. I need to head to the office." He finished off his coffee and stood up from the table. "I've got a meeting with the crew first thing. Some of them have been acting like assholes recently and I'm not happy with the quality of the rehab work we've been doing."

"TJ, I've been telling you for months that there's something wrong with your crew. That Robertson seems like a real hothead. Why do you keep that guy? Looks like he's out of work more than on, he can't be doing a good job."

TJ immediately regretted having said something to Margie, since he knew she was correct. He also knew that she knew she was right. There had been problems on the crew for some time that TJ had not addressed. Today he was set on grabbing these guys by their balls and squeezing until they got the message. But he didn't want to say anything more to Margie about it now, there would be plenty of time to talk later.

"You're right as always, Margie."

Hugging her lightly as he walked by, he gave her a quick kiss on the lips and on her cheek, then headed for the back door.

"See you this evening, honey. Unless you need me at the office I'll be here. See you around seven?"

"Yep," was all he said, Margie hearing him clearly through the screen door.

As TJ headed to his truck, Margie went downstairs to put a load of clothes in the washing machine. She looked at the clock and realized that she needed to check on Frank to make sure he was up and ready to eat something. Although school was over, he had secured a job until he started with the Coast Guard.

When Margie returned to the first floor from the basement she went over to the kitchen sink, where she could look through a window and see a corner of the driveway. She noticed that TJ's truck was still sitting in the driveway, which was odd, unless he was sitting there writing up some notes. She didn't hear the engine running, the only sounds she could hear were birds and the occasional car passing by.

Curious about what could be holding TJ up, she walked outside. Turning the corner on the walkway that led from the driveway to the house she stopped. In fact, everything seemed to stop.

Margie could not see TJ's head from where she was standing. He seemed to be leaning over to his right toward the passenger's side of the truck. What she could see was shattered glass and jagged edges of what remained of the driver's side window. As she inched closer, her heart pounding, nothing got any better. When she opened the driver's side door, she found TJ lying on the passenger's seat with part of his head blown off.

Margie Smith's scream pierced the air, startling the birds into flight.

2

Detective Vincent Amato from the Barnstable County Police drove up to the home of TJ and Margie Smith. With the number of people walking around the driveway studying the truck and searching in nearby bushes, it almost looked like a convention.

Standing at 6'1", with dark hair and wearing a sharply pressed dark suit, Amato was an imposing figure...until he smiled. The talk around the police department was that Amato's smile and charm were enough to get witnesses and suspects alike talking. Amato always had a good joke to offer and could quickly connect with almost anyone. If he chose to.

Looking at the scene, he caught the eye of Officer Peter Shea. Shea was an older officer, very personable, though a bit timid in dealing with detectives. Shea immediately walked over to Amato.

"Talk to me, Shea," Amato said, casting his eye across the murder scene.

"Well, detective it looks like this." Shea pulled out a small notepad and looked at his notes. "At approximately 6:45 AM Missus Smith noticed that her husband's truck was still in the driveway. He was supposed to have gone to work. She approached the truck, opened the door and found him lying dead."

Amato walked over to the truck while Shea, walking to catch up, explained more about the apparent circumstances. The coroner was examining the body and preparations were being made to remove it to the Office of the Medical Examiner.

"Where'd the shot come from, Shea?" Amato asked.

"Well, sir, that's not entirely clear. From the angle as best we can tell, in that row of trees and bushes on the other side of the road, but there's nothing we can find that confirms that." Shea had his face pointed toward the possible point of origin.

On the opposite side of the two-lane street was a small forested area stretching at least one hundred yards, bordered on both ends by two single family houses. The foliage was thick, making it impossible for anyone in either of the bordering houses to see anyone more than two feet from the roadway. Amato stood, studying it from a distance.

"No shell casings?" Amato asked.

"None, sir. We think we know where the shooter positioned himself, but it was really well done. When the medical examiner gets finished we'll have a better idea, but for now, all I can say is, by the distance to the target, it was a high-powered rifle."

Amato turned from the wooded area to his colleague. "Have you spoken with the...widow?"

"Yes, sir. She's a mess. Her son is in there with her. She didn't have much to say that was very useful." Shea continued with his report.

Amato nodded to Shea and walked toward the front entrance of the Smith home. He knocked on the screen door, opened it and walked inside. Sitting on a sofa next to a young man was the woman he assumed to be Mrs. Smith. He guessed the young man with his arm around her was her son.

"Missus Smith?" Amato asked cautiously and respectfully.

A red-eyed face turned up toward him. The young man—who looked to be in his late teens or early 20s—looked up also, though with skepticism and annoyance.

"Yes," she answered, tears running down her face.

"Missus Smith, my name is Detective Vincent Amato.

I can't tell you how sorry I am about the loss of your husband. May I take a few moments to talk with you about what happened?"

Amato addressed her formally. He was self-conscious of his Providence accent, living on the Cape and knowing it did not quite fit into the environment. Sometimes in conducting official business he would have to slow down his speaking and make an effort to be more precise.

Trying as best she could to straighten up and compose herself, Margie Smith took a tissue and wiped away the tears. Her son looked at her, trying to will her his support.

"Yes, Detective. What do you want to know?"

"I'm told you didn't hear anything, but you did see that your husband's truck hadn't moved and that you went outside. Is that correct?"

"Yes, that's right. I heard nothing." She looked down at her lap half-way through her statement, as if her grief had weight.

Amato waited a moment before continuing. "Missus Smith, is there anything, no matter how insignificant it may seem, that you heard or saw that you think might be useful for us to know?"

Margie sat still for a moment. Amato could tell that she was reliving the moment she discovered her husband's body in the truck, perhaps trying to mentally force time backwards so that she could do something to prevent this tragedy.

"Detective, for the last few hours I've been thinking and thinking about that very question. I tell you, I didn't notice anything. There was a car or maybe two that passed by, but I couldn't give you a description. Something that sounded like a motorcycle but, you know, I hear those things all the time. Nothing sounded unusual. I didn't see anyone walk by. Nothing out of the ordinary. Maybe if I had walked out with my husband this wouldn't have happened. Maybe the killer would've been scared off or—"

"Ma, listen," said Frank, "there was nothing you could have

done. Dad wasn't killed by accident, someone was out to get him. You couldn't have saved him."

"Missus Smith, your son is correct, there really was nothing that you could've done." Amato paused for a moment. "Let me ask you both a question. Did Mister Smith have any enemies? Anyone, and I mean *anyone* who might've been angry enough to kill him?"

Margie and Frank looked at each other for a moment, then, in despair shook their heads 'no'.

Amato thanked them both and excused himself, exiting the house and walking back to Shea, who looked at him quizzically.

Amato shook his head. "Nah, nothing. You were right. Damn, this is ugly. This wasn't some murder after an argument. Someone wanted to make sure this guy was dead."

Before Shea could respond, they both noticed a young brown-skinned man with a short Afro haircut and a pen stuck behind his right ear walking up the driveway. The man was in his mid-twenties, wore a sports jacket and slacks but no tie, and carried a notebook.

"Gomes!" exclaimed Amato, pronouncing the name so it rhymed with"homes." "How the hell did you find out about this so soon?"

David Gomes was a reporter for the *Cape & Islands Gazette*, a weekly newspaper whose owner and editor had set her sights on becoming daily. With a small staff, the *C&IG* could not compete with the Boston Globe or, for that matter, the Cape Cod Times, but it was a feisty paper that addressed issues on Martha's Vineyard, Nantucket, and Cape Cod, including both sides of the Cape Cod Canal.

Amato flashed on a memory of breaking down on Route 28 near Mashpee in a rainstorm. He had shown up on Cape Cod just out of high school, never explaining why he left Providence. He could not figure out for the life of him what was wrong with the car, and no one showed the slightest inclination to stop and help.

Sitting in his car in the midst of that cold April rain, he saw in his rearview mirror a car pulling up behind him. Police? No. A young man wearing a baseball cap got out of the car, ran to Amato's car and tapped on the window.

"Hey, buddy, you in trouble or just waiting for someone?" the young man asked. Amato could not make out much about him, though he could tell that he was 'colored,' and quite wet.

"My car conked out. I need to get to a gas station and get a tow."

The young man said, "Let me give you a ride. My dad owns a station not too far from here, he can get someone to come back here and help with your car."

From that day David Gomes and Vincent Amato became fast friends. While Amato lived in Hyannis and Gomes in Mashpee, they spent a good deal of time hanging out. Even after returning to the Cape from the military, they were able to keep their friendship going.

"You know me, Vinnie," Gomes replied with a smile to Amato. "I keep my ear to the ground." Gomes and Amato shook hands like they always did.

"I have to keep you out of the way while we finish up. It's ugly." Amato angled his head in the direction of the truck.

Gomes took out a pad and pulled the pen away from his ear, his facial expression turning serious. He could tell that while Amato was glad to see him, he was clearly disturbed by the crime scene.

"The long and the short of it is this, Gomes. The decedent is one T. J. Smith. That is, Thomas J. Smith, a contractor whose office is here in Osterville. This morning he went to his truck to drive to the office and was shot and killed by what appears to have been a high-powered rifle fired from over there." Amato pointed toward the trees and bushes across the street.

"No witnesses, Vinnie?" Gomes asked.

"Not only were there no witnesses, but no one heard

a sound, except for some background traffic. Not even the man's widow heard anything." Amato and Gomes stared at each other.

"A silencer?" asked Gomes.

"That's my best guess. This was a professional hit, if you ask me. One shot, no damage to anything or anyone other than the deceased. Bang, and the guy's dead."

Gomes was generally able to read Amato's face. Although the detective wasn't giving much away, Gomes saw that this killing was unsettling for his friend and not something that Amato was used to on the Cape.

"Listen, Gomes, do me a favor and just hang out here on the driveway or in your car for a few minutes until we clean things up. Then, if you want to go speak with the widow, fine. I don't want any problems with my superiors." Amato walked off to speak with some of the officers on the scene.

It was too warm a day to sit in his Volkswagen Bug, so Gomes walked to the end of the driveway and looked over at the area where officers were combing the bushes. He made a few notes on his pad and then saw the police were packing up and leaving, the body already on its way to the morgue.

Amato signaled to Gomes with a two-fingered half salute that they were done and it was okay to go speak with Mrs. Smith.

Gomes approached the front door of the house, anxious about the sort of welcome he would receive. He dreaded this part of a reporter's job: interviewing the widow, the pain that he saw always made him sick.

3

The screen door of the Smith house was closed, but the inside door remained open. Gomes knocked lightly on the screen door. He could hear a fan whirring inside the house. A young man appeared from the living room wearing a plain white T-shirt and jeans.

"Yeah?" said the young man, sounding tired, frustrated, and like he would rather that Gomes go to hell.

"I'm sorry to disturb you. My name is David Gomes and I'm with the Cape & Islands Gazette. I wonder, could I speak with you and Missus Smith regarding today's tragedy?"

Frank Smith stood for a second weighing his options.

"Listen," Frank started to say, hesitating as if he was not sure how to address Gomes. "Ah, Mister Gomes, as you can probably guess this is not a great time for me and my ma. What about you coming back some other day?" Frank was not particularly rude, but he clearly wanted Gomes to leave, and he began to turn away from the door.

"Mister Smith, I'm so sorry about today's tragedy. I will return another day, but I feel like I owe it to our readers to get your immediate feelings about what happened and your best guess as to why. I really won't take up a lot of your time."

Frank was getting ready to reply when a woman's weary voice called out from another room. "Frank, let him in."

Frank opened the door and pointed in the direction of the living room, saying nothing further. Gomes entered and saw Mrs. Smith sitting on the sofa. She was no longer crying, but her eyes were red and she seemed sapped of energy. Neither mother nor son paid any attention to the television playing in the background.

"Missus Smith, thank you so much for giving me a few moments of your time...and your son's." Gomes looked at both Margie and Frank.

"Please sit down, Mister Gomes. I'm not sure what I can tell you that the police haven't already told you."

Gomes was struck by how polite and welcoming Mrs. Smith was, particularly under the circumstances.

"Missus Smith, the police indicated that you heard nothing, but that you became curious and went outside, where you discovered that your husband had been...killed." Gomes was uneasy about using the word "killed" but could think of no other way to describe what happened.

"Mister Gomes, would you like something to drink?" Margie asked abruptly. She turned to her son. "Frank, would you be a dear and go into the kitchen and get us all some lemonade?"

Frank got up with a grunt and went to the kitchen. While he was there Margie said nothing. She stared at her hands and moved them around. Gomes silently looked around the room, occasionally looking over at Mrs. Smith. Middle-aged, with smooth skin, slightly tanned and with hair just streaked with grey, under other circumstances she would have been described as an eye-catcher. She wore a light blue shirt buttoned nearly to the top tucked into what looked like white painters pants.

Gomes heard ice clinking as it was being deposited into three glasses. He also heard the pleasant sounds of a light wind blowing outside of the house, ringing chimes on the outside porch. Returning with the lemonade, Frank handed glasses first to Margie and then to Gomes.

Margie took a sip and looked over at Gomes. "Mister Gomes, I have no idea what happened or why. All I know is that I kissed my husband good-bye expecting to see him for dinner this evening. I went to put a load of clothes in the washing machine, came upstairs and discovered that he'd been killed. I heard nothing. I didn't see anyone running away, walking away or driving away. I'm totally in the dark."

Frank sat sipping the lemonade. Before Gomes could say anything, Frank put the glass down and said, "Just so you know, Mister Gomes, I heard nothing. I was asleep. I woke up when I heard my mother screaming. I went running out of the house and saw..." Frank's voice trailed off to a melancholy silence.

"Did your husband have anyone who held a grudge? An unhappy customer or a lawsuit against him?" Gomes asked cautiously, looking back and forth between his pad and her face.

"Let me tell you a few things about TJ. He was one of the nicest and most generous people that you'd ever meet. His clients loved him. He was a good neighbor. He offered major support to a local little league team and a hockey team. He hired people who were down on their luck, and kept some that he should've let go."

Gomes sat taking notes. It was clear he would not get anything more out of this. Not to be cynical about it, he thought, but TJ was "Saint TJ." If there was a bad side to him, Gomes would not hear about it today. Just as he was getting ready to close up shop and head out he changed his mind.

"Missus Smith, when did you and Mister Smith marry?"

Margie's face changed abruptly. "Oh, well, TJ and I married in late forty-six. We got married in Boston and then moved to the Cape."

"How did you meet your husband?" Gomes asked, a bit more animated.

"We met at a dance early the same year. He had gotten home from the war. I had moved to Boston in forty-two to work during the war. I grew up in Lawrence."

Gomes could tell from her accent that she was not originally

13

from the Cape, though there was a little 'Cape' there. Margie continued. "You know how they talk about 'love at first sight'? Well, my relationship with TJ was *anything* but that."

Margie smiled slightly. Frank sat looking incredulous that his mother was having this discussion at this moment, but he slowly relaxed as the discussion lifted his mother's mood.

"When TJ and I met at that dance, he seemed nice enough, but quiet. I guess I didn't find him particularly exciting. He was not a great dancer and he just seemed to...want to be around me or something. At a certain point, I got up, excused myself, and figured that was going to be it.

"Well, TJ didn't give up easily. A couple of days later my roommate told me that TJ had come looking for me. I didn't know what to think. I arranged to meet him for coffee after work. He was working on the docks at the time. You know, longshore." As Margie looked over at Frank seemingly to get the 'ok' on the discussion, Frank nodded his head affirmatively.

"It was a different TJ. Or maybe it was just a differ-ent moment, I don't know. I had been working in a factory during the war and after that, they let me go." She paused for a second. "But then I was hired by this clothing factory, so, I wasn't all dressed up for work. Neither was TJ, he had just gotten off his shift. So, in a funny way we weren't trying to impress each other."

Margie stopped for a second and drank some more lemon-ade. "I realized that TJ was a really smart and a very nice man. From that point on we started seeing each other and eventu-ally we got married. In Boston he tried to put to use what he'd learned in the War, but he couldn't get any good work, so we moved down to the Cape and started from scratch."

"Which branch of the military was TJ in?" Gomes making notes.

"The Air Force."

"The US Army *Air Corps*, Ma! There was no *US Air Force*

until after World War Two." Frank's frown indicated he had made this point many times in the past but it never seemed to register.

"Yes, the Air Corps. He was over in Italy."

Margie's mood suddenly plummeted without warning, and Gomes realized that he needed to bring the interview in for a landing.

"Missus Smith, I want to thank you and Frank for your time. Your family will be in my thoughts." As Gomes got up to leave, Mrs. Smith attempted to give him a smile, but it quickly collapsed. As Frank moved over to sit next to her, Gomes showed himself out, feeling both sad and perplexed. Despite the demand that he, as a journalist, be objective, the tragic circumstances tore at his heart.

4

Detective Amato turned his car onto Tower Hill Road in Osterville and looked for a place to park. He got out of the car, buttoned his suit jacket and walked across the street to the small office with a sign proclaiming "All-Cape Construction." Through the plate-glass window he could see a number of people scurrying around.

As Amato opened the door to the office, a doorbell chimed. A gray-haired man with a pasty face and not much hair stood behind a counter, his work shirt with the name "Sam" stenciled above a pocket. Sam was on the telephone, walking back and forth, pulling a long cord and looking overwhelmed.

Sam held up a finger to Amato to signal that he would be off the phone in a second. Not bothering to listen to Sam's end of the conversation, Amato walked toward the back of the office, where he could hear several voices.

"How can I help you?" asked Sam, hanging up the phone.

"Detective Amato. I'm here about the Smith killing. Who may I ask are you?"

"Sam King, Detective. I'm sort of the second in command here, and with TJ's murder, things are just going to hell." At that point the telephone rang. Sam looked over at it and then let it ring, mumbling, "Someone else will have to pick it up."

"Mister King, as you can imagine, I'm trying to figure out who might've had a motive for this killing. What can you tell me?"

King moved his right hand down across his face, casting his eyes down at the floor. He seemed to use the counter to hold himself up, looking completely exhausted.

"I've no idea who'd want to kill TJ. He was a good businessman. We have a good crew...well, a *pretty* good crew." King smirked. "He was really active in the community. You know, he was a stand-up guy. Of course, there were times when people would get pissed off about this or that, but it was never that serious."

Amato looked over his notes for a moment, then turned his head toward King. "Everyone show up for work today?"

King shook his head. "Two of the guys apparently decided to extend their weekend. Everyone else was here. Most are on a job in Chatham, a couple of guys are doing some electrical work on a house in West Yarmouth."

"Would you give me the addresses for the jobs along with the names, addresses and phone numbers of the two guys who didn't show up today?"

"Certainly, Detective. Hold on, I'll write it down."

Amato waited while King pulled out a piece of paper and copied the information from an address book.

Amato scanned the paper. "The two no-shows were this Bob Robertson and Teddy Shepherd? What about addresses for these guys? Next to Robertson it says 'girlfriend' and an address, next to Shepherd it has a PO Box and a telephone number with the word 'messages' next to it. What's that mean?"

King looked embarrassed. "Sorry, Detective, that's all I have. Robertson told us that he stays with his girlfriend in Hyannis. We've seen her so we know that she exists." King smiled, suggesting the girlfriend was a looker. "Now Teddy Shepherd — 'Mister Clean' some people call him because of his bald head—is a different sort. A damned good worker, detective. We don't know where he lives, to tell you the truth. He's very private. Friendly enough and always polite, but he doesn't give away a lot of information. He's got that Mashpee PO Box. The number is a restaurant in Mashpee where he picks up messages."

Amato gave King a skeptical look.

"Detective, I know this sounds odd, but you have to understand the construction industry. We get guys who move in like locusts at certain points and then disappear. They don't stay long enough to put down roots, so they get a room somewhere or shack up with some girl. This may look odd, but it really isn't."

Amato shrugged. "If you say so, Mister King. Thanks for the information. Listen, if you think of anything, and I mean *anything* that you believe might help us, please get back to me. Here's my card."

He handed the business card over and began to leave. Suddenly turning around, Amato said, "One more thing. What sort of shape is the business in?"

King looked a bit puzzled, not seeming to understand where the question came from. "We're in good shape. The regular debts that you'd expect with any business, particularly one that's up and down the way that construction is, but right now we're doing well. We have the two projects I mentioned, plus some pickup work here and there. We also have a good chance on some work on a new mall over in Bourne on the other side of the Canal that we just bid on. If that comes through, we'll have to do some more hiring." King made the final statement with pride, shaking off some of the depression that he had clearly been feeling.

"Got it. Thanks, again."

Amato exited the office and headed to the car. He radioed in a request that some officers go interview the crew and track down the two missing workers. He sat there for a minute and leaned against the steering wheel just looking out, lost in thought. *No apparent motive, no real suspects. Damn!*

5

The next morning Vincent Amato was sitting at Emily's, a breakfast and lunch diner at the east end of Main Street going towards Yarmouth, reading the paper, his jacket off sitting next to him. Emily's was a regular hangout for cops and, in the summer, for tourists looking for good, inexpensive food.

Amato had a hard time focusing on what he was reading since he kept thinking about the TJ Smith murder.

"A penny for your thoughts?"

Shaken out of his pensiveness, Amato looked up into the face of David Gomes. "Early morning, Gomes?"

"Nothing comes to a sleeping man but dreams, Amato. You above anyone else should know that." The reporter, dressed as he normally was for work with a jacket, khakis and a shirt with no tie, smiled and sat down at the table as Amato moved a few things out of the way.

"Okay, Vinnie, what do you make of what happened yesterday?" Gomes searched for the waitress so he could order.

A young, blonde woman with pale blue eyes in her early 20s came over and presented Gomes with a smile that brightened the room.

"Morning, Lucy. Can I have some coffee, fried eggs and potatoes?"

"Some day surprise me, David, order something different, will ya?" With a grin Lucy headed towards the kitchen. Gomes watched her for a moment walking away.

"You looking to change your luck, Gomes?" Amato had a mischievous look. The two of them often kidded one another about the women they each found attractive.

"Yeah, yeah, cut the crap, Mister Detective."

Amato chuckled and took a sip of the coffee. "The hell if I can figure out what happened yesterday. This whole thing is damned curious. This stuff that we discuss has got to be off the record, you know."

They knew the drill. Amato provided Gomes with detailed and accurate information, almost always background that Gomes would have to otherwise confirm. When he could, Gomes provided Amato with information without revealing sources. Neither one had ever compromised the other in their working relationship.

Amato said, "The widow thinks the deceased was the moral compass of the Cape, or something. Apparently his second-in-command at the company does as well. In fact, so does his entire crew, at least the ones we were able to find. Officers interviewed all of the crew except for two who didn't show up yesterday. But I'll get to that in a second. The crew was at their job sites on time yesterday and working from seven AM on. There was no way any of them could have gotten from TJ Smith's place in Osterville to their work locations by seven."

Amato stopped to finish the food on his plate, which coincided with the waitress bringing Gomes his breakfast. Gomes immediately dug into the fried eggs and potatoes, saying, "Funny how the wife didn't hear a shot."

"She says all she heard was the usual traffic on the street." Amato signaled for more coffee. "Now, the two guys that didn't show up, that's where it gets interesting. One guy is, what would you call it nicely...a drunk. I'm told he's a good worker when he's sober, but you can never count on that. Well, my guys tracked him down. He and his girlfriend decided that a two-day weekend wasn't long enough, so they took yesterday off to go to the beach and continue partying. He didn't bother to call in, which appears to have been part of a pattern. When we caught up with them they had nothing useful to say, they were both passed out at the time TJ was shot."

After finishing his coffee and then signaling the waitress for a refill, Amato continued. "Now, this other guy, Teddy Shepherd. He has a Mashpee PO Box, but no one knows where he lives. He didn't show up and didn't call in, either. We called the place where you can leave messages for him—some restaurant. Actually, you might know it since you live in Mashpee, it's called..." Amato turned a page in his notebook. "Bob's Teepee."

"Yeah, I know it, it's a family-owned place. Good food. Opens early and stays open pretty late for Mashpee. I know the owner. Not well, just enough to say hi and chat with him a bit."

"Well, they take messages for this Shepherd. My guys checked, they haven't seen Shepherd for a few days and have no idea where he is and where he stays. This morning I called the company's office to see whether Shepherd had shown up and they said they haven't seen any part of him."

Amato pointed at some egg stuck on his friend's cheek. Gomes wiped it away with a napkin. "What does anyone know about Shepherd?" Gomes asked, placing his knife and fork on the empty plate.

"Not a whole hell of a lot. They say he comes from California. Apparently a very good, hardworking type. Was always looking for overtime. Never said no to any assignment. Rode a motorcycle. Pretty much kept to himself, though it doesn't sound like he was stuck up, just quiet."

Amato and Gomes sat in silence for a moment staring at their coffee cups.

"So, Gomes, we put out a description and we're looking for the guy. I don't know whether this is a dead-end or not, but it's the only lead we've got for the moment."

"But no motive?" said Gomes.

"Correct. We have no idea what the motive could be."

"Well, Vinnie, I've been doing a little of my own checking. So far, nothing is popping up, but if I hear anything, you'll be the first to know."

After ordering a coffee to go, Gomes put some money on the table to cover his breakfast and stood up. Amato gave him a send-off salute.

Gomes exited Emily's after looking back at his waitress-friend, Lucy. She smiled in return with a flirtatious look. Gomes shook his head as he opened the door and headed back to his world. His thought quickly shifted from Lucy to his being handed this murder mystery. It wasn't the sort of story he usually worked on, but it was damned peculiar and he was determined to get to the bottom of it.

6

On the way to his office at the *Cape & Islands Gazette*, Gomes decided to make a stop at the Hyannis Hobby Shop on Winter Street. As Gomes opened the shop door he heard the ring of the bell announcing his entrance. He looked around the store, which had one of the best collections of model trains, planes, cars and ships he had ever seen. At this time in the morning there were few, if any, customers in the store. As he closed the door all he heard was a fan.

Standing toward the back next to a small office area was a large, not very tall man in his late 30s with thinning, light brown hair, sleepy blue eyes and thick moustache. The guy looked like a wrestler, a solid black T-shirt covering his muscular body. In contrast, there was something about his face that seemed much softer than the rest of him: maybe it was something in his eyes. Making eye contact with Gomes, he smiled, put down a pad and signaled for his visitor to come over to the counter.

Hank Matthews was a most unusual person and friend. He and Gomes had a ritual: Gomes would drop by for a visit—which he did at least once a week—and always bring coffee. Gomes could not remember ever showing up without it. In the summer it might be iced coffee, but it would be coffee. Today it was hot coffee, 'regular,' New England for cream and sugar.

Ex-military, Matthews was circumspect about what he had done for the US government. Though he admitted to having joined the Army, it was not clear that he ended his military career in that service. He had traveled to several far-away parts of the world and was an incredible military historian. You could ask Matthews about virtually any war, and he would weave together a compelling and illuminating story, explaining the reasons for the war, the relative strengths and weaknesses of both sides, and much more. Having watched Hank captivate small audiences with his stories, Gomes urged Hank to write his stories.

"David! Have you put a ring on the finger of that girl of yours yet?" Hank approached his friend, a big smile on his face.

Here we go again, thought Gomes.

"No, Hank, no ring. When we're ready I'll get to it, and you'll be the first to know."

Hank shook his head, his smile fading. This exchange was a regular discussion between them about his friend's relationship with Pamela Peters.

"David, I know you're tired of hearing me say this, but Pamela is special. If you keep waiting around for the right moment, she'll slip through your fingers."

With his focus on the TJ Smith murder, David did not want to get into another discussion about his relationship with Pamela. "Hank, I know you care for Pam, but let me figure this out on my own time. Okay?"

Hank turned and walked toward the back of the store, throwing his hands in the air. For some people this would have been interpreted as rude. That was not Hank's intention. It was his way of signaling that the discussion had ended and it was time to transition to another subject.

Hank settled into his office chair, indicating to Gomes to do likewise. Gomes handed him the coffee, for which Hank thanked him, and sat down on a chair facing him.

"So, David, as the kids say these days, what's happening?" Hank sat back in his chair and took a sip of the coffee.

"Did you hear about the murder in Osterville?"

"Yeah, that was a shocker. No surprise you're involved."

"I'm covering the story. It's creepy, Hank, the guy was shot with a high-powered rifle. From a distance. You know, like a sniper."

Hank looked back and forth between Gomes and his own coffee. "Yuh know, when I set up this store, that guy's company handled most of the rehab. They did good work."

"Did you ever meet the owner?"

"Nah, I can't remember the name of the guy who came by and worked with me on the design and everything. But he was good. Do the cops have any idea why he was killed?"

"They have no damned idea, Hank. I spoke with the widow and the son, they both think that the guy was mister perfect, which I can sort of understand. The widow didn't know of any enemies. Nothing."

They sat in silence for a moment.

"How many shots?" Hank asked.

Gomes looked up from his coffee, a bit surprised by the question. "One shot, Hank. Only one shot, fired from across the street and behind some bushes."

Hank nodded his head for a moment. "Then the assassin was good. He knew about Smith's morning pattern, and he must've used a scope, given the distance. I hate to tell you this, kid, but it sounds like a professional hit."

"I know," Gomes replied, a little nervous.

Hank sat there sipping what was left of his coffee.

"David," Hank offered, suddenly switching gears, "in all seriousness, I know that I kid you a lot about you and Pamela. And I know that it sometimes pisses you off, but—"

"Hank, enough already! I know you're not trying to mess with me. It's just that this is complicated. I don't think that you have ever been—"

Gomes stopped in mid-sentence, as if an invisible hand had covered his mouth. He and Hank both realized that Gomes was getting ready to say something that would have been factually wrong and emotionally painful.

Hank looked at his friend with no anger in his eyes. Just sadness, though he tried to cover it over with a smile. They quickly changed the subject. Hank told him about some new models that he had on inventory. One he had just assembled was an F-4 Phantom II jet fighter-bomber, one of the planes the US was using extensively in the Vietnam War. Hank stood up and led Gomes over to the assembled model. It was an incredible job. Gomes could see that Hank was proud of his work. The model looked like it could take off at any moment.

Gomes looked at his watch and saw that it was getting late. He shook hands with Hank, said his good-byes. As he headed off to work Gomes couldn't escape the feeling that Hank had more to say about the Smith murder but as usual was keeping his cards close to his chest.

7

The Cape & Islands Gazette was located off of Main Street in Hyannis on the west end of town. The offices of the paper were in a two-story house. The first floor was entirely occupied by the paper, while the second floor was an apartment where Jacqueline Reynaud, the Quebec-born owner, publisher and C&IG managing editor lived.

Susan O'Hara, the receptionist and administrative assistant, greeted Gomes as he walked into the building. Susan was in her 40s, with flaming red hair and porcelain skin that would make a model envious and a voice that could make an opera singer jealous. She always knew how to welcome a guest with charm and humor.

"Good morning, *Mister* Gomes," she said, being intentionally formal as she almost always was in the morning when she wanted to kid him. O'Hara was very good at picking up on signals. If she sensed something was wrong, she would take a different and more serious tone.

"My dearest Missus O'Hara, how delightful it is to see you this morning," Gomes replied in his own kidding way. He had never met 'Mr. O'Hara' and was never quite sure whether the husband existed, now or ever. Taking a more serious tone, he continued: "Is the boss in, Susan?"

"Yep, she's in, and I think she's waiting to see you." As soon as Susan replied there was an incoming phone call she had to answer. She smiled at Gomes as she shifted her attention to the incoming call.

Gomes headed to his work area. When the building had

been rehabbed, the walls dividing up the space on the first floor had been eliminated, leaving just a few structural beams in a wide-open space. Several desks were scattered about. Jacqueline Reynaud was sitting at her desk near a large window. She glanced up, smiled and then continued with something that she was writing. Gomes walked to his desk, dropped off his bag and then went to speak with Reynaud.

In general, people would sit at her desk. If the matter was really private she would invite them outside or, alternatively, take them upstairs to her apartment, where she had a small, comfortable sitting area for confidential meetings.

Gomes thought of Reynaud as a genius. She had some money in her family, but how much nobody could say. Incredibly creative, she seemed to be able to weave gold from straw, the paper being a prime example. The gossip was she came to the Cape to get away from her family and set off on her own, but nobody knew for sure.

Gomes found Jacqueline's dark features very attractive but he tried not to think of her in such terms. Gomes would periodically compliment her on her wardrobe or how her hair was styled, but that was it. At about 5'8", she had long, dark hair that she usually tied up in a bun. Her eyebrows were equally dark. She tanned well in the summer, sometimes making it difficult for people to identify her origin. When she looked at someone, it was as if she was looking into their soul. At least, that's how Gomes felt.

Above all, Reynaud was about business. She was not a terror, but she was someone who defied you to be any less than honest with her.

"Good morning, Jacqueline. This a good time to talk?"

"Always, David, mon cher," her Quebecois accent always giving him a warm feeling. Reynaud addressed him by his first name unless he had really screwed up. At that time she would make it known to the world that there was a storm brewing by calling him "Monsieur Gomes."

Gomes sat down in front of her as she put down her notebook and stuck her pen in her hair. As she moved her notepad aside and eased back in her chair, Gomes said. "This case that I picked up yesterday could be something big, Jacqueline. I just wanted you to know because it could take up a good deal of my time."

"What is your angle, David?"

"Well, as you know, this construction contractor was shot and killed while he was getting ready to go to work. The shot was nothing short of perfect. This doesn't look like a crime of passion. One shot, possibly with a silencer. Nobody reported hearing it. It could be a sniper."

"Do the police have a suspect yet?"

"They're looking into one of the victim's crew, but he's disappeared." The last statement caught Reynaud's attention.

Gomes leaned forward in his seat. "I want to continue looking into this, Jacqueline. I want to try to find the missing construction worker. I'm wondering whether there's something illegal going on with this guy's construction company, though so far everyone seems to think the world of the deceased. In any case, this feels like a hit."

Reynaud looked him dead in the eyes. "David, have you gotten carried away reading The Godfather? This is Cape Cod. We're not in Boston or New York. We're not even in Providence."

Although some might have taken his boss's tone for sarcasm, Gomes knew that was not the way she operated. "Yes, Jacqueline, I just finished reading The Godfather, but that's not what's going on here. It's not my imagination, this man was shot and killed silently, from a distance. There was no shell casing left. All I ask is that you let me look into this. If it turns into nothing, we can just drop it and I can go back to reporting on whale sightings off Provincetown."

Gomes ended his statement with a smile on his face so that Jacqueline knew he was not being an insubordinate smart ass. Reynaud made note of something on a fresh piece of paper in front of her.

"Bien," she said. "I need you to develop a profile on the deceased. Who was he? See what you can find out about this man that you say disappeared. I must ask you to be very careful. *Faites attention.* Maybe this was a jealous lover or an angry customer, but if it is anything along the lines of what you are suggesting, this could become most dangerous."

Gomes nodded and thanked her. He excused himself, got up and went to his desk to plan out the day. When he looked over at Jacqueline a few minutes later he caught her looking at him with what seemed a look of sadness in her eyes.

Or was it fear?

8

Late on Friday morning Vincent Amato sat at his desk listening to music on the radio and reflecting on his recent meeting about the Smith murder case. In the few days since the murder, the situation had not become any clearer.

First, there was no news on missing construction worker Teddy Shepherd. No one could identify where he lived or where he had gone. He was last seen leaving work the Friday prior to the Monday murder after a routine work day.

Amato had tried checking into Shepherd's residence in California, but the information was scant. The man had a California driver's license, indicating he lived or had lived in Los Angeles. There were no outstanding warrants for him, no other important information. He apparently worked construction in Los Angeles before coming East. There did not seem to have been much of a job history. He had told a co-worker that he served in Vietnam at some point. Beyond that, there was no useful information.

The disappearance of Shepherd irritated Amato. He wanted results, and he wanted them now.

The second development was even more unsettling. While Officer Shea was conducting an inspection of the All-Cape Construction offices the day after Amato had visited, he stumbled across an unregistered handgun in the office that had been occupied—exclusively—by TJ Smith. Shea would never have discovered the gun, a fully loaded .38 caliber pistol with filed down serial numbers, had he not accidentally dropped a pen.

Shea had taken a pen out of his pocket to make note of something. He fumbled it, the pen fell to the floor and rolled under TJ's desk. Shea went down on his knees to get it and realized that there was something taped to the bottom of the lower drawer in the desk. He angled himself and realized that the object was a gun.

After getting a flashlight and looking at the drawer, Shea was able to see that a pistol had been secured with industrial tape but was positioned in such a way that someone sitting in the chair at the desk could lower their right arm, grab the gun and pull it loose from the tape. It would not necessarily be easy, but a right-handed person like TJ Smith, would be able to do it, particularly if they had a little advance warning that they needed the weapon.

Upon discovering the .38, Shea's curiosity increased. He and another officer carefully looked around TJ Smith's office. In a file cabinet with office supplies, the other officer discovered additional cartridges for the .38 hidden in a box marked "staples."

Amato checked with Mrs. Smith and her son Frank about the gun. They both appeared shocked. Neither of them had ever seen TJ with a gun or heard him make any mention of using a weapon, let alone buying one. No one in the office seemed to know anything about the gun, either.

It was clear that the office door was almost never locked, so someone else could have gotten into the office and placed the gun there. But why plant a weapon under his desk? That made no sense.

Someone like TJ should have had no problem buying a legal gun, so why would he obtain a stolen handgun? If he felt that his life was in danger or if he wanted some protection, he could have gotten a permit for a gun and purchased it legally. He had no criminal record that Amato could discover.

Amato was trying to process all of this information when the intercom buzzed. "Detective Amato," said Francine

Almeida, Amato's secretary, "there's a Mister Thomas Abbott from Cape Cod Savings & Loan on the line for you."

Amato twisted his face with some annoyance. "Who the hell is Thomas Abbott, Francine? Is he returning a call that I made to him, the name doesn't ring a bell?" Amato needed more coffee.

"I don't know him, Detective. He said that he was calling about the TJ Smith murder case."

"Put him right through, Francine. Sorry to growl at you," he quickly added. Francine knew Amato well enough to not take it personally. A moment later Amato's line rang.

"Mister Abbott, this is Detective Amato. I understand you're calling in connection with the murder of Thomas J. Smith in Osterville."

The voice on the other end of the line was both formal and cautious.

"Detective Amato, thank you for taking my call. I was not sure whether to contact the police, I was afraid I might be bothering you, but my wife encouraged me to call. She's a more responsible person than I am."

"Not a problem, sir. Please tell me what I can do for you."

"Well, Detective," Abbott started, "I saw the story in the paper about the murder of Mister Smith. This is very horrifying. Things like that are not supposed to happen on the Cape. That was one of the reasons that I moved here in the first place. Forgive me for going on a tangent."

Abbott cleared his throat. "Well, when I read about the killing it got me thinking. The name rang a bell. Now, I know that may sound strange, since 'Smith' is such a common name. But you see, I'm the branch manager for my bank here in Falmouth. I'm not going to bore you with all of my duties, but one of them is to look at new accounts and see whether there is any activity on them, whether the client has obtained whatever services he or she is supposed to have gotten from our bank. You know what I mean, Detective?"

Amato was tapping his foot. "Yes, Mister Abbott, I understand. And you don't need to apologize for calling me or about whether any of this will be relevant. Leave that to me. Okay?"

Abbott cleared his throat, thanked Amato and continued with a story that became increasingly intriguing. Some weeks earlier, Abbott had been going through various reports and happened to notice that there was an account for a Mr. Thomas J. Smith from All-Cape Construction. The account had been opened within the last several months, but the only activity were deposits of no less than $100 at any one time, often larger amounts, but all at different branches of the bank from around the Cape. There were ten deposits, with the account going from $500 to over $5000 in those few months.

Abbott noticed that Smith had never requested checks for this account. This seemed odd since Smith was the head of a construction firm and the account was a business checking account. Smith, according to the records, had specifically declined a savings account. The other thing that Abbott noticed was that there were no withdrawals at all.

"When I notice something odd, Mister, I mean Detective Amato, I not only make a note of it, but I call the customer. In this case it appeared that there had been some sort of oversight and that he hadn't been properly served by our branch. I mean, after all, someone gets a checking account and deposits money but there are no withdrawals and no checks! It made no sense to me, so my first impulse was that someone in our bank had dropped the ball." Abbott stopped for a moment. Amato could hear what sounded like him taking a sip of something. Abbott cleared his throat again and continued.

"I called Mister Smith at All-Cape Construction. I didn't get him but I left a message with someone at their office and Smith called me later that day. When I explained to him why I was calling, his reaction was most strange, Detective. He got very silent. He asked for the location of my branch and told me that he would come down to meet with me right away. Well, that was not going to work because we were nearly at the closing hour, so he agreed to meet me the following morning. I told him that there was nothing urgent but that we wanted to make sure he received the best service from our bank. Mister Smith simply replied that he would see me the next morning and he hung up! How rude!!"

As Amato listened, the tapping of his foot increased.

"The next morning, not more than five minutes after we opened, Mister Smith appeared. He had his construction clothes on and was shown to my office. I went over the information again. He looked at me quite seriously and said that he had *never* opened an account in my bank and that he had *no idea* what I was talking about.

"Well, I didn't know what to say. I provided him with the information that I had about his application, including his signature. He looked it over and shook his head. He claimed that it was not his signature, though he admitted that it looked a lot like it, and that he had never opened the account. He said that no one was authorized to open such an account. No one in his family had opened it either.

"I didn't know what to do or say. I told him that the money was legally his. All of the information that we had was accurate, including his social security number, and we had no indication that this was fraudulent. I told him that I would take this up with my superiors and that we would report it to the police.

"Well, Detective, at that point, Mister Smith became very quiet. He said that I should do nothing, that he was going to do some checking on his own. He said that maybe there had been a mistake made by someone in his company. I told him that I would still have to make note of this to my superiors but that I would await further instructions from him. His demeanor changed quite dramatically. He stood up and politely thanked me for my assistance, and then excused himself. That was the last that I ever saw or heard from Mister TJ Smith."

Amato had been taking detailed notes. When Abbott finished he asked: "Mister Abbott, how long ago was this meeting with Mister Smith?"

"About two weeks. May 19th to be exact, which is why this is so clear in my mind. And the account, before you ask, was set up..." Abbott hesitated, probably looking at something, "... five months ago. You know, Detective, this could simply have gone by had I not had a relatively free day to go through our records. I cannot tell you how often things like this happen and no one notices for the longest time."

Abbott continued talking and explaining what it was like to work as the branch manager in a bank. Amato tuned Abbott out, but sat there processing the information and trying to decide whether he had any further questions before he let Abbott go.

"Mister Abbott," Amato interrupted, "thank you so very much for this call. This information is potentially very valuable. Please give me your telephone number in case I have further questions."

Amato made note of the number, thanked Abbott and hung up. He stared at his notes for a moment, pondering the implications of what he had just heard. He wrote a question in his notepad: *Did Smith open the account and lie about it, or was it someone else? And what connection was this to the murder?*

9

On Wednesday the following week, David Gomes drove his car into the beach parking lot at Centerville's Craigville Beach with his radio on listening to a Boston Red Sox game. Since it was a nice day, beachgoers were out in force, some wearing jeans, others wearing bathing suits, and most wearing sun glasses. The long, wide beach was dotted with brightly-colored umbrellas, with the sea breeze muffling the shouts of children and their laughter.

Over-dressed in his oxford shirt and khakis, David rolled up his sleeves and smiled as he locked his car and proceeded over to Tony's, one of the many clam shacks that appear during the summer months on Cape Cod beaches. Gomes loved fried clams, and Tony's did them well, along with great French fries, hot dogs, and fish and chips.

Gomes saw that Amato had already secured a bench and was sitting there with his back leaning against the table, jacket off and sleeves rolled up, his face turned upward, a pair of sunglasses reflecting the bright sun.

"Afternoon, Mister Sunshine," Amato said, turning to look at his approaching friend. "So, what was so urgent that we needed to meet here instead of at Emily's?

Gomes did not take the bait. "Doing well, sheriff," Gomes replied. "Let's get some food and then we can talk. How much time do you have?"

"Plenty," Amato replied, which normally meant 30-60 minutes when he was on duty.

Amato and Gomes both ordered fried clams, French fries

and soda. After paying, they sat down at the bench and waited for their order to be called. They had ordered just in time, as a small line of teenagers was forming behind them.

"Alrighty, Gomes, let's get down to business."

"Vinnie, a little bird told me that this Smith case has taken a weird turn."

Amato sat there with his sunglasses on looking directly at his friend. Gomes could not read any expression on Amato's face. "I've been told, Vinnie, that you're doing a criminal investigation into Smith himself. That you now think there may have been something less than honest going on with his company."

At that moment their orders were called and the two of them got up to get their food, looking over their shoulders to make sure no one grabbed their benches. After getting their food plus plenty of ketchup, tartar sauce and napkins, they returned to the bench and dug in. Neither said anything for a few moments while they savored the delicious clams.

"Off the record, Gomes, we discovered a handgun at Smith's office, hidden along with a set of bullets in some office supplies. The gun's serial number had been filed off."

"Not registered, then?"

"Correct. Then something weird happened. I got this call out of nowhere informing me that Smith had set up a bank account separate from his other accounts, into which about $5000 had been deposited, but with *no* withdrawals. When asked about this account by someone at the bank a few weeks ago, Smith denied that he ever opened it."

Amato took another mouthful of clams, wiped his mouth and then grabbed several French fries, dipping them one at a time into the ketchup. A crying seagull passed over them heading to a garbage can to scavenge. Gomes let Amato take his time, knowing the detective never liked being nudged.

"Why would the guy open up a separate business bank account in his own name, deposit money, and then deny that it was his?" Gomes asked as he joined Amato in devouring more French fries.

"Well, David, that's the question that me and my people have been trying to figure out. He didn't seem to have been living beyond his means, but he had this gun and it was placed in a location where you literally had to hunt for it in order to find it. In other words, it was not left in the open for all to see. And then, Smith, after being asked about the account and denying that it was his, didn't want the bank to do anything about it, like call the police."

The two friends continued eating.

"Vinnie, this doesn't add up. Maybe someone was trying to set him up. Either that or the guy lost his mind." Gomes popped another French fry dripping with ketchup in his mouth.

"I doubt that he was nuts," Amato said. "Maybe it's a little 'mix and match.' What if Smith was up to something? He went and got this gun because he might need to do some dirty work and he doesn't want it traced back to him. The guy was a veteran, we know that he had weapons training."

"Yeah, maybe, " said Gomes. "How many people know about this?"

"You tell me, my friend, you're the one who told me what you heard. Before you told me a 'little bird' had informed you about the investigation I would say only a handful of people know."

Gomes finished eating and sat sipping his soda, looking over at the beach and pondering the new info. He turned back to Amato. "Look, Vinnie, I wanted to ask you about this stuff for two reasons. One, I wanted confirmation, that's my job. Two, you have a leak somewhere. Now, the leak may not be malicious, but it could also be someone who's trying to tarnish the image of TJ Smith. I don't want to sound paranoid, I'm just saying, you know? I'm going to do some snooping around and see what more I can uncover. Oh, by the way, anything more on the missing construction worker?"

Finished with his food, Amato nodded his head. "Shepherd? The guy's vanished. Maybe the Starship Enterprise beamed him aboard." Great fans of Star Trek even though it had gone off the air, the two friends grinned.

Becoming more serious, Amato said, "Dave, we don't have a clue about Shepherd, the guy is gone. We still have no idea where he was living, and the California information wasn't very helpful. Apparently he lived in California but he has no record and there's very little information on him other than he was a construction worker. It's like we're hunting a ghost. Our current theory of the case is that Shepherd was the killer, though we have no evidence to prove it and no motive. We also have a line of folks who say that he was as wonderful as the fresh donuts at that market on Route 28."

Tossing his paper plate and cup in the trash, Gomes said, "Listen, Amato, I appreciate the briefing, but you didn't give me the name of the bank or the person who provided you with the info." He knew he was pushing the detective, their friendship got him only so far.

"I'm going to hold onto that for now, I don't want this individual getting panicked and changing his story. When we decide on our next steps I'll fill you in. You understand, yeah?"

Gomes nodded. "Guess I'll have to find some more little birds to chirp, chirp in my ear." They shook hands and headed for the parking lot.

Gomes sat in his car for a moment thinking. *Who the hell was this guy, Shepherd?* His gut told him that TJ was being set up, but who was this mystery man who so easily vanished, and why would he want to murder a simple construction contractor like TJ Smith?

10

Gomes read the headline in the *Telegraph* with disgust: "Murdered Osterville Contractor under Investigation: Possible Criminal Wrong-doing reported" He threw the paper down on his desk, cursing under his breath. At lunch the day before Amato had asked him to be careful in his investigation. Now, one of their rival papers, the *Cape Cod Telegraph*, had grabbed the story, including a report on the mysterious bank account and the unlicensed gun in the victim's office.

Gomes rarely read the *Telegraph* because of their right-wing editorial policy. Also, he found their coverage pretty weak. Despite the fact that *Cape & Islands Gazette* was a weekly, they had made a name for themselves by providing quality journalism.

But today he had received three calls, including one from his boss, Jacqueline Reynaud, about this story in the *Telegraph*. Gomes had been reluctant to publish anything outside of his initial report on the murder until he had a more complete picture. Jacqueline was beside herself.

"How did this happen, David? How would a paper like the *Telegraph* get ahead of us? You were on the scene within minutes after the incident! You have a relationship with the detective in charge of the investigation!"

Gomes could tell from her deep, low voice that morning that his boss was not only angry but disappointed with him. He felt embarrassed and, more than anything else, that he had let Jacqueline down.

Gomes picked up the phone and called Amato. Amato's assistant, Francine, said he was out in the field and would be calling in for messages. Gomes thanked her and went back to reviewing the article.

The whole piece was ugly and entirely speculative. The article provided little information that Gomes did not already know, although it did mention the name of the bank in which TJ had his mysterious account. The article made a lot of the hidden gun, and it cast aspersions on Smith, suggesting there may have been some illicit deal between Smith and the dis-appeared construction worker, Shepherd. Some people the reporter interviewed questioned how Smith had sustained his business during economically rough times. An hour later when Detective Amato returned Gomes' call, he pounced.

"Vinnie, what the fuck is going on?! You asked me to be cool on this story and I open the damn Telegraph and see a front-page story on the Smith case! In fact, I didn't have to open the paper, my boss called me this morning and ran me over the coals Vinnie, I don't—"

"David," Amato interrupted, "look, I feel terrible about this." Amato rarely sounded as unsettled and embarrassed. "I have no damn idea how this story leaked. I've been trying to find out all morning. Someone on my team obviously made the connection with the Telegraph. I didn't lie to you, you know that. If I find the person who leaked this story I'm going to drill them another ass-hole, I'm so pissed."

"I sure hope so!" Gomes began to calm down. He knew that Amato would not have messed with him, but that didn't make the situation with his editor any easier. He was fuming. Jacqueline had questioned his actions as well as his judg-ment. His relationship with Amato put him on the inside track. How could he have been scooped by the *Telegraph*?

Sensing that matters were not resolved, Amato switched gears and tried joking with Gomes. Gomes half-heartedly chuckled, but when it became clear that Gomes was still upset, the detective told him that he owed him big-time and that drinks were on him the next time that they got together. With that, Amato hung up.

◇

Gomes was working on a local story about homeless vets sleeping on the beach. He was typing up his notes from interviews of three men arrested for camping on private land when the receptionist buzzed to tell him Margie Smith was on the line. Surprised to be hearing from the widow, he took the call.

"Missus Smith, how are you getting along?"

Margie told him she needed to meet with him right away, she was terribly upset by the article in the Telegraph. "The article makes TJ look like some kind of a crook! Mister Gomes, you must print the truth about my husband. Please, will you meet with us?"

Suggesting a local diner, Gomes agreed to meet in an hour. He hung up with competing emotions: anxious about interviewing the woman who was in so much emotional pain, but excited that he might find some new angle on the Smith murder that would earn him a reprieve with his boss.

11

Gomes sat in the booth of the local diner as the Smith family sat down across from him. Mrs. Smith, a pleasant smile on her face, looked to be in better shape than the last time they had met, wearing a black, nicely fitting dress as if she were going to work in an office. Her son Frank looked casual and restless, as if he was at this meeting under protest, wearing a Boston Red Sox T-shirt and looking away from Gomes. His sister Antoinette, who David had not previously met, appeared relaxed while at the same time keenly observant. She looked at the menu, then at her mother. Though the physical resemblance between mother and daughter was striking, Antoinette was dressed much less formally, wearing jeans and a light purple blouse.

"Missus Smith, this is your meeting," opened Gomes. "What can I do for you?"

Margie looked at her kids for a moment. "Mister Gomes, I know that you've been following the case of my late husband. He was barely in the ground when his reputation came under attack. This illegal gun in his office. This questionable bank account. It all came as a shock to the three of us, and none of us believe any of it to be true. After the article in the Telegraph, the situation has gotten very ugly."

Margie stopped for a minute, on the verge of either tears or fury. As she was about to continue, Antoinette put a hand gently on her mother's shoulders, saying, "Mister Gomes, our lives feel like they're going to hell. Our father's reputation has been destroyed. The business is now under threat because people want to break their contracts with the company. They say they're uneasy about what my father might have been up to. We have friends that...well, at first they expressed their sympathy and support, then they started asking questions. Now they don't want to come around. Some won't even return our calls!"

Pretending not to notice the tears welling up in Margie Smith's eyes, Gomes looked over at Frank. The young man was squirming in the chair and beginning to turn red. He was also fingering the table knife in front of him as if he were going to use it on some one. "Frank, what are you thinking?" Gomes asked, feeling as if he was defusing a bomb.

"What I'm *thinking*? You have to be shittin' me, Mister Gomes. My father is getting smeared from one end of the Cape to the other. I can't believe it! My father was a good man, everyone knew it, but they won't come forward and say so. These fuckin' cowards are ready to let his reputation go down in flames and let the company and my family go to hell. Sorry about the language, Mom, but I'm sick of this shit."

Margie sipped her ginger ale, a tear running down the right side of her face. All of them looked at Gomes.

"I understand what you each are saying. I've also been very concerned about what I've been hearing and reading. But I'm not sure what I can do." Gomes looked at each of them.

"Well, Mister Gomes," said Antoinette, "you can start by telling people the truth about our father. You can get to the bottom of what happened. The police seem to have given up trying to get the real story."

"I'm sorry, Miss Smith, but that's simply not true. I know the lead detective, Vincent Amato. He's not given up at all. He's busted his tail on this case, if you'll forgive my language."

Antoinette sat back in her seat, surprised by Gomes's response. "Well, it *feels* as if they're no longer interested. You would think they would've gotten to the bottom of this by now, or at least not let that *paper* destroy my father's reputation!"

Gomes paused before responding. "Miss Smith, I really do have a sense of what you feel. Believe me. But these things take time. This is a very strange murder case. It's not the sort of thing that happens here on the Cape. As much as I respect my detective friend Amato, I'm not sure he has the resources to get to the bottom of this.

"I know that the Telegraph story was irresponsible. I exploded when I saw their article and I called Detective Amato immediately. He doesn't know who was responsible for leaking the information, but he's doing his best to find out. In either case, your family is paying the price and you shouldn't have to go through this."

The three Smiths were silent until Antoinette leaned forward. "We need you to clear up this mess, Mister Gomes."

"I'm not a private eye, Miss Smith, I'm a reporter. A journalist. Yes, I investigate, but I have other stories to work on and an editor who expects finished copy on her desk." Seeing the disappointment on Mrs. Smith's face, he added, "You might want to consider hiring a private investigator. PIs and the cops have methods that I simply don't."

Gomes wanted to be supportive, but he wasn't sure what else he could do. In some ways—and he kicked himself for feeling this—he felt put upon.

Margie Smith said, "Mister Gomes, we understand your position. We really do. We're not trying to make life difficult for you. You've been honest with us from the start. We feel a private eye would be too expensive, we simply don't have the funds for that. We're asking you to help us get to the truth. We obviously hope that my husband's name can be cleared. But we really need to understand what happened and why. You have to help us, Mister Gomes, there's no one else."

Before Gomes could repeat his inability to help, Antoinette gripped his arm with a fierce determination. "Mister Gomes, my mother shared with me a story that you did about some illegal dumping that was going on in Wareham. You dug into that story until you got the answers. That's the sort of approach we need to understand what happened to my father."

Gomes felt the opposing pull of his sympathy for the family and the demands of his editor to move on to other stories. After a painful pause, he said, "If I do this, you each have to be ready for the truth, *no matter what that truth is*. I cannot guarantee that Mister Smith will come out of this smelling like a rose. Are you ready for that? I mean, *really* ready?"

As he looked directly into their eyes, each member of the Smith family nodded 'yes'.

"We're ready," Antoinette said emphatically.

"Alright, I'll do what I can." Gomes sat up straight and took a deep breath. "Let's start with the three of you painting a clearer picture of who Thomas J. Smith was. Hold nothing back."

The mood changed immediately. Margie, Antoinette and Frank all started talking, so Gomes had to stop them and tell them that they needed to speak one at a time. They provided Gomes with plenty of background, along with a list of friends and business associates he could contact. When Gomes asked about the .38 that had been found in TJ's office, they insisted they knew nothing about it. Margie flat out stated: "When TJ returned from the War he wanted nothing more to do with killing. A gun in his office? I don't believe it for a minute."

Gomes asked if the business was in trouble, mentioning the curious cash deposits in the suspicious checking account. Margie, who handled the books for All-Cape Construction, asserted that the fiscal practices were sound and that it was a competitive business. None of them knew anything about the mysterious checking account.

A waitress refilled their coffee cups while Gomes tried to put everything together in his own mind. Frank told the waitress he wanted some French fries, and Gomes made it an order for two.

"Missus Smith," Gomes began, "in the weeks prior to your

husband's murder did you notice anything different about him? Anything out of place? It may not have seemed particularly important at the time, but maybe it does now?"

Margie shook her head 'no.' As the waitress brought over the French fries, she said, "No, TJ seemed pretty normal to me. He—"

"No, Mom," said Frank, a french fry in his hand, "that's not true." Margie and Antoinette looked at Frank with surprise. "About a month before he was killed, I noticed something going on with Dad. His mood changed. I would sometimes find him in the backyard by himself seeming like he was lost in space. And, Mom, you remember when Mister and Missus Gierek visited? Dad and Mister Gierek would go out for long walks. And they were never very happy when they returned."

Antoinette knew nothing about any of this since she had been away at school. Margie Smith closed her eyes for a moment. When she opened them, she looked at Gomes.

"Frank's right. Maybe I was just putting that out of my brain, I don't know. I figured it was just business problems. For a few weeks he *was* a bit distant. The visit by the Giereks was nice and I thought that it would bring TJ out of whatever he was dealing with. Well, Jennifer—that's Al Gierek's wife—and I just spent a lot of time together."

"Who are the Giereks?" asked Gomes.

"I'm sorry. Al Gierek and TJ fought in the War together. They were on the same plane together in the Air Corps."

"It was a B-24 Liberator," said Frank. "A bomber. Did you ever hear of the bombing of the Ploesti oil wells in Rumania, Mister Gomes? Those were the bombers that were used."

Gomes nodded his head affirmatively. He knew a little about military history and was familiar with the famous raid that targeted a major oil source for the Nazis.

"Anyway, Al's family lives outside of New Haven. Al and TJ were fast friends. We would visit one another at least twice a year, and every so often they would come here during the summer so that our kids could play together. They're really good people, though their oldest—Mike—is a bit much, but then—"

"Excuse me," Gomes interrupted Margie, "do you have any idea what TJ and Al were discussing on these walks that Frank mentioned? Did TJ say anything to you?"

"I have no idea, Mister Gomes. I just figured that it was men talking, you know?"

Frank looked at Gomes as if he had something weighing on his mind. "Frank?" said Gomes. "Something bothering you?"

Frank said slowly, "I don't know what was going on with my Dad exactly, but I can tell you that one day I found him in the basement. He was going through some junk. He had tears in his eyes. He didn't notice that I was there until I said something. He was sort of startled. There was no one else around so I asked what was bothering him. At first he said that nothing was bothering him and everything was fine. He tried to crack a smile and just said that there was some basement dust in his eyes."

"You didn't believe that."

Frank shrugged. "A few minutes later he started lecturing me on how terrible the War had been. You know, World War II, and how there are no heroes and that all of my friends that have thought going into the military was so cool were 'full of shit.' Those were his words, by the way.

"I felt like I was stung by a bee or something. I was just trying to make sure he was okay, and he blew up like that. Anyway, later, before I went to bed he apologized to me and just said that I'd caught him at a bad time. But he never offered anything close to an explanation as to what was going on."

"What did you think?" Gomes asked.

"I really didn't know what to think. I knew deep down he wasn't angry with *me*. He seemed worried and sad, I'll be damned if I know why."

Gomes thought for a second. "Let me ask you, Missus Smith and Frank, did TJ's behavior change at any point, for better or worse?"

There was silence at the table for a moment. Frank went first. "I don't know about you, Ma, but Dad seemed to come out of it—whatever 'it' was—about a week before he was killed. He seemed almost back to his old self."

Margie Smith nodded in agreement. "Yes, you're right. It's all such a blur, I confess that I put a lot of this aside, but I think you're right, he *did* seem to regain some spunk or something."

Gomes suggested they had covered enough ground for the day. He asked them for contact information for the various people they had mentioned, particularly the Gierek's. He emphasized again that he had *no idea* whether he would be able to come up with a thing, but he would give it a try.

As they left the coffee shop, Margie Smith gave Gomes a hug, thanking him for all that he had done. As the three Smiths turned to walk away, Gomes headed back to the office, wondering if he had bit off more than he could chew, and worrying that his investigation might turn up the kind of nasty dirt on TJ that would tear a family apart.

12

When he got back to his desk, Gomes called Amato. "Vinnie, you got a moment?"

"Sure, buddy, what's up?"

"Listen, I just met with the Smith family. A few things came up. I want to ask you something to look into. Within the last two weeks before TJ Smith's death were there any unsolved killings or anything that might have had a relationship to this?"

"Why are you asking?"

"Frank and Margie Smith indicated that something happened that put TJ into a depression or fear or something. Then, about a week prior to his death, he came out of it. Something happened. I don't know whether it has any relationship to the killing, but I wanted to flag it for you."

"Much appreciated, Gomes. The only thing out of the ordinary that could be tied to Smith was that weirdness with the bank in Falmouth. But I'll do some digging."

"Great. I'm going to try to find out where that damn Teddy Shepherd lived."

"If someone in Mashpee knows, they sure as hell aren't saying. It's like the guy lived in a cave." Amato paused. "Got anything else for me from the Smiths?"

"Well," began Gomes cautiously, "they think that you've dropped the ball on this case. Or, at least that you've given up on finding real answers. I defended you, but they didn't buy it."

The detective was silent on the other end. "This happens

a lot, my friend. People watch too much TV. They think that the answers come quick, like you can get someone to confess by grilling them. I can't worry about it, but sometimes it gets to me. In this case, yeah, it definitely gets to me."

Amato let out a long sigh. "I've never handled a case like this before. It has all the marks of a professional killing. That's never happened on the Cape."

"No, it hasn't," said Gomes. "Until now."

◇

After making a series of phone calls to friends, family members, business associates, employees and a couple of TJ's neighbors, Gomes reviewed his notes. He learned that as a teenager, TJ had played with the wrong crowd and was often in trouble. His life changed when he went into the Army Air Corps during the War. When he came out he was responsible, caring and generous. He also turned out to be a good business man.

The last person on his list of contacts was a man who knew TJ during the War: Al Gierek. After a series of phone calls, Gierek consented to talk on the phone to the reporter.

"I'm sorry that I couldn't speak with you sooner," Gierek began in a friendly voice that sounded younger than his actual years.

"Mister Gierek, I'm very sorry about the death of your friend. I'm trying to do a story that captures who TJ actually was."

"Where to begin?" Gierek said, his voice mournful and reflective. "We met in Italy during the War. You know that, I suppose. He was a very capable airman. A hard worker, and a great friend. When we would go on leave, we often hung out together.

"Listen, Gomes, is all this on the record? I don't want to say anything that's going to put TJ in a bad light."

"Mister Gierek, we can put as much of this on the record as you want. Otherwise, it's just background."

"The reason I ask is that TJ and I would, well, you know, we would do a bit of gambling and hanging with those Italian ladies. They were gorgeous. Some of them were low on food, so we'd give them a thing or two and, well, they would take care of us, if you get my meaning?"

"Of course. I understand."

After telling a few war stories, Gierek said, "You know, Gomes, TJ and Margie were classy people. When they moved to the Cape and we couldn't afford a vacation, they opened their home to us so we could get away from the rest of the world."

"Did TJ have any enemies?"

"Nah, everybody liked TJ. *Everybody.*"

"Why would he have had a gun, do you think? The police found an unregistered gun in his desk."

"That makes no sense to me. The last time I saw TJ with a gun was in the Service. He didn't talk about guns, he didn't joke about them, and, as far as I knew, he didn't own one."

Switching subjects, Gomes said, "Frank Smith told me that during your last visit, you and TJ spent a lot of private time together. He suggested there was a lot of sadness. In fact, Frank and Margie said that for the last month before his death, TJ was depressed. Does any of this ring true for you?"

"Ah, well, you know, there are some things that a guy doesn't want to discuss with his wife. Certainly not with his son." Gierek stopped talking and sounded as if he was drinking something. "TJ was concerned about business. He was feeling overstretched. He had a big deal coming down the road, but he wasn't sure that he could hold out. He didn't want to talk with Margie about it, he didn't want her all worried and upset. Nothing illegal, Mister Gomes, it's just that in the construction industry it sometimes takes a while for a contractor to get paid. Sometimes the developer or the general contractor takes their time on payment. Things like that."

Gomes thanked Gierek for giving him so much time. Hanging up, he made a note to follow up on the financial angle. Maybe Smith had borrowed money from people with short tempers and long knives. The kind of debts you failed to pay at your peril. Maybe. But there was nothing in Gierek's voice that sounded ominous.

13

With the information from Gierek that TJ was sweating his business finances, Gomes decided to go after the Cape Cod Savings & Loan matter. He didn't know who in the bank had given the story to Detective Amato, but he had a contact there, Theresa Smalls, a childhood friend.

The bosses at the bank had always underestimated Theresa Smalls, a University of Massachusetts graduate in economics. On the shorter side, with deep brown skin and an Afro, Smalls was quiet, attractive and soft spoken. Though Theresa could have been running Cape Cod Savings & Loan, given her sharp organizational skills, management limited her to the role of teller. A keen listener and observer, she let very little get past her at the bank.

Although Theresa worked at the main branch in Hyannis, she was able to identify the branch where TJ Smith opened his account. In short order she determined that two persons at the branch were the most likely ones to provide Amato and the Telegraph with information. Of the two, one was on vacation, the other was a Thomas Abbott.

Gomes thought he might get a better 'read' on Abbott if he spoke with him face-to-face, so he wound his way down to West Main Street to Route 28, passing the Cape Cod Melody Tent. Despite the summer tourist traffic, he liked the interplay of sunlight and shadows from the abundant tree stands and forests that lined Route 28, hiding the many ponds and the herring-filled tributaries that emptied into the ocean. Passing the Old Indian Church and Burial Grounds as he made his way through Mashpee on the way to the Falmouth Bank branch, he was reminded of a potential news story about a possible tribal land reclamation suit by the Wampanoag that might slow the relentless development of the Pomponeset-New Seabury area. Right now, though, his focus was on TJ Smith.

Gomes had no trouble finding Abbott. As he entered the bank he approached Miss Higgins in the customer service area, who directed Gomes to a luncheonette down the street. Higgins was absolutely correct in her description of her boss. Sitting by himself reading some papers was a well dressed man looking as if he was preparing for a business meeting. Every hair was in place on his head and every stitch was tight on his suit.

"Mister Abbott, I presume?" asked Gomes politely to the otherwise startled man. Abbott dropped his fork and picked up his napkin to cover his mouth as he attempted to swallow his food.

"May I help you, sir?" asked Abbott. "Do I know you?"

"I'm sorry to bother you, Mister Abbott. A young woman in the bank told me that you were at lunch. I sort of…implied that you and I had a meeting scheduled."

Abbott looked angry and flustered.

"I will have to speak with the staff when I return to—"

"Sir, please don't hold that against them. They were attempting to be of service to me."

Abbott sat back, beginning to relax.

"Well, sir, you have the advantage of knowing my name. Who, may I ask, are you?"

Gomes pulled out a business card and put it before Abbott. Without asking permission to be seated, he sat down at the table. A waiter came over to the table looking concerned, but Abbott waived him off.

"A reporter, Mister Gomes? How can I be of help?" Abbott was nervous, looking down at the card and not at his visitor's face.

Gomes apologized for interrupting Abbott's lunch, then explained the story he was working on. Abbott's eyes widened.

"The police told me this would all be kept in confidence," Abbott asserted with some degree of indignation.

"Please let me explain, Mister Abbott. After the story of the questionable bank account appeared in the press I came up with you as the person who spoke to the police through looking over the bank personnel. I can promise to identify you as an 'anonymous source'. Would that work for you?"

Abbott sat silently for a moment, then nodded his head in agreement that Gomes could go forward. "Mister Abbott, I'm trying to figure out why TJ Smith would open an account that he didn't use, and then deny that he had ever set it up."

"*That* is precisely what I have wondered about since I first discovered that his account was growing but never used. And that he never requested a set of checks. For a *checking* account!" Abbott was becoming more invigorated as the discussion progressed.

"Did Detective Amato interview the bank employee who opened up the account?"

Abbott cleared his throat and took a sip of water. "Yes, but I don't think that she was of much help, as she was new to the bank. She said that the person she met with was an older man with a work-shirt that had stitched on it the name All-Cape Construction as well as the man's name, TJ Smith. He had all the appropriate identification. She didn't pay attention to the way he looked. When she was shown a picture of the actual TJ Smith, she denied that was the person who opened the account."

"Was this employee able to provide anything more?"

"No, that was all of it. She said that the man was very polite and had little to say, though he did ask whether he could make a deposit at any branch. Which, of course, he could."

Gomes thought for a moment. "Wouldn't this individual

have received some temporary checks? Wouldn't the bank have automatically mailed him his permanent checks?"

"Excellent thinking, Mister Gomes," said Abbott, showing surprise and respect. "That *is* the way it is *supposed* to work. So, yes, point one, this person DID receive temporary checks, and point two, he asked that the bank hold off on sending permanent checks because, according to our employee, they would soon be moving and they wanted to put the new address on the checks. She believed his explanation, so she let it go."

"And Smith never made out any of the temporary checks."

"That's right!" Abbott took another sip of water. "Just so you know, the police asked a sketch artist to draw a picture of the man that our employee met with. I got the sense that it didn't help."

Starting to get up to leave, Gomes asked Abbott if the police showed the bank employee a picture of a Teddy Shepherd. Abbott said he didn't recall such a picture, who is Teddy Shepherd?

Gomes said that was the same question he'd been asking since he took on this case.

◇

Before going home, Gomes dropped in on Hank for a late cup of coffee. Instead of quiet, Gomes found a madhouse of young boys, some with their parents, looking at the models or making purchases. Gomes walked around the store looking while Hank was up to his neck in customers.

He soon found a box containing the parts of the model of a German Tiger tank, a weapon made famous to younger audiences in the Henry Fonda/Robert Shaw film Battle of the Bulge. He could not believe the level of detail in the model.

"Finally," Gomes heard, seeing Hank standing behind him. "Dave, it's been crazy busy most of the afternoon. I don't know

where all those kids came from! No end of tourists since the Kennedy family put this place on the map!"Gomes handed Hank the cup of coffee—his ticket of admission—though it had lost much of its heat. They walked back to Hank's office, where Gomes gave his friend a brief summary of his progress in the investigation. Hank, as always, listened carefully.

"How's Pamela, Dave?" he asked in a non-sequitur.

"She's fine, Hank," Gomes replied, afraid he was about to get a lecture.

"Do you have a picture of that construction guy who disappeared? Maybe he impersonated the murder victim at the bank."

"I don't have Shepherd's picture, Amato should have it. My guess is that the picture doesn't match the guy at the bank, but I'll ask him anyway."

"Good idea. I'm just wondering, if Shepherd opened the account, why in Smith's name? And just as important, why leave the money there? Why not take it out?"

They both sat in the quiet of the store, the fan running in the background. Hank was the person—besides his own girlfriend, Pamela—that Gomes sought out to talk through hard issues. Hank always asked the right questions.

Before leaving the store Gomes asked if he could use the phone. Hank nodded his head and left Gomes alone to talk while he walked through the store going over inventory.

"Amato, this is Gomes," he said as soon as he was connected with the detective. "A quick question."

"Make it quick, David, I have a meeting I have to run to."

"Vinnie, have you gotten a picture of Shepherd?"

"Funny you ask. Yes, we got a copy of the picture from his California driver's license, but it didn't help us with the bank, which is what I assume you're really asking."

"You caught me, Vinnie. Yeah, I found Abbott and met with him. He told me that the police used a sketch artist to try to identify who set up the account."

"Yeah, and it was useless. The guy the girl at the bank described could have been almost anyone. We showed her a picture of Shepherd later and she said it wasn't him, so, we're back to ground zero."

"Okay, Vinnie, thanks. I don't want to hold you up."

Gomes hung up and headed out, thanking Hank as he the door chimes rang on his way to the street.

14

The following morning Gomes went to Bob's Teepee on Route 130, a favorite hangout with good, inexpensive food and an owner who didn't chase people out as soon as they were finished eating. Some older members of the Mashpee community— Wampanoag, Cape Verdean, and white—spent hours at the restaurant, sometimes playing chess, checkers or dominoes.

As he walked in, Gomes heard jazz playing softly in the background and breathed in the sweet aromas of fresh pies and cakes. Karen Costa, the hostess, greeted him. Karen, a little darker than Gomes wearing a well-shaped Afro, was a part-time college student. Every man who was not blind flirted with Karen. She was always friendly, even charming, but would never lead anyone on.

The owner, Bob Sampson, was a tall man in his late 40s with yellow/brown skin. He claimed to be part Wampanoag, part Cape Verdean, part Black American, and part Portuguese. With the look of a warrior—it was rumored he had a black belt in some martial art—Bob kept an eye on his establishment and made sure there was never any trouble.

Bob always provided flyers and newspapers from assorted organizations for all to see and read. He was especially proud of material about the struggles in Africa against Portuguese colonialism and white minority rule, as well as material about the struggles of Native Americans. If you wanted to get Bob talking, all you had to do was to mention the PAIGC (African Party for the Independence of Guinea-Bissau and

Cape Verde) and he would talk about how they were kicking the asses of the Portuguese.

"Morning, Karen," Gomes said with a smile. "Bob around?"

"Good morning, David. Yes, the boss is in the back. Why don't you check in his office?"

Gomes thanked her and proceeded down a small hall until he reached a door with a sign sporting the picture of a soldier pointing a rifle at you. The sign said "HALT!" Every time that Gomes saw the sign he had to chuckle. He knocked on the door.

"Yeah?" came a deep voice from inside.

Gomes slowly opened the door into a small office that felt like a cave, except for a nice sized window looking out onto a wooded area. Bob was sitting at his desk in a space just big enough for two people to sit comfortably.

"Gomes, what can I do for you?"

Bob, dressed more like he worked in a warehouse than running a restaurant, rarely asked customers how they were doing, he always wanted to get right down to business. Not unfriendly, he was just not someone who would give you a hug.

"Bob, I've been doing some follow up on the TJ Smith murder in Osterville. I wanted to speak with you about Teddy Shepherd."

Though Bob's facial expression didn't change, his eyes took on a guarded look. "Well, Gomes, I spoke with the cops about him. I didn't really know the guy. I mean, I met him a couple of times, but never to really speak with him...at least at any length. We just took his phone messages." Bob sat back, his face a mask.

"Yeah, that's what I heard. But let me ask you a couple of things, if you don't mind?" Bob remained still, not objecting, not agreeing.

"Why did you take messages for the guy in the first place? He wasn't from around here, he was a drifter."

"He was a veteran, Gomes, you should appreciate that. He

was a veteran and a construction worker. He came in here for his meals. He would get an early breakfast, usually to go, and then dinner almost every day. About a week after he started the routine he pulled me aside, said that he didn't have a phone where he was staying and asked if I would take messages. I told him 'sure.' He seemed like a decent guy. He said that if it put us out to not worry about it, so we took messages for him, but there were never many."

"Do you have *any* idea where this guy lived? That seems to be the mystery of the hour."

"No. Like I told the cops, he told me that he had a room with no phone. That was it." Bob turned his head to look at something he'd been reading when Gomes entered.

"Bob, one more thing. Do you mind if I speak with any of your people here about Shepherd?"

Without looking up, Sampson replied: "Talk with whoever the hell you want to, Gomes. Just don't keep them tied up too long, we're running a restaurant here, not an information bureau."

As he thanked Bob and left the office the owner acknowledged Gomes's exit with a grunt.

Gomes first asked Karen about Shepherd. She indicated that she spoke with him when he came in, but she never spent any time with him. She added, "David, you might want to speak with Anne Lang. She was seeing Shepherd from time to time. Or so I hear."

Karen pointed toward one of the waitresses. Blonde, in her 20s, standing about 5'5" in her waitress uniform, Anne was talking with a customer at one of the tables. She turned and walked towards Karen and Gomes.

"Anne, meet Mister David Gomes," Karen said. "Mister Gomes is a reporter for the Gazette. He wants a minute of your time."

"Nice to meet you, Mister Gomes," Anne responded, looking nervous. "Karen, are you sure that it's okay with the boss?"

"If Mister Sampson had an issue with it, Mister Gomes wouldn't be standing here," she replied with a half-smile.

Gomes suggested they sit down at one of the tables. There were few customers at the moment. "Miss Lang…"

"Call me Anne." She looked at him with cool blue eyes, pronouncing her name 'Anna.' Before he could begin again, Lang said: "Mister Gomes, I know who you are. I read your stuff. You've written about the murder of that guy in Osterville, the murder they want to pin on Teddy Shepherd, right? "

Gomes was surprised by her knowledge of him and his work, as well as her accent, which sounded like she was from the northern Midwest.

"Wow, Miss Lang…I mean Anne. I didn't realize you knew so much about my work. So, let's start by your calling me David." Gomes smiled, receiving no response from Lang.

"Anne, I'm continuing to work on a story about the murder of TJ Smith. Teddy Shepherd worked for him for about six months and disappeared at the same time that Smith was murdered."

"He did NOT 'disappear,' David. He left." Lang's look was a hard-edged challenge.

"I stand corrected, Anne. *He left*. If Shepherd *is* as innocent as you believe, the more I find out about him, the better I can clear him of any charges. Right?"

When Anne silently shrugged, not denying the reporter's assertion, Gomes said, "What kind of person was Shepherd?"

"Are you asking everyone these questions, David?"

"I am. I'm trying to create a picture of the people around TJ Smith, whether his family, friends, co-workers…whoever."

Lang stood up and walked over to the soda fountain for a cola. She returned to the table with the glass and sipped it. "Teddy and I went on a few dates. And we would talk sometimes when he came in here for his meals." She took another sip of the soda.

"He was a *perfect gentleman*. He was kind, considerate and

generous. I would see him helping some of the customers who had problems with their cars. I remember him giving a kid some money for a soda. He would always pay for me whenever we went out. And he understood whenever I would say *no*. A lot of men don't."

Anne stared at him, no smile. Gomes decided to shift gears, asking her personal questions about her background, growing up in Minnesota, and eventually moving to the Cape. When Gomes saw that she had relaxed he returned to the topic of Shepherd. "Did you meet Shepherd here?"

"Yeah." Gomes could hear the Scandinavian accent now. "He came in one day for breakfast and we just started talking. He was very nice. He wasn't coming onto me, he was very polite. Eventually he asked me out. We went bowling in Hyannis, and then just hung out for a while. We would do things like that."

"Where did he stay?"

Lang shifted in her seat, her expression changed. "Like I told the cops, I have no idea where he was staying."

"That seems strange, Anne. You know, to see a guy for a while and not know where he lives." Gomes gave her a questioning look.

Lang looked down at the table. "Yeah, it *was* a little strange. But he said his landlady was sort of old-fashioned. She didn't like the idea of women visiting men outside of marriage." Anne smiled after the last statement, the first smile Gomes had seen on her face. At least now he had a clue: Shepherd had a *landlady*.

"What else can you tell me about Shepherd? What made him interesting or nice?"

Anne looked over his shoulder toward Karen, though she didn't seem to need to rush off. "I don't know, David, he was just a *nice guy*. If he had stayed around, I would've wanted to try a real relationship." A light came on in her eyes. "I suppose you knew that he had a motorcycle. Well, when he came to pick me up on the bike, he always made sure I put on a helmet, and we would take off."

"That's thoughtful."

"One night we were supposed to go out and it was raining cats and dogs. I wanted to see him, but I didn't want to ride on that motorcycle in the rain. All of a sudden I heard a horn and saw these lights flash. When I looked outside, there was this black car with Teddy inside. I went running out to the car and got inside. He told me that he had borrowed the car from someone because he didn't want me soaked. Like I said, a really nice guy."

"Whose car was it?"

"He didn't say. He just said that he borrowed it from someone who didn't use it very often. When I got into the car it seemed almost new. It was clean with no smell of cigarettes or anything. Teddy told me that there weren't a lot of miles on the car."

Gomes made a mental note of his second clue: a black car, low mileage, well maintained.

When Lang looked over Gomes's shoulder again he realized it was time to end the interview. "Anne, thanks so much for your time. I really appreciate this."

"Sure, David. I don't think that I was particularly helpful, but if there is something that you can use, great."

"One more quick thing," Gomes said cautiously. "In the beginning you said that Shepherd didn't 'disappear' but that he 'left.' What did you mean?"

She seemed surprised by the question. "That guy Smith got killed on a Monday, right? Well, a few days before that Teddy called to tell me he needed to go back to California for family reasons. He said he hoped to be back to the Cape, but was really not sure when it would happen. He was very apologetic about it. I told him I understood and that I hoped to see him again, but I never did."

◇

As he drove back to the office, Gomes thought about the information Anne had given. He now knew that the guy had a landlady and, more than likely, a black car with low mileage. That was something to go on, though it was thin. Would Jacqueline continue to support his work on this story? He hoped so, it was just getting interesting.

15

Gomes always looked forward to Sunday dinner with his folks. While he didn't go every Sunday, he went enough that it was a semi-ritual. Sometimes there would be family or friends in attendance, other times it would be just the three of them, David being an only child. And every so often Pamela would join him at the dinners.

Joaquim "Jack" Gomes was a tall, 6'3" coffee-colored man with wavy black hair. Family members and friends rarely called him "Joaquim." Early in life, in order to fit in with non-Cape Verdeans and non-Portuguese, he allowed himself to be called "Jack." The name stuck and, despite his parents' misgivings, he became *Jack Gomes*.

After serving in World War II, Jack Gomes returned to his birthplace, New Bedford, Massachusetts, where he found it difficult to pick up where he left off, having seen a bigger world. He re-connected with Helena Alves, someone he had been dating in high school. Helena was the product of a Portuguese mother and Cape Verdean father. Life at home had been difficult for Helena. Her mother had been shunned by Helena's grandparents and siblings for marrying some-one 'colored.' Despite the love between her parents, there was a tension in the household throughout Helena's childhood. The entire Portuguese side of her family shunned Helena, whose father burned with resentment.

Helena was and remained a radiant beauty. She was 5'2", with auburn, curly hair and a pure, golden complexion. Though she had gained a few pounds over the years, she still caught the eye of every man she passed .

Jack and Helena moved to the Cape to start fresh. With what he'd learned in the motor pool in the Army during the war, he worked in an auto service station and, eventually, bought his own station at the Mashpee traffic circle where Rt. 28 met Rt. 151 and Rt. 130. He was a good businessman, able to build the station and eventually hire two Air Force veterans who had been stationed at Otis Air Force Base. They proved to be excellent mechanics, making Jack's station the go-to location for auto repair.

David's father was not much for conversation. He wasn't cold, just pensive. He was a study in contrast with not only his wife Helena, but also his younger brother Al. Helena, always the life of the party, was smart and ambitious. She first worked as a domestic and part-time worker in a textile mill near New Bedford. When Jack and Helena moved to the Cape she continued the domestic work while working toward her college degree. Because so many parents asked her to tutor their children, she decided to go into teaching.

David parked his car in his parents' driveway around 5pm. Since there were no other cars in the driveway, David assumed that dinner would be with his parents alone. He let himself into the house, which smelled of steak cooking on the barbecue grill outside. A master of the grill, on Sunday Jack usually took the lead in cooking.

Helena greeted David with a warm hug. They chatted as David grabbed a beer from the refrigerator and Helena chopped up vegetables for a salad. He walked onto the porch where his father was tending the grill.

"Welcome home, son," Jack said with an easy grin. "Just you, me and your mother. Hope you're not disappointed."

David smiled and shook hands with his father, as they normally did. They chatted for a few minutes, then Jack moved the steak and potatoes inside.

Jack and Helena did not drink much but, on Sundays they

generally enjoyed wine with their dinner.. Jack had, over time, experimented with different wines and tonight they were going to enjoy a *tinta roriz*. The three of them sat there enjoying dinner on a pleasant summer evening when Helena asked David about work. This was frequently not a pleasant discussion since Helena and Jack always wanted David to become what they called a 'real' professional. David resisted this, telling his parents that as a writer he *was* a professional. Tonight, however, the clash did not unfold.

"So, what's the story with the murder case you've been writing about?" Jack asked.

David took them through what had transpired. He also expressed his frustration about not being able to get closer to the bottom of the case. He told them he was preparing to publish a story about TJ Smith, based on his investigation and interviews, and that the Smith family would be quite happy with the story, though that was not the intent. Nothing that David had come across suggested that TJ was anything other than a stand-up guy.

"Okay, Davey," his mother interjected, "you have found out that the dead man was legit. Now what?"

"The problem I'm having is that this guy Shepherd was staying somewhere here in Mashpee but no one will come forward and admit it." David picked up his glass of wine and finished what was left in it. He put it down and sat there for a moment.

"Well, son, you know that the killer had a landlady. I would assume that the black car that you mentioned was hers," opined Jack.

"Why'd you assume that, Dad?" David responded.

"Simple. You have this guy who moves into this area within the last year. He doesn't know anyone, at least as far you can tell. His girlfriend tells you that he has a motorcycle, but then he shows up with a car that is barely used. That tells me the car probably is owned by a retiree and my guess—and I could be wrong—is that his landlady was a retiree. The other thing that your story tells me is that wherever this guy was staying, the landlady is either scared to admit that he was there, doesn't know that the cops are looking for him, or she thinks the guy is worth protecting."

"Wow, Dad," David exclaimed, "you should give up the service station and come to work with me. Or go into being a private detective!"

Helena sat for a moment smiling with pride at her husband. Then she stood up to clear the table. David jumped up and told her that he would take care of that. He cleared the table and began washing the dishes while thinking over what his father had raised. Jack remained at the table, where he took out a cigar—one of his rare treats—and lit it. The sweet smell of the cigar wafted into the kitchen.

Jack, cigar in mouth, stood up, looked outside as if mulling something over, then walked to the telephone. He grabbed a pad of paper from the drawer underneath the phone. Pulling the phone with its long cord to the dinner table, he dialed a number.

"Father Collins? Hi, this is Jack Gomes. Sorry to bother you on a Sunday evening but I was wondering whether you could help me with something."

David and Helena listened quietly to the conversation. At first it was just pleasantries between Jack and Father Collins, the priest from St. Matthew's Catholic Church, the Gomes's family church in Mashpee. David sensed his father getting ready to shift gears in the conversation.

"Father, you know my son, David? Of course. Well, among other things, David is writing a story about people on the Cape who rent out rooms or homes to guests. You know, folks who come here for the summer or others who might be here to work for a few months and then leave...Yeah, exactly..."

Jack moved the cigar in and out of his mouth, puffing occasionally as he listened to the priest. "Father, I was wondering whether there are folks in Mashpee that you think that David should interview. He's not thinking about someone who owns a cabin or motel, but more folks who have a spare room or an addition to their house that they might rent out...Yeah, exactly, Father...exactly."

Jack shifted in his seat and began writing feverishly, saying nothing except a few "yeah's" and "thank you's." After a few minutes Jack looked up, his eyes shifting between Helena and David. He closed off the conversation, thanking Father Collins for his time and the information he provided and hung up the phone. Jack took a long puff on his cigar and blew a perfect smoke ring.

"What was that about?" David asked.

"I'm not trying to do your work for you, son, but it occurred to me that Father Collins, probably more than anyone else knows folks from Mashpee who are renting out rooms or who have spoken about it. I've seen the notices posted at the church about rooms available. So I figured that I'd ask him. I decided to change the story a bit because if the whole thing seems too sinister, Father Collins might clam up."

"Well, Dad, maybe you *should* have my job," David responded with a tremendous grin. "What did he give you?"

"A list of about fifteen...well, maybe about twenty people who are renting rooms or portions of their house. Some of them have tenants and others are vacant. I figured that this would be a start."

David picked up the list and gave his father a hug. Jack was not great about accepting hugs, though when he received them from his son they were always welcomed.

"I'll get on this first thing tomorrow! Thanks so much, Dad."

Helena smiled at her husband, who never ceased to amaze her. Jack was proud of himself as well. He took a puff from his cigar and they continued chatting long into the night.

16

On Monday morning David headed to the office first thing. Draping his blazer over the back of his chair, he pulled out the piece of paper on which his father had written the list of names provided by Father Collins. There were about twenty names and phone numbers.

After prioritizing women in his search for the "landlady," Gomes thought about what he was going to tell people. To avoid any trouble, ethical or otherwise, he pulled out a file folder and wrote on it: *The challenges for landlords with temporary tenants.* He then put two pieces of paper in the typewriter along with a carbon sheet separating them. He typed a "memo to file" indicating that he was going to begin working on a story that examined the challenges faced by landlords on the Cape who offer temporary rentals. He further explained, in the memo that his line of inquiry was that there were security issues, matters of payment, and the condition of the rental unit after it has been occupied that presented challenges to landlords. He then took the papers out and handwrote on the carbon copy a message to Jacqueline, saying: "FYI." He dropped the memo in her in-box and returned to his desk to start making phone calls. Now, if anyone asked, he was working on an *actual* story.

The phone calls took some time. Not everyone was home. Two people that he reached did not want to talk. A couple of those called were not home. But he was able to arrange some interviews. He also made note of those who did not want to speak with him, figuring he would come back to them later.

The appointments were complicated to arrange. It was clear he would need several days to conduct all of the interviews. Nevertheless, he found that the stories people told about renting out rooms or homes were quite interesting and varied. There were funny stories, such as a family that seemed to keep adding people to the space that they rented; predictable stories, such as renters who ducked out without paying or having damaged some of the property; and there were a few disturbing stories, such as a very well-dressed man who rented a room and then went outside and hung himself from a tree.

Gomes realized that he had the basis for a legitimate independent story that he could come back to later, though that had not been his main objective in doing the interviews. So far he had not identified anyone who might have rented to Teddy Shepherd.

At the completion of his ninth interview with an older Mashpee couple who had been renting out space for years, Mrs. DeMaris, who was in charge of the renting asked Gomes an innocent-sounding question: "Mister Gomes, you said that you're interviewing quite a number of us old timers in Mashpee who have rented. Do you have Violet Johnson on your list?"

Gomes did not see the name on his list.

"No, I don't have her. If you have her address and phone number I can try to set up an appointment."

"She lives not far, down off of Route 130, it's just a hop, skip & jump from here. Give me a moment and I'll write it all down. She had a very nice young man renting a room until just a few weeks ago. Such a wonderful woman," Mrs. DeMaris said this with a gleeful chuckle. "She's been renting to people for years and I know that she has stories to tell!"

Mrs. DeMaris stood up and went to the kitchen, returning with an index card container. She picked through the cards, then pulled out one and read off the address and the phone number. Putting the card back in the box, she smiled and held her husband's hand while the two of them waited to see whether Gomes had any further questions.

Gomes looked at his watch and realized he had enough time for another interview before returning to his office in Hyannis. After thanking the couple for their hospitality, he asked to use their phone and called Mrs. Johnson. The phone rang busy. He decided that since her house was so close he would just drop by.

Gomes drove off with a rough idea where the Johnson house was, but he nearly missed it due to the tall shrubbery in front. The house was situated on a slight incline and was nearly impossible to see from the road. Gomes turned into the driveway and slowly drove up the hill toward the house.

He stopped the car a respectable distance away from a turn-around area in front of a garage, got out of the car and walked up the pebbled driveway. The door to the two-car garage was wide open. There sat a 1967 black Ford Falcon, along with various gardening supplies. Gomes noticed that on the side of the garage there was a metal staircase going up to the door of an attic or apartment above the carport.

It was very quiet except for the occasional car driving by and the sounds of birds in the woods around the house. The abundant plants in the garden beds abutting the house rustled in the breeze. Gomes walked over toward the enclosed porch sheltering the main entry to the house. He rang the doorbell outside the porch door and waited. No sound within. He stood there for a moment trying to decide whether to leave a note for Mrs. Johnson.

"May I help you?"

Gomes turned around and looked into his own reflection on sunglasses worn by a striking, dark brown African American woman, probably in her 70s, with a wealth of thick gray hair beneath a straw hat. She wore blue jeans, a loosely-fitting cotton work shirt and carried a trowel in her right hand.

"I asked, *may I help you?*" she repeated, polite but firm.

"I'm very sorry...you sort of surprised me. I didn't hear you approaching," Gomes replied.

"I surprised you? Well, think of it from my point of view. I walk around my house and run into a young man standing at my door." She had a wry smile on her face that accentuated her beauty and somehow calmed the situation.

"Please forgive me," Gomes began. "My name is David Gomes and I'm with the Cape & Islands Gazette." Gomes handed her his business card. "Are you Missus Violet Johnson? I tried calling you from the DeMaris home, but your phone line was busy. I wanted to ask you for a few minutes of your time regarding a story that I'm working on."

"Cape & Islands Gazette? Never read it." She tucked the business card into a back pocket. "I was out back working in the yard. When I'm outside I take my phone off the hook." Opening the porch door, she added, "You look thirsty, Mister Gomes. Why don't you come in and join me for some iced tea?"

Entering the porch, Violet Johnson directed Gomes to sit on an old wicker chair. "I'll be right back." She walked into the house and soon returned with two glasses of iced tea along with a small sugar bowl and two spoons. They both prepared and then sipped their ice tea. Gomes was struck by how refreshing it was.

"The tea is excellent, Missus Johnson," he exclaimed. "I don't say that just to please you. Often tea is bitter. This has real flavor!"

"My own brew, Mister Gomes. I mix in black tea and mint that I grow here. In fact, I have so much mint that I give most of it away! If you want some, I can prepare a little bag for you."

"I will take you up on that, thanks very much." After another sip Gomes explained his cover story to Violet Johnson. She listened quietly, nodding occasionally to indicate that she understood what he was saying.

"Well, Mister Gomes, my late husband and I moved here from New York City in 1960. I was a secretary in a company and he worked in a warehouse. He had a good union pension and we had saved up some money. We decided to move to the Cape before we were too old to enjoy it. We started a small business together that brought in a little money. Not a lot, but enough. Then my husband died about five years ago."

She stopped for a moment, looked off into space, then lifted the glass to her lips and took a sip. "My husband was a great man, but he didn't take care of himself. He kept denying that there was anything wrong with him. Well, by the time we got him to the doctor it was too late. Smoking killed him and I could never convince him to stop. Even when he knew that he was dying he found a way to sneak out of the house to smoke a cigarette." She closed the story with a small, ironic smile, shaking her head in a silent conversation with herself.

Gomes asked her about her experience renting, the sorts of renters and why she even started. They created the extra room on top of the garage, it was comfortable and private, and started renting soon after moving to the Cape to bring in extra income. They rented to all sorts. Her experiences with tenants had been generally positive.

"The only bad experience I had was not with a renter but someone looking for a place. This man, who was white, came here from Hartford, Connecticut. He worked in an insurance company, if memory serves me. He seemed nice enough. I thought that we were on the verge of a deal, but then he said, 'Do I sign an agreement with the owners?' Well, Mister Gomes, I was a bit stunned. I pointed out that I was the owner. He seemed a bit taken aback and stumbled on his words. He thanked me and said that he would be in touch. I never heard back from him."

"What was your most recent rental experience, Missus. Johnson?" Gomes threw out the question casually.

"I had a young man here. A construction worker. He was

with me for about six months. He was a wonderful tenant and a perfect gentleman. He paid on time and did me so many favors. If my car was acting up, he would take a look at it. He helped me around the house from time to time. And, you know, he would never ask anything in return." She looked both pleased and a bit sad when she completed her words.

"When did he leave?"

"Oh, he left back at the end of May. I was sorry to see him go. But he said he had to go back to California. So he packed what little he had and got on his motorcycle and took off."

Gomes was trying to contain his excitement. "But it's summer, Missus Johnson. Why haven't you rented out the apartment? I'm sure there are people who want to be on the Cape over the summer."

Johnson smiled, "A few problems that I needed to take care of in the apartment before I let anyone have it. The biggest thing is a plumbing problem that Teddy discovered but couldn't repair. He told me 'I know that you think that I'm Superman but there are some things that I cannot do.' He figured that it would not be a big job but that I needed to get a plumber. In any case, I took care of it and next week I should have someone moving in." She finished off her iced tea.

Excited at hearing the name 'Teddy,' Gomes knew he had to proceed carefully and not give away his actual agenda. "Missus Johnson, you mentioned that your tenant's name was Teddy. Was he by any chance the Teddy Shepherd who worked in Osterville?"

Violet looked up at him with surprise and happiness. "You know Teddy? Did he do some work for you?"

Gomes cleared his throat and adjusted himself in his seat. "Missus Johnson, I'm not sure how to put this. The police want to find Teddy Shepherd. Did you follow the story about the contractor in Osterville who was killed some weeks back?"

Violet looked startled. She shook her head. "No, I don't follow the news on the Cape. Never have. I go down to the store to get my New York Times and read that. I'm a real New Yorker, Mister Gomes." she said with a half-smile. The smile faded. "Teddy wanted by the police? For what? There must be some mistake."

"Mrs. Johnson, Teddy Shepherd was working for the man who was killed. On the day of the murder Shepherd disappeared. He didn't report to work and hasn't been seen since."

Violet looked at Gomes as stunned as if she'd received a blow to the back of her head with a blunt object.

17

After waiting for Mrs. Johnson to recover from the news about her former tenant, Gomes continued, "I'm going to suggest *two* things. The first is that you call the police. I can give you the number of Detective Amato who is handling this case. The second..." he thought for a moment and then continued, "...the second is that you call a lawyer. Do you have a lawyer, Missus Johnson?"

Violet nodded her head in the affirmative. She looked through the screens in the porch as if recalling some moment in her life. Gomes gave her Detective Amato's number. She looked at it and then looked outside again.

"There must be some mistake, Mister Gomes. I cannot believe that my Teddy would have done anything wrong. I *certainly* did nothing wrong. I gave him a place to stay."

Gomes saw that her composure was crumbling. She was frightened and confused.

"Missus Johnson, I understand," Gomes said softly, "but you need to call the cops and your lawyer. This is a very serious situation. The cops have been looking for Shepherd for weeks. They have nothing to tie him directly to the killing but his disappearance makes them suspicious."

"He *didn't disappear*," Violet said emphatically, her fear replaced by anger. "He left town and went home. He told me he was going to leave and he left. It's not like he slipped out of town during the cover of nightfall."

"I was not trying to offend you, Missus Johnson. I was just trying to be straight with you. I hope you understand."

Violet Johnson put her glass down on the table, stood up and walked into the house, leaving the door ajar. Gomes sat there trying to decide what to do. He hoped that he hadn't gone too far. He heard her dialing a number on her rotary phone, followed by silence. Then he heard her voice but could not quite make out the words. After a short conversation he heard her dial another number. Again, he could hear that she was talking but could not make out what she was saying. A few minutes later she returned to the porch with fresh glasses of tea.

Mrs. Johnson sat quietly, lost in thought. Occasionally she looked at her watch but said nothing more for several minutes.

"Well, Mister Gomes, now that you have startled me to death, do you have any more questions?"

"No, thank you. I've probably overstayed my welcome. If I think of anything else, I might give you call, if that's okay?" Gomes tried smiling to lower the tension between them. He wanted to ask her more about Shepherd but he could tell that she was no longer in the mood to answer any questions. He also realized that he would be unable to trust her answers now that she understood that Shepherd was a wanted man.

"Mister Gomes, if you don't mind, would you just stay here a bit longer?" Her request surprised Gomes.

He looked at his watch. "Certainly, if you wish."

Gomes was unclear why she just wanted him there as company, presumably as she awaited the police. She just sat there quietly saying nothing, seemingly lost in space. Gomes turned to another page in his notepad and began writing up this visit and his impressions. Eventually he heard the low rumble of a car coming up the driveway. Gomes looked up and saw a Dodge Charger pull up into the driveway near the black Falcon in the garage and away from Gomes's car.

An elderly white man with gray, poorly combed hair who stepped out of the vehicle seemed to not fit the muscle car he was driving. Gomes was pretty certain it was a '69 Charger, a car that anyone who loved to drive fast hungered for. Yet the driver was very non-descript, dressed casually and not the sort of person you would associate with such a car. Gomes watched him pull the seat forward, lean into the car and pull out a briefcase and a blazer. He shut the door and walked over to the porch.

Violet stood up and called the person—she referred to him as "Nate"—to enter the porch.

"Mister Gomes, this is Nate Wellington, a long-time friend of mine and my late husband. He is also my lawyer. Nate, meet the gentleman I mentioned on the phone, David Gomes from the Cape & Islands Gazette. Nate, would you like an iced-tea?"

"Violet, you make the best iced-tea on the Cape, you know I can't say no to that fine offer. I'd appreciate it." Nate smiled as he found a chair, while Mrs. Johnson walked inside to get the iced-tea.

"Well, Mister Gomes, you're the person who broke the news to my friend Violet that she'd been harboring a fugitive?"

Wellington was casual, friendly, and unsettling. There was something about this guy that he could not quite put his finger on. He explained to Wellington how the conversation had progressed and watched Wellington, who did not take any notes, absorb it all. At that moment Mrs. Johnson reentered the porch and handed Wellington some iced-tea, which he graciously accepted and began to drink. He nodded his head thanking her, a broad smile of satisfaction across his face.

"Mister Gomes, Nate is, as he likes to say, a 'semi-retired' attorney. For years he practiced law in Boston and, from what I hear, was one heck of a labor lawyer. He had quite a firm."

"Mister Gomes...do you mind if I call you David? Please call me Nate." Gomes nodded his head in agreement. "David, Violet tends to exaggerate my attributes, but, yes, I was in Boston for years. Now I live here in Mashpee and practice a little law, mainly wills, some real estate and a few other things." He paused for a moment to drink some more of the iced tea. "David, would you mind if I borrowed Violet for a few minutes? I understand that the good police of Barnstable County should be here soon and it would be useful for the two of us to chat some."

Gomes offered to leave but they both insisted that he stay and relax. He said he would walk around the yard until the police arrived. Everyone smiled, though clearly no one was happy. Gomes then exited the porch while Nate and Violet went inside and closed the door.

A few minutes later Nate called out to Gomes, inviting him back to the porch. He noticed that his glass had been refilled with iced tea. Violet seemed to be inside. Nate pointed to the seat for Gomes to sit down.

"So, David, you apparently pulled...what do they call it...a 'foolly' on my friend Violet," Nate offered with what, under other circumstances, would appear to be a genuine smile.

Gomes was unclear how to respond and looked puzzled.

"My friend Violet may not keep up with the news on the Cape but I sure do. In fact, I read your paper every week. As soon as Violet mentioned your name on the phone I knew who you were. You've been investigating the murder of that contractor from Osterville. And you showed up here today using some cover story. Very smart, Mister Gomes." Nate lifted his glass of tea in a toast to the wily reporter.

Gomes thought that this guy must be a terror in court. He could imagine the cross-examinations that he would give, tearing a witness apart.

"Nate, I appreciate your reading my paper, but if you do, then you know that I cover a number of stories. Yes, I've been interviewing people for a story about renters but, sure, I've been trying to figure out what I could about Teddy Shepherd. I was stunned when Missus Johnson revealed that he had been her tenant."

Nate nodded his head affirmatively, never changing his demeanor. "I'm sure, David, I'm sure. And, please understand me, I would probably have done the same as you."

"I don't look at Missus Johnson as guilty of anything," said Gomes. "That's why I suggested that she contact her lawyer so that–"

"*And* call the police, David. Correct?"

"Of course, I suggested that she contact the police. This is a murder case."

Nate sat there looking at Gomes, the smile never leaving his face, but the eyes remained piercing. With the sound of a siren approaching, Missus Johnson rejoined them on the porch. As the sirens went silent, they heard the sound of two cars coming up the driveway, their lights flashing. Gomes opened the porch door and stepped out.

Amato jumped out of the driver's side of the first car as soon as it stopped and walked to the porch. Another officer Gomes did not know — a young, redheaded fellow looking like he'd just returned from Marine Corp boot camp—got out of the passenger's side to follow the detective. Two other officers, in uniform, got out of the second car and walked toward the garage.

"Okay, Gomes, what's the story?" Amato's voice was clipped and all business.

"Hello, Vinnie. Mrs. Johnson is on the porch with her lawyer. This is where Shepherd was staying. He was lodged up there." Gomes pointed toward the apartment on the second floor of the garage.

Amato looked up at the apartment, a look of annoyance on his face. "Alright, I'll start with her. You said her *lawyer* is here?"

"That's right. When I realized this was the place, I suggested that she call you immediately and call her lawyer."

Amato rolled his eyes, clearly irritated that he would not be speaking with Mrs. Johnson privately. "Well, there's nothing that I can do about that. In any case, Gomes. I need you to take off. I'm going to ask her about some things that I'm not ready to release to the press, even off the record. Got it?"

"Got it." Gomes knew his friend was annoyed that the police had failed to find the Johnson house. "Just let me introduce you to her, she's pretty shook up by what I told her. Okay?

With a sigh, Amato gestured for Gomes to lead the way. As Gomes, Amato and the young officer entered, Violet Johnson and her attorney stood up.

"Missus. Johnson, let me introduce you to Detective Vincent Amato from the Barnstable County Police. Detective Amato, this is her attorney, Nate Wellington."

The three shook hands as Amato told them the young officer's name, Tanner. Wellington was cordial, but wary, Violet Johnson was clearly nervous, alternating between looking at Amato, Wellington and the floor.

Amato glared at Gomes, who made his good-byes, headed to his car and drove back to Hyannis wishing he could be a fly on the wall of the porch...with a notepad.

18

Standing on her porch looking nervously at the two police officers, Violet offered her guests some iced tea. Amato and Tanner accepted; Nate signaled he had had enough. Nothing was said while Violet was inside getting the iced tea.

For the next thirty minutes Amato asked Violet about Teddy Shepherd: how he paid for his room, where he was from and where he had gone, about his relatives and friends, and if she ever saw him in possession of any weapons. Whenever Violet looked over to Nate prior to answering, Nate encouraged her to speak forthrightly. Amato took few notes, though Tanner wrote steadily.

Johnson's answers gave Amato nothing useful. The man was a ghost, sharing little with his landlady. She had never seen him with a weapon of any kind, just the tools of his trade.

"Missus Johnson, would you mind if we went up to the apartment, looked around and checked for finger prints?"

Nate opened his mouth to reply but was preempted when Violet asked: "Do you have a warrant, Detective?" Nate smiled but said nothing.

"Ma'am, we're in the process of getting a warrant. I just thought you might want to cooperate with us in getting to the bottom of this mystery." Amato was trying to be respectful, though he might have come across a bit condescending.

"Maybe we should just wait until the warrant arrives. I wouldn't want any…suggestions later on that I did something wrong. I still don't believe that Teddy was *your* murderer."

After that Violet sat quietly, hands folded, looking Amato directly in the eyes.

Nate seemed to be getting a charge out of the exchange. He leaned over to Violet and whispered something to her. He could tell that Amato was about to become unhinged. Violet slowly nodded in the affirmative.

"Detective Amato," said Wellington, "what if we do it this way? Missus Johnson has a legitimate concern that there could be some sort of misunderstanding. I believe she would be comfortable with you starting a search of the room if we were there. I promise you, we will not get in the way."

Amato shrugged. "Sure, I have no problem with either or both of you being there while we do the search. In fact, I think it would be helpful. Just please don't touch anything."

Wellington leaned closer to Violet and said, "Fingerprints."

19

August was always a strange month on the Cape. Everyone had the sense that summer was coming to an end. There was a certain frenzy among tourists as they tried to get in as much Cape-for-the-summer as they could. People who had delayed their vacation were rushing to the Cape to get a few good days of the best beach time and seafood New England had to offer.

Two weeks after Gomes interviewed Violet Johnson he was sitting across from Jacqueline at her desk. The response to his article on TJ Smith had been favorable. He argued in the article that there was no substantial proof of any malfeasance on the part of TJ Smith and that the man may have been set up. The Smith family was overjoyed by the article and each member—Margie, Antoinette and Frank—called Gomes to thank him.

Gomes had written a second, briefer article that had just been published, revealing that the lodging of the major suspect in the case had been discovered and that there was no indication he had been in hiding. Gomes chose, and Jacqueline agreed, to not mention Violet Johnson's name. There was no need to unsettle her life.

As he and Jacqueline were discussing a new controversy on the Cape about reopening passenger rail service to the Cape, the phone on Gomes's desk rang. He decided to let it ring, planning to just check with Susan later for messages. He wanted to wrap up his discussion with Jacqueline and work out a plan for the story that they would do on the passenger rail controversy.

The phone on Jacqueline's desk rang. She looked at it for a moment and then walked over to answer. "Oui...yes...yes, I will tell him," she said looking at Gomes and hanging up the phone.

"David, Detective Amato is trying to reach you. He says it is important. Susan is holding the call."

Gomes walked over to his desk, where he hit the intercom button and told Susan that he was back at his desk to receive the call. The phone rang.

"Gomes, we need to do lunch. How is 1:00? We can meet at Craigville, if you're not tired of the clams."

"No problem, Vinnie, but is it urgent? I'm sort of in the middle of something. I'd have a bit more time tomorrow or the day after."

"I don't need a lot of your time, but I need for you to put your thinking cap on, this one can't wait."

There was something in Amato's voice this particular morning that conveyed an urgency Gomes could not ignore. "Okay, Vinnie, I'll see you at the beach at 1:00."

Gomes looked over at Jacqueline, who was looking at him with curiosity. He returned to her desk, where they wrapped up their discussion on the article.

<><

Gomes arrived at Craigville Beach on time but, as usual, Amato had gotten there first. Getting out of his car, removing his blazer and dumping it in the back seat, he walked over to the clam shack where Amato was sunning himself at one of the tables. Several teenagers were at the shack waiting in line for food, radios playing, ignoring Amato. As was also usual, when Gomes approached, Amato greeted him without ever turning. That always brought a smile to Gomes's face.

"Well, Detective, I have arrived!" Gomes said with a joking voice and a grin. Amato turned towards Gomes and shook his hand, though he did not look like he was in a great mood. The two of them went over to order some lunch. As they sat at their table waiting for their food, they watched a few beachgoers hovering around the table looking to see whether they could share it. Every time someone looked like they wanted to sit down, Amato gave them a fierce look, chasing the interlopers away.

"Things have gotten complicated, Gomes," stated Amato after consuming a good portion of a clam roll. He took a sip of his ginger ale. "This discussion is very much off the record, by the way. I mean *really* off the record. Got it?"

Gomes nodded his head in agreement while Amato finished off the clam roll, noting that Amato seemed so serious he wasn't enjoying the clams.

"Well, my friend, fingerprints from Shepherd's apartment at Missus Johnson's place came back. Would you believe, Davie old boy, that we have the fingerprints of a dead man?"

Gomes stopped eating his coleslaw mid-bite. "How's that?"

Amato had a twisted smile on his face. "Just what I said. We took prints from that apartment. 'Shepherd,' as he called himself, did an excellent job cleaning the apartment in Mashpee. He really cleaned up the place before leaving. But more importantly, he wiped the place down. Must have assumed that we would find the place at some point. He was probably counting on his landlady finding another tenant quickly. If she hadn't needed to do that plumbing she would have rented the place already and we'd be stuck. In any case, we found some clear prints and put them in the system."

Amato stopped for a second to taste a few French fries, though he didn't bother dipping them in ketchup. Or even taste them. "The report on the prints came back this morning. They are for an 'Antonio Da Silva.' Da Silva was presumed drowned about a year ago off of a place south of L.A. called Laguna Beach. We checked with the Laguna Beach Police, they said that the guy was reported missing while swimming, his personal stuff was left on the beach, his body was never recovered."

Gomes began to say something but Amato held up his hand to stop him while the detective finished his French fries. "Gomes, the story doesn't end there. The guy was ex-Air Force. Had been in Vietnam a few years back. Decorated, for God's sake. He was in something called the Air Commandos, which I understand is an elite unit. So now the F.B.I. come in. The higher-ups think this guy could be some sort of contract killer."

Amato looked down at the empty plate, considered ordering more fries but decided against it. "So, the overall situation is this. This guy created a fictitious *persona*, including a false driver's license. He didn't die from drowning. He was trained to kill, and he disappeared, just like at Laguna Beach."

"Vinnie, this is incredible! But why would this guy kill TJ Smith? Who would even hire somebody?"

"That's part of why I called you. I need to know whether you came across anything that would explain it. There's no indication that they knew each other before 'Shepherd' went to work for Smith, so *somebody* wanted him dead."

As Amato stood up to throw the trash away, Gomes confessed he hadn't found anyone with a serious grudge against the victim.

"Well, there's one other thing that you should know," Amato said, looking Gomes straight in the eyes. "Antonio Da Silva aka Teddy Shepherd didn't come from California. He was a neighbor, Gomes, he's originally from Fall River."

"Fall River!?" Gomes was surprised.

"Yeah, Fall River. In fact, I went there to interview his parents. Didn't get much, though. His parents thought he was dead. They were shocked that he was still alive. They hadn't heard from him since before he was reported drowned." Amato sat down again, apparently having just needed to stretch; or maybe it was just nerves.

Gomes watched people walking over to the beach, carry-ing towels and joking, crossing the road from the clam shack and the saltbox cottages a few hundred yards down the road. Just as he got ready to say something, Amato offered another comment.

"Listen, Gomes, there's one other thing I need to tell you." Amato's voice was low and flat. "About the FBI. In some ways they seemed a bit more interested in *you* than they were in the case."

"Interested in *me?*" Gomes was flabbergasted.

"Yeah. Remember last summer you did that article about those Black Panthers going to Martha's Vineyard to raise money? Well, that article that you wrote and a follow up came to the FBI's attention. Then there were those other Black militants you know in Boston; that guy Malik Monteiro and his crew. Then, your name surfaced in the TJ Smith case and these guys started asking *strange* questions."

Amato had been cleaning his teeth with a toothpick in between comments. He let it sit there in the right-hand corner of his mouth.

"*My articles* on the Panthers got their attention? And Malik? Yeah, I know those guys, but so what? You're shittin' me, Amato!"

"I wish I was. No, they asked me a lot of questions about you. At a certain point I told the bastards to 'let up'; that you were not the focus of this investigation. They looked at me like I was an idiot."

Amato and Gomes sat on a bench looking out at the water, with its white foam glistening in the noonday sun. Gomes told Amato about his experience with the Panthers and the articles he had written. In the summer of 1969 he was invited to Oak Bluffs on Martha's Vineyard to a Saturday afternoon event with two Panthers from Boston who were visiting the summer home of a jazz musician. The musician was spon-soring a talk by the Panthers as well as using it to raise funds for the legal defense campaign of Panther co-founder and Minister of Defense Huey P. Newton.

The two Panthers were a man and a woman, both in their twenties. The man acted like the leader and gave a fairly rhetorical, though heart-felt talk. During one of the breaks, Gomes had gone over to speak with the woman, who was standing by herself drinking a soda. She had beautiful brown skin, possessed twinkling eyes and a well-shaped Afro. She had not had a lot to say until Gomes started asking her questions. He was very attracted to her but pretended that was not the reason that he approached her.

The woman's name was Claudia. He could not remember her last name. He started asking her about this event and about the Panthers. He was surprised by the depth of her analysis, far deeper and more enlightening than that offered by her male colleague. She laid out a critique of the Civil Rights leaders, as well as a critique of individuals such as Ron Karenga who she described as "cultural nationalists," a term with which Gomes was unfamiliar. She talked about police brutality but went beyond that to an intense and compelling critique of capitalism, particularly focusing on the limitations of what President Richard Nixon called "black capitalism."

Gomes was deeply attracted to Claudia, but more than anything else, he was profoundly impressed. Since his article about the event reflected this impression, the FBI more than likely picked up on that. He never saw Claudia again, though he certainly wanted to and—truth be told—tried to figure out a way to track her down. He wrote a follow up article on the Panthers, discussing a July 1969 conference that the national party held about building what they called a united front against fascism. He interviewed some Panthers who were in the New Bedford area, and did a phone interview with the same male Panther from Boston who visited Oak Bluffs, whose name Gomes could not at present remember either.

"Do I need to worry about this, Amato?" Gomes asked.

"I don't know. Maybe. I just wanted to make sure you didn't get caught flat-footed. If I were you, I'd assume that your phone is tapped. I can't believe they think that you are somehow involved in this mess, but they may have decided to take advantage of this situation to do a little probing. To be honest, Gomes, I would keep a little distance between yourself, the Panthers and that other group in Boston, just to be on the safe side."

Amato looked out to sea, saying nothing more. The two never talked much about politics. When they did, things would sometimes become tense. A couple of times it blew up into loud exchanges. Amato was no racist, but he had the politics of a sort of liberal Republican. Gomes had only recently started to think of himself as a leftist, though he was not a member of any organization. He had been reading the Black Panther Party newspaper , and read a few progressive magazines from time to time, like *Monthly Review* out of New York. And he would have political discussions with people, such as Malik Monteiro and people around him in a group called the Movement of February 21st, commemorating the day that Malcolm X was murdered. Despite all of that, politics was not central to his life.

They had plenty to talk about, whether crime, baseball, or scuba diving, which they both loved. After a big blowup, Gomes decided to leave left-wing politics out of the equation. That said, he appreciated Amato looking out for him. He had never spoken with Amato about Malik, so he assumed that the FBI had raised it, perhaps to get a rise out of Amato.

"Amato, I need to speak with the parents of this guy Shepherd, or Da Silva. They're not going to want to speak with me. I need to call in a major favor, old friend."

Amato looked down at the remnants of a sand castle, now just a few lumps in the wet beach. "Alright, let me do this. I have a friend from Providence, a cop in Fall River. Another *paisan."* Amato smiled. "His name is Carlo Salvucci. Carlo is a stand-up guy. I think that he could put in a word for you with the Da Silva family, he helped me when I went there to interview them. But like I said, don't expect a lot. They didn't give me much information. They lost touch with their son and were in some level of shock. Maybe they know more, but they weren't coming out with much information."

Gomes thanked Amato and asked him to give him a call after he reached Salvucci. Amato wanted any information that Gomes came up with that would be relevant to the case. Even though Gomes would not violate his ethics, he understood that he had an obligation to his friend...and to the truth.

20

That afternoon Gomes stopped by a coffee shop on Main Street in Hyannis. He picked up two coffees to go, put them in a bag, and walked over to Winter Street to visit Hank at the hobby store. Gomes opened the door into the shop and heard the ring of the bell announcing his entrance. He looked around the store and saw several teenage boys wandering around the store looking at the various models.

Hank was standing at the back watching the boys as they roamed the store, pretending to be reviewing his inventory. When he gained eye contact with Gomes he signaled for him to come over to the counter.

"David, how the hell are you?" asked Hank with a smile. He stuck his hand out to take the coffee that Gomes had brought him.

"Doing ok, Hank, though this case is taking some strange turns," he said, taking a sip of his own coffee.

"How's Pamela, David?" Hank asked. This was another part of their routine.

"She's good and sends her best. Look, I know you think I should move to the next level with her, but I just think that I'll get in her way, man. Anyway, that's not why I came by today. Besides enjoying your wonderful personality, I need some advice."

Hank was not going to let Gomes switch subjects that easily. "David, I've seen the way that girl looks at you. You are the one she wants and if you don't watch out, it'll all vanish. You may not get a second chance."

Seeing a dark look in his friend's eyes, Gomes understood that every time Hank brought up Pamela, he was bringing up the memory of his lost love.

Hank got up and walked to the office, giving Gomes a chance to compose his thoughts. Through his prodding, Hank had been forcing Gomes to think about his relationship with Pamela, making him think more than he wanted to.

Gomes watched Hank look around the store to make sure that the boys were not doing anything mischievous. "Hank, I need some help thinking about this case. There are a few things that have come up," he said to shift gears and to get Hank refocused. Gomes did not want to discuss Pamela at the moment and was tired of getting pounded by Hank on the matter.

Gomes took a sip of his coffee and looked up at his friend. "Hank, tell me about the Air Commandos."

Hank took his eyes off the teenagers. "The Air Commandos? That's a hell of a change of subject! What the hell do you want with the Air Commandos? Are you planning a new career that I don't know about? Have you been speaking with the Air Force recruiter on Main Street?"

Though Hank had a smile on his face, Gomes could tell that his friend was both curious and concerned.

"This has to do with the TJ Smith case out of Osterville. It turns out that the main suspect in the case had once been in the Air Commandos. Amato told me that they were like Special Forces, but I had never heard of them before."

Hank got up from his stool, lifted the counter flap and walked over to check on the kids. Gomes heard him ask them whether there was anything that he could do to help them. A conversation started, followed by Hank and the boys walking back to the counter. He stood at the cash register and waited for the boys to put a model airplane kit on the counter. They were purchasing a kit for an X-15 rocket plane, visibly excited by their choice. Hank offered them a few hints on how to make the model even more attractive. The boys were half paying attention, but Hank smiled anyway. When the transaction was completed they left the store, proud of their purchase, the door chimes ringing as they departed. Hank returned to his stool and relaxed.

"Alright, Gomes, now, back at the ranch. You were asking me about the Air Commandos. They were known as the First Air Commando Wing, then re-designated as the First Special Operations Wing. Amato was basically correct. They are the Special Forces for the Air Force. But they're an unusual bunch. They're organized for counterinsurgency *and* covert operations. They are responsible for certain types of air missions, but they're also responsible for being combat meteorologists...weathermen, so to speak. They help with rescue operations, a range of things. They are a very tight, well-disciplined operation, and they operate in the shadows." Hank finished off his coffee.

"So, a guy would have to be pretty damn good to become an Air Commando, right?"

"No question about that, David. And if this guy is somewhere in his 20s, it's quite surprising that he would have left them. Was he on leave or something?"

"No. As far as I understand, he resigned from the Air Commandos. He was supposedly in California and died in a swimming accident. Then he appears on the Cape under a different name."

Hank mulled this over for a minute, staring at a model of a B-52 bomber. "David, listen. Someone coming out of the Air Commandos is going to be a skilled killer. They can do a lot of other things, but killing will certainly be one of them. You think this guy became a contract killer, is that it?"

Gomes shook his head. "As far as I can tell, there's no reason to believe this was some sort of mob hit. I think the guy who was killed was being made to look bad, for sure, but that was a dodge, the man was clean. "

"Then I don't know what to tell you, David. This guy would have been well trained and well disciplined, so unless he lost his mind, there was a mission behind this murder."

Gomes stared at the floor for a few moments. "Hank, here's the other thing. The FBI has taken an interest in yours truly."

"An 'interest' in you?"

"Yeah. They were called in to assist with the TJ Smith murder case. I guess because this crossed state borders or something. But they started asking Amato about me, the Black Panthers, and other things. It makes no sense."

"David," started Hank, "Is Amato looking out for you?"

"Amato *is* the person who flagged this for me. He's not trying to put me under. I'm just not sure how to handle this."

"You need to speak with the lawyer at your paper. If the FBI is messing with you, you need to know how to play this. How they would jump from the TJ Smith to you and Panthers is beyond me."

"I know, it doesn't make sense, unless the FBI is trying to make use of this situation to do something deeper."

"Hoover and his FBI hate the Panthers and the other radicals. They'll make use of any excuse to mess with them. You may be a tool in all of this."

The two of them sat there for a few minutes in silence. As Gomes rose to leave and Hank grabbed his arm. "David, seriously, watch your back. You have the FBI on you. But this former Air Commando is a lot scarier. This guy's been trained in more than just using a weapon. He knows covert operations. He's trained to be in the shadows. You've been in the military, I know, but you don't hold a candle to this guy in terms of his capability to pull something off. So just be careful, okay?"

"Understood, General," Gomes responded with a smile, but also acknowledging Hank's concern. They shook hands and Gomes exited the store as a family was entering. A young boy, probably around 10, was telling his parents about a great model that he had to have, the McDonnell Douglas F-4 Phantom.

21

A day after his conversation with Hank, Gomes left the office for home a little early in preparation for his trip to Fall River. Since he had arranged for an evening meeting with the Da Silva's, he figured he deserved a few minutes rest to take care of some things and then get on the road. He wanted to put on a fresh shirt and even wear a tie with his blazer for the meeting.

He was looking around his place to see if there was anything more that he needed to bring with him to Fall River when the doorbell rang. Through the glass surrounding his door Gomes saw the profiles of two men. He could not make out much other than one was black. Although he didn't have time to speak with some Jehovah Witnesses trying to save his soul, he opened the door.

"Yes?" Gomes said, "May I help you?"

The white man in a black suit opened the screen door, saying, "Agent Paul Jameson from the FBI, Mister Gomes, can we come in and speak with you for a few minutes?"

Gomes was flustered and, without thinking, invited the two men in.

"This is Agent Oscar Mason," said Jameson, pointing to the black man who, also in a black suit, stood there looking at him with a completely unemotional face.

Gomes pointed to two chairs and sat on the couch, using the time to get focused. Both men looked to be in their 30s. They both had short hair and were well-built. The black agent had a broad face, was on the lighter side and looked ex-military. The white agent had black hair and eyebrows that looked somewhat Neanderthal, reminding him of the actor Robert Lansing from the TV show, *12 O'clock High*. Gomes could not tell for sure whether he was ex-military. They both seemed to take control of the room, though Gomes could not quite figure out what led him to feel that way.

"Mister Gomes," started Jameson, "the FBI has been asked to assist with the investigation of the murder of the contractor, TJ Smith. We understand you have in your journalistic capacity been engaged in investigating this killing."

"Yes," Gomes responded, asking himself why he had allowed the agents into his apartment. "I've written a few stories on the killing."

The two agents made notes on a pad. "Do you have a theory about the case?" asked Jameson.

"I'm not sure that I'd call it a 'theory,' Agent Jameson, but it appears that a man named Shepherd has turned out to be a former Air Commando named Da Silva who was brought up in Fall River. He worked for TJ Smith under the name Shepherd and disappeared around the time of the killing. I have no idea why he would've carried out such a killing. There was no connection between the two as far as I've been able to find."

Gomes looked at his watch. He was starting to get uneasy about whether he would be able to make it to Fall River at the agreed time.

"Mister Gomes," opened Agent Mason, looking like he was getting ready to growl, "Are you familiar with something called the "Transit Company?"

"The 'Transit Company'?" he asked back at them, somewhat startled. "Do you mean, like the agency that runs the buses here?"

Jameson broke into a smile but Mason's face remained stone. "No, I'm referring to an underground network that gets draft dodgers and deserters out of the country and into Canada."

Gomes put on a perplexed look, though he was well aware of what the 'Transit Company' was, having explored a story about them. They seemed to be an outfit in the New England states with ties to a network in Canada that helped resettle young men trying to avoid the Vietnam War.

"I've never heard of something like that. I know that there are folks who are helping people get to Canada, but that name doesn't ring a bell."

"I see," replied Mason, looking up toward the ceiling. "We'd been led to believe that you started an investigation into them."

"I have an interest in those who are trying to avoid military service. That may have been what you heard."

Mason shook his head in a way that indicated that he did not believe what Gomes said, but he didn't challenge the reporter on it.

"Do you think that there could be a connection between this killing and the Weathermen, Mister Gomes?" Jameson asked in a softer tone than his colleague, inquiring about the quasi-military leftist organization.

Now Gomes really was perplexed. "Why would there be any connection with the Weathermen? This has no markings of a political killing. It feels like you guys are barking up the wrong tree!"

Gomes was getting edgy. He couldn't figure out where this was going, and he needed to throw these guys out.

"Mister Gomes," began Mason, "You have documented ties to the Black Panther Party and this Movement of February 21st. I'm thinking that blinds you to the possibility of a left-wing connection to the murder."

Gomes stood up, almost without thinking. "Gentleman, thank you for visiting me today. I have an appointment in Fall River. If you want to follow me there to ensure that I'm not meeting with the Panthers or the Weathermen, by all means, do so. But for now, I must ask you to leave."

Jameson and Mason put away their pads and stood to leave. They both started to speak at the same time, but Mason was first. "Thank you for your time, You don't seem to appreciate the terrorist danger that may be facing Cape Cod. We don't believe for a minute that this Da Silva is operating on his own. Your sympathies with those radicals is well-documented, and you really don't seem that interested in helping us better understand what may be going on here. We regret that. You will certainly regret that as well."

"Have a nice evening," Jameson added for his partner. The two agents walked out and crossed the street to their car. Gomes sat down and waited to hear the engine start and the car take off. He continued to sit there, listening to the birds and processing this interaction, then he left the apartment and headed to his car, scared that the god-damned FBI was monitoring everything he did.

The bastards.

22

As he drove towards Fall River, David Gomes used the solitude of driving to reflect on recent developments. He kicked himself for letting the FBI into the apartment. He should have told them to contact the lawyer for the Gazette. They rattled him and that fact alone angered him. Their questions were stupid and provocative. How any serious law enforcement outfit could assume that the TJ Smith murder was a political killing was over the top. They were either idiots or that had a political agenda of their own. He had a hunch it was the latter.

As Gomes got closer to Fall River, he thought about his phone call with Lt. Salvucci from the Fall River Police. Salvucci had been polite, if not warm. Gomes could hear in his voice that he was taking this call strictly as a favor for his friend, Amato. Having known Bruno Da Silva for several years, he agreed to inform the Da Silva family that Gomes was legit. But the officer warned Gomes that the Da Silvas had been visited by law enforcement and the press and were not likely to give much information to a new reporter.

Gomes expressed his appreciation to Salvucci for setting up the meeting. He called the household and spoke with Bruno Da Silva, who reluctantly agreed to the visit but said it would have to be around 6:00 pm after he got home from work. He did not indicate whether Susana Da Silva would be there. Gomes decided to leave that alone and hope for the best.

Gomes was unfamiliar with Fall River, having never spent much time there but for a few visits when he was a kid. At

5:30 he turned off of Route 6 and pulled over so to re-read the directions, leaving the engine running. He realized that the directions he was given by Da Silva were more vague than he had thought when he took them down. He looked around and noticed a man probably in his 50s walking down the street. Gomes leaned over to the passenger side and rolled down the window.

"Excuse me, sir, I think I may be lost. Would you tell me how to get to this address?" Gomes read off the address and pointed to the paper on which it was written. The man, with deep eyes, ashen skin and black hair, looking as if he had just walked off a cargo ship, had a skeptical look on his face. "Why you want to go there?" he said in a heavy Southeast New England accent with a Portuguese undercurrent.

Gomes was taken aback by the question. It was not what he was expecting. "I have a meeting there in a few minutes, sir, and I don't really know Fall River."

The man kept staring at Gomes, displaying no expression. "You sure this is the neighborhood you're looking for? There aren't many of..." The rest of what the man raised was lost in his mumbling voice.

Gomes rolled up the window and decided to keep looking. He discovered he was two blocks away from the Da Silva's street. Quickly finding the house, he pulled up just past some boys playing stickball on the street. The boys looked at him to make sure that he was not driving further down the block.

The Da Silva house was a white single family with two floors and a triangular face to the front. Gomes saw a pickup truck in the driveway not far from a garage. The flags of Portugal and the US flew side-by-side on the porch.

Gomes walked up to the main entry. Before he could get to the door, it was opened by a balding man in his late 40s. Gomes could see through the screen that he was a bit over-weight but generally in good condition.

"I'm assuming you're that reporter, Gomes," said the man,

holding the screen door.

"Yes. You must be Mister Da Silva."

"I am. Come on in."

Gomes walked into an entryway with a staircase to the second floor in front of him. To the left was a dining room, and beyond, a kitchen. To his right was a living room with a fireplace, television, sofa, a couple of comfortable looking chairs, a glass-encased large map of Portugal, and a table. Da Silva directed Gomes there.

Gomes sat on the sofa, Da Silva sat across from him. In the background Gomes could hear some glasses clinking in the kitchen. Saying nothing, Da Silva picked up a magazine from the table and flipped the pages. A moment later Gomes turned to look as he heard footsteps approaching.

Every so often you can look at a person and see precisely how they appeared when they were young. When Gomes looked at Mrs. Susana Da Silva he knew that as a young woman she had been a striking beauty. She remained very attractive in her late 40s, with olive skin, black hair streaked with grey, wearing designer glasses and a loose-fitting, flowered dress that made her look older than she was. Gomes immediately stood.

"Please sit down, Mister Gomes. I'm Susana Da Silva. You've met my husband, Bruno." Her smile would quiet an unruly crowd. "Can I offer you something to drink? Some coffee or tea, perhaps?"

"Either would be great, Missus Da Silva, I have to a drive back home this evening."

Susana Da Silva went back to the kitchen, where Gomes could hear her working. Bruno Da Silva indicated no particular interest in talking, so Gomes decided to await Susana's return. He sat on the sofa making some notes on his pad.

Susana Da Silva returned a few moments later with a tray of coffee for three. She placed the tray on the table and began to fix her coffee. Gomes did likewise. Bruno Da Silva continued to read the magazine. Eventually he put it down, though he did nothing with the coffee.

"Mister and Missus Da Silva, thank you for taking this time to speak with me. As you know, your son Antonio is at the center of an investigation of the murder of TJ Smith, from Osterville, Massachusetts, so if I could just ask you—"

"These accusations are a load of crap! We shouldn't even be talking to you." Bruno's eyes were slits of rage.

"Now dear, that nice Detective Salvucci *did* say Mister Gomes could be trusted to get our story right."

After a moment of silence, Gomes tried again: "When did you find any of this out? About Tony being wanted for questioning."

Bruno Da Silva jumped right in. "The State Police came knocking on our door. They brought along that cop from the Cape that you know, Officer..."

"Amato. Detective Amato is from the Barnstable County Police," Gomes said.

"Yeah, Amato. They came by and explained that Tony's fingerprints had been found in a house on the Cape and that he had disappeared after this Smith guy was shot. We told them we hadn't seen Tony in a long time. We understood he was killed in a swimming accident, though my wife here never believed that."

Now animated, Bruno turned toward Susana, who nodded her head in support.

"Forgive me for asking this, but do you think that your son could have carried out this killing?"

"No fuckin' way, Gomes. I can't believe he would've done this," said Bruno, crossing his arms. Susana stared at Gomes, her face a mask, saying nothing.

Wanting to mollify Bruno, Gomes said, "Of course, it sounds impossible." Hearing nothing more from the couple, he continued. "I understand your son served two tours in Vietnam. After that he resigned from the Air Force. Do you have any idea why he resigned? He was in an elite branch of the military."

Bruno shook his head. "When Tony came home after his last tour he was shaken by the war. He decided that he wanted to get on with his life. That's all I can tell you."

Gomes realized the interview was getting nowhere. "Well, can you tell me how long he stayed with you when he left the service?"

Bruno looked over at Susana, who was looking down at the floor, avoiding eye contact with either of the men. "He was here for a few months. He didn't do very much."

Gomes turned toward Susana. "Missus Da Silva, did Tony see his friends while he was here? Did he have a job or do anything special?"

Susana got ready to answer when Bruno cut in. "Tony's friends pretty much took off after high school. Some folks stayed around Fall River, but others went to college, enlisted in the service or just moved away. For the most part they were gone. Tony hung around the house, went to a few bars, walked around. Didn't do much. And then he told us that he was moving out to California."

Bruno crossed his arms again and sat there looking at Gomes. Suddenly Susana stood up, surprising both Gomes and Bruno. "Mister Gomes, would you like some more coffee?" she asked pleasantly, though with an edge in her voice.

"Absolutely. I may regret it when I get home tonight and can't sleep, but you make some good coffee."

Susana turned to her husband. "Bruno, would you mind coming into the kitchen and helping me?"

"How can I help you? You didn't need any help with the first pot."

"Bruno, *please* come into the kitchen." Bruno shrugged his shoulders, got up and followed her into the kitchen.

From a distance Gomes could hear whispering that started low and increased in volume. Every so often he could make out a word or two, but he couldn't hear entire sentences. Suddenly Gomes heard Bruno say in a loud voice, "Alright, have it your way!" This was followed by some rattling noises. Gomes then saw Bruno with a tool box in hand walk to the front door and out of the house, slamming the door as he left. A minute later Susana returned with two steaming cups of coffee and a pleased look on her face.

23

"My apologies, Mister Gomes," Susana told Gomes once Bruno had left them. "My husband had a number of things on his mind and had some work to do outside on his truck. We can continue." She took a sip of her coffee, crossed her legs politely and looked over at Gomes. Her body language was changed: she sat up taller, stuck out her chin. Was she taking charge? He wasn't sure.

"Missus Da Silva, I'm trying to understand who your son is so I can draw a fair picture of him for my paper. People on the Cape who knew him described him as serious and 'the perfect gentleman.' He was also called a good worker."

Susana sipped more of her coffee, lost in thought.

"My son always wanted to go into the Air Force. He loved military airplanes. Any airplanes, for that matter, since he was a child." Susana told Gomes more about her son's history, with Gomes asking questions about Antonio as a boy and Susana easily responding. Gomes started to get a picture of an athletic and smart boy who loved to swim. When he was a teen-ager, he became a baseball player. He built models— particularly model airplanes—well into his teen years and always hoped to be able to fly planes.

When discussing her son, Susana seemed to become a different person: younger, less inhibited. She recounted how after high school graduation he had immediately joined the Air Force. While enlisted he wrote to her, but when he became an Air Commando his communication became less frequent. She could tell by some of his letters that he was deeply shaken by his experiences in Vietnam, though he did not go into detail. After leaving the service and coming home he said little about what had happened. Susana tried getting him to talk, but he was reluctant. Every so often she would hear him in his room crying.

Susana was not surprised when Antonio announced he was moving to California. When she heard that he disappeared and was presumed dead from drowning, she did not believe it because he had been such a good swimmer.

Susana had shown Gomes a few pictures of Antonio in an album from when he was a boy. There were pictures of other family members, including the Da Silva's daughter, who was a few years younger than Antonio.

Gomes knew that Mr. and Mrs. Da Silva needed to eat dinner. He started to put his things away when Susana asked, "Would you like to see some of the models that Tony made? I think that you'll be impressed."

"Of course, I'd love to see them," he said, though he was ready to get on the road back to the Cape. But it would have been impolite to refuse the offer.

Following Mrs. Da Silva, Gomes walked up the stairs, taking a U-turn at the top and walking a few feet down the hall to a small bedroom. Susana stood to the side and ushered him into the room.

There were two rows of shelving on the wall filled with an amazing variety of model planes. The shelving ran the length of the room and then a 90 degree turn, with shelving at the end of the room. Beneath the longer shelving was a desk. Opposite the desk, a couch. Gomes assumed the guest room had originally been Tony's bedroom.

The models were primarily military aircraft. Gomes recognized many of them. They started with World War I vintage planes, the rest were World War II and Korean War vintage. He looked at the models in utter amazement. The level of detail that had gone into building them was astounding. His attention was drawn to a model of a P-51 Mustang, one of the best pursuit fighter-planes of World War II, right next to, and Gomes could hardly believe this, a Me-262, the German jet plane that briefly saw service at the end of World War II. Gomes had never seen a model of the 262. There were bombers, including a B-17, B-24, B-25, and a B-29. Gomes noted that the models were placed in historical order. Near the entrance to the room were the most recent models from the Korean War period and afterwards. There was a Chinese-marked MiG-15 and MiG-17, as well as an F-86 Sabre Jet, each looking as if they could take off from the shelving itself.

"What an amazing collection!" Gomes exclaimed. "I have a friend that runs a hobby store in Hyannis and, let me tell you, he would be very impressed!"

A smile of pride on her face, Susana described how her son had worked long and hard on each model, taking them all very seriously. She also noted that he was VERY protective of his models.

"You know, Mister Gomes, once we had a relative living with us. They were going through some hard times and needed a place to stay, so they slept downstairs. In order to help around the house they did the cleaning. Well, one day they were cleaning in this room and they knocked over one of Tony's models. The model was cracked. When Tony got home he was beside himself. He yelled at this relative—who, by the way, was twice his age—and nearly went after him with a baseball bat. My relative was so upset that he left the house for the night. From that point on, Tony kept his door closed and cleaned his own room."

Susana shook her head in what appeared to be a mix of disbelief, humor and sadness. "And then he came home from the war. He didn't make any more models and he didn't discuss his planes. I asked him one day whether he wanted me to do anything with the models. His only reply was, 'Do what you want, Ma,' and that was it. He never spoke about the model planes again."

Still mesmerized by the models, Gomes nodded his head in thanks for letting him enter this museum. It was time to go.

Gomes would later ask himself whether it was a reflection from one of the lights in the room or whether it was just chance, but something to his left caught his eye as he was getting ready to leave the room. He stopped to look at a picture on the desk of a soldier encased in a glass frame. Gomes hadn't noticed it earlier because his attention had been riveted on the models.

The picture was of a young man, looking both serious, but mischievous, in a World War II uniform. The face looked familiar. "A relative, Missus Da Silva?" Gomes asked, curious.

Susana looked at the picture. "That man, Mister Gomes, was Antonio Tavares. He was my first husband and the natural father of my son, Tony. He was killed toward the end of World War II."

Gomes noticed tears welling up in Susana's eyes. He knew now was not the time to ask another question.

24

Gomes was seated on a stool in the kitchen listening to Susana Da Silva speak. She was standing with her back to him preparing a salad.

"Tony Senior was the love of my life, Mister Gomes. We were high school sweethearts and could not wait till we graduated so we could get married. But Tony was also in love with the idea of flying. He insisted that he needed to join what was then called the Army Air Corps. So, we graduated, got married, and he joined the Air Corps. He came home after training when he was on his way to Europe in late 1944. Well, let's just say that it was a nice visit and the next thing I knew, I was pregnant with Tony, Junior, or Little Tony as we called him. Tony Senior was killed in March 1945 in Italy trying to save the crew of his bomber. Tony Junior was born later that year and there I was, a widow with a baby.

"In 1947 I met Bruno. We got married and we had our daughter, Olivia. Bruno adopted Tony and raised him as his son," she added, chopping carrots; chopping them, suddenly, quite forcefully.

Gomes felt the depth of her sadness. Now a few pieces were coming together. "Missus Da Silva, was the fact of Tony Junior not being Mister Da Silva's natural son a problem between the two of them?"

"You're damned right it was!"

Startled by the voice, Gomes and Susana turned towards the entrance to the kitchen. They had no idea how long Bruno had been there. Clearly he was in a foul mood. "You're pretty fuckin' smart, Gomes. I knew that you were no dumb monkey when I first saw you."

Dumb monkey thought Gomes. Is this guy for real? But when Gomes looked into those very red eyes he realized this was going to get very complicated.

"That kid never gave me a fuckin' break. He never let me forget that I WAS NOT HIS *REAL* FATHER. He wouldn't let up. When he first found out that his *REAL* father had been a war hero, my God, he couldn't get over it. I mean I heard about it over and over. I had been nothing more than a GI during the war. I saw combat. I had bullets flying at me. but that wasn't enough for him to have a bit of pride in *me*. A bit of respect for what I'd done. But you know what, Gomes? What was worse was that any time I did ANYTHING that the kid didn't like, he'd lash out, saying things like *'My REAL father wouldn't have done that.'* I had to listen to that crap year after year.

"Any time I tried to discipline him or even instruct him, man, he would go running to his mother and complain that I was some ogre. And his *mother*," Bruno said looking directly at Susana, who had turned away from him and was completely silent. "His mother would come and tell ME I had to be more understanding. I mean, Gomes, what the fuck was I supposed to have done? I was trying to take care of the brat and all I got was that thrown back in my face."

Bruno stood there silent for a moment. Gomes could not tell whether he was awaiting a response. The lethal mix of anger and sadness in the man was overwhelming. Gomes didn't know what to say or do.

Bruno turned around and headed back out of the house, slamming the door behind him. Susana let out a sigh. "I apologize for that, Mister Gomes. Bruno did his best to raise Tony, but they had some difficult moments. You could see that in what he said. I've had the same discussion with him over the years. Bruno provided a home, clothes, and food for me and

Tony, and Olivia, of course, when she was born. But Bruno and Tony were like oil and water. When Tony needed something, Bruno would be there for him. But Bruno is no teddy bear. That's just not who he is. When Tony injured himself playing baseball at a game, Bruno took him to the doctor and sat there well into the night, even though he had to get up REALLY early the next morning."

Gomes thought that this was as good a time as any to excuse himself. There were many thoughts that came to mind, but emotions were running high. He thought perhaps he could pursue some of his questions later. He thanked Susana for her time and left the house. Her eyes were red and welling with tears.

It was dark and Gomes was not looking forward to driving home, particularly on an empty stomach, but he had no alternative. He stood on the porch for a moment, thought about how to get home and then started walking towards the car. Bruno Da Silva was sitting on the tailgate of his truck, seemingly looking off into space. Gomes said 'good night,' thanked him and kept walking towards the car.

"Hey, Gomes. You got kids?"

Gomes was startled by the question. He was not expecting Bruno to say anything to him. He turned towards Da Silva. The house lights illuminated the left side of Bruno's face.

"No, sir. No kids, no wife, and only sort of a girlfriend." Gomes tried to sound friendly and non-defensive.

Bruno got off of the tailgate and walked slowly and unstably over to Gomes. "It's no joke, Gomes. I married that woman when probably few other guys would've, despite the fact that she was a knock-out. She's *still* a knock-out." Bruno looked back at the house. "Most guys wouldn't have wanted to inherit a kid. You want your own kid. Well, I took on the kid, he was part of the package, you know? And I did my best, damn it. I did what I could to make sure that he was taken care of. But he kept getting in the way. He kept fuckin' with me. There's no other way to put it. He kept comparing me to his REAL father. Gomes, you can't compete with a ghost, particularly the ghost of a fuckin' hero!"

Gomes could see that Da Silva was really torn up. He couldn't tell if the man had been crying, but he could hear in his voice so many different emotions. Heard the pain and the sorrow.

"Did you love him, Mister Da Silva?" Gomes asked quietly.

Bruno stood there for a moment completely frozen in time. "What the fuck are you talking about, Gomes? I took care of the little snot."

"No, I was asking something else. Do you think that he felt that you cared about him?"

Da Silva then turned away and went back to his truck. Gomes walked over to his car, got in and started it up. He looked over at the house and the truck but saw no sign of Bruno Da Silva. Gomes made a U-turn and headed back to Route 6, and home. Preoccupied with thoughts about what he had just experienced with the Da Silva family, he did not notice a car turn on its headlights and follow him at a safe distance.

25

That next Sunday was a beautiful August day. Gomes and his 'sort-of' girlfriend Pamela Peters were driving to his parents place for dinner. Usually in jeans, Pamela's shapely legs and arms were on display in a knee-length green shift dress that highlighted her dark skin color and hazel eyes. She smelled of jasmine, which Gomes always found intoxicating.

David kept thinking about his using that term—"sort of girlfriend"—with Bruno Da Silva. David's parents adored Pamela and had been pushing him to make a commitment to her, but David was not sure. It was not that he felt unready or unprepared for marriage, he was more than in love with Pamela. He was not sure that Pamela really wanted marriage. She was a brilliant photographer, not able to make a living at it, so she had various odd-jobs to sustain herself. But her passion was photography and it was clear that she yearned to be a full-time professional photographer.

He was worried about getting in the way of Pamela's career. His parents did not really believe him when he tried explaining this, so when the issue came up, he would grow silent.

Though born on the Cape, Pamela grew up in Boston. She was Wampanoag and Black American. The Wampanoag had a high degree of inter-marrying with Black Americans, thus raising for some people the question as to what it meant to be Wampanoag, or for that matter, Black American.

Pamela was gorgeous. She was identifiable as 'black' but there were features of hers that were different. Her skin was the color of dark chocolate, and her black hair was wavy, not curly. Her eyes were hazel green, and there was something about them that was always friendly. She was the sort of person everyone wanted to be near, and every man wanted to love.

Some members of David's family were not as sanguine about his relationship with Pamela as were his parents. It was all about color. For several of his relatives, she was too dark. At a family gathering one of his relatives commented that her only saving grace was her "good hair." David walked away and left the affair.

But today was different. Uncle Al and Aunt Flora would be joining them. In the old days, Uncle Al—the brother of David's father—would have been described as a "race man." He and David's father were roughly the same color—a milk-chocolate brown—but Uncle Al was always ready to self-identify as Black." He was very proud of his Cape Verdean heritage, and let everyone know it. He was another person who always spoke about PAIGC leader Amilcar Cabral. About the same color as Uncle Al and with a pretty face, Aunt Flora was a real activist. She was involved in her union, the Amalgamated Clothing Workers of America. David often found leftist organization pamphlets at their home. Although Uncle Al could REALLY talk, Flora had one of the sharpest minds he had ever encountered. As a result, hanging out with his parents, Uncle Al and Aunt Flora was always exciting and interesting, filled with debate.

David turned into the driveway and saw Uncle Al's blue Chevy Impala. At the sound of the little Volkswagen, David's mother opened the door and greeted them with a hug and a kiss. She grabbed Pamela's arm and pulled her toward the kitchen while David walked into the living room. His father and Uncle Al were sitting there with the television on, a baseball game in the background while Aunt Flora went back and forth between the kitchen and the living room with drinks and snacks. She loved both baseball and football games and knew more sports statistics than both his father and Uncle Al combined.

David gratefully accepted Flora's offer of a beer as he relaxed on the couch. Al and his father were discussing the latest news about the Vietnam War. No one supported the war, they only differed on what it would take to get the USA out.

Absorbed in thoughts about the Smith murder, David realized he was more focused on the game than anything else. Pamela came out of the kitchen and joined them. Though not a sports fan, she got a tremendous kick out of how animated everyone would get. And she admired how Aunt Flora always settled any baseball dispute with a sharp observation of the play.

Soon David's mother announced dinner was ready. This Sunday they were treated to "polvo a modo ze de lino" (octopus stew) along with salad and beer. The dinner was terrific. Although David had learned to cook, more or less, he realized whenever he visited his parents that he was nothing in comparison to his mother. Or father.

His uncle and aunt had brought a pie along for dessert, but before they could dig into that David and Pamela cleaned off the table and began washing the dishes, drying and putting them away. They teased each other while completing the clean-up operation.

From the living room Uncle Al asked, "Well, nephew, are you working on anything that will win you a Pulitzer Prize?"

Uncle Al was only half joking. He had a strong admiration for David's writing, reading every article and asking questions about them. Uncle Al was more supportive of David's writing than his father, who pushed him to become a lawyer, while Uncle Al urged him to think about what was next after the Gazette.

"David is still working on the contractor murder story in

Osterville, Al," said his mother proudly.

"Yeah, Uncle Al, I'm still working on it. It's gotten a bit... complex. I'm not sure how much longer I can spend time on it, though the whole mystery is fascinating." David was speaking from the kitchen where he was washing dishes.

"Explain," said David's father from the living room, always a man of few words.

David walked away from the sink with a clean pot in his hand. He started to describe the latest steps he'd taken, choosing not to mention the meeting with the FBI over his stories about the Panthers and some Black radicals in Boston.

David took them through his discovery of the Da Silva family in Fall River. David's mother set out coffee cups and saucers, cream and sugar, Flora brought in the pie. "The big discovery is that the suspected killer was the child of a war hero from World War II named Tavares. A guy from New Bedford."

There was an episode from The Twilight Zone that David remembered where everything stopped for a moment in time and then, just as suddenly, time moved forward. There was the same sudden silence in the household. Pamela noticed it, too. Uncle Al's hand holding a coffee cup froze mid-way to his mouth. "Did you say, *Tavares*, nephew?" His voice was shaking.

"Yes, sir. Antonio Tavares was the name of the father *and* the son. When his mother remarried, her second husband adopted him and he became—"

"Da Silva." Uncle Al put his coffee down. He and Aunt Flora looked at each other, then at David's parents. There seemed to be a kind of telepathic conversation among the four of them in a period of, perhaps, five seconds.

"Antonio Tavares from New Bedford? Are you sure?" asked Uncle Al, while David's father looked over at him with a strangely supportive glance. Uncle Al looked very unsettled, moving back into the kitchen to get some more water.

"Yes, sir, that's the one. If you all don't mind my asking,

what's going on?" asked David.

"David," said Aunt Flora, "Antonio, or Tony Tavares as we knew him, was your uncle's best friend. And I was..." She stopped for a moment, collecting herself. "I was a good friend with his wife, Susana."

Uncle Al put an arm around Flora. David's parents kept silent, knowing that the story Al was about to tell would be difficult. And painful.

Uncle Al told David that he had been in the same high school class as Tony Tavares in New Bedford. David's father Jack, two years older, knew Tavares, but was not close with him. David's mother, Helena, never met Tavares. Aunt Flora, who was not yet involved with Al, though she knew him, was very close with Susana (at that time, Fonseca).

Al and Tavares both graduated high school in June, 1944, knowing they needed to go into the service. Tavares had always wanted to fly planes and was set on going into the Army Air Corps. Al assumed that he would go into the Army as an infantryman.

"After graduation we had to make our final decision about going into the service. We weren't going to wait for a draft notice. Well, Tony and I had been drinking and joking around, but then I got serious. I told him that 'Colored' flyers, as Blacks were called, had a unit that was trained in Tuskegee, Alabama. I joked with Tony that he was a 'Northern Boy' and I wasn't sure how well he'd get along in the South.

"Something happened in that moment. It was as if something snapped in him. I'd never seen this part of Tony before. We'd had serious discussions in the past—like when he told me he was going to propose to Susana after graduating. He started yelling that he wasn't really 'Colored' and that he was not going to serve in some *'Nigger'* unit. *His* words, nephew.

"Let me be clear, that Tony was Portuguese only in the way that many Cape Verdeans used to think of ourselves. He was Cape Verdean but *very* light-skinned. If you saw him you would not assume that he had any of *us* in him. You know, any African, but that's another story. Everyone in our community knew he wasn't white."

Al looked over at David's father who nodded his agreement with Al, then he looked at Flora. "Nephew, Tony said some things that night I'll never forget. He said that no one was going to tell him where to go. He started accusing me of being a coward and said some other really shameful things."

Al got up and walked back to the kitchen. Flora said, "David, the day after that fight between Tony and Al they ran into each other. Tony offered him a strange apology and patted him on the back, literally. They went their separate ways and never saw each other again. Al went into the infantry, fighting in a Black unit in Italy. Tony went to Italy, too, but in the Air Corps."

Al returned to the room with a glass of whiskey. His eyes were downcast, his voice, laden with sadness. "Tony came home after training before he was deployed overseas. He and Susana were already married. They'd had a small wedding after graduation. Only invited family.

"When I was in Italy I got word from Susana that he'd been killed. It was some sort of accident. What I didn't realize is that the guy had saved his plane by knocking a bomb loose in the bomb-bay of his B-24. In the process he lost his footing and fell to his death."

As Al took a needed sip of the whiskey, Flora added, "The Army presented Susana with a medal on behalf of Tony. Anyone and everyone who could speak Portuguese and Krioulo showed up. Everyone was so *proud* of him. They named a street after him, and later on, a library."

"What a sad story," said Pamela. "I guess there were a lot of them from the war, like today. Viet Nam."

Al said, "I don't think your aunt has ever been able to come to terms with what happened next."

Before Al or Flora could continue, David's father leaned

forward. "Son, it's hard to explain what happened after the War. I mean, you've seen people come back from Vietnam, but it was different. Suddenly all these veterans were returning, pretty much at the same time, and trying to get on with their lives, but, you know, some people never returned home. All these guys coming home reminded women like Susana of what they lost. She just came apart. I didn't know her well, but I saw that the lady was in a lot of pain."

"Susana gave birth to Little Tony," Flora said. "She asked me to be the godmother and asked your uncle to be the godfather. He and I had started to date after he returned from the War. Of course we accepted that responsibility. And we took it seriously! We both did what we could to support her and the baby, Susana was living with her parents. Your uncle loved Little Tony almost like a son."

The warm smile on Flora's face faded. "In early '47, Susana was working in a grocery store not far from Route 6. This guy came into the store, a truck driver, and struck up a conversation. It was the guy that she eventually married. Bruno. He lived in Fall River but drove a truck in southern New England for some company, and stopped in New Bedford every so often. He started to drop by the grocery store and speak with her. Eventually they started to date.

"Susana felt a little guilty, she had been so much in love with Big Tony. She never thought she could love again. But she was a war widow and this guy, he was sort of good looking for a white guy, took an interest in her. So, she decided to go forward.

"Susana introduced me to Bruno. Look, I was excited about meeting him and I was happy that she was happy. But when I met him it was strange. He looked at me oddly, like with no feeling, even though he knew I was Susana's best friend. He was polite but had little to say. Susana could sense that something was wrong and she kept talking, like she was speaking for both of them.

"After that, it just kept going downhill. I thought maybe Bruno had been in a bad mood, so I suggested that the four of us go out together. Well, it didn't happen. She told me that Bruno was kind of private, so I dropped the matter. I kept trying to see Susana, because we were good friends, she never seemed available, or if she was, only for short periods of time."

"It even got difficult for me to see Little Tony," said Al. "There was always an excuse, like Little Tony had to go to the doctor, or Bruno was taking him out or something."

"Well," said Flora with a sigh, "it all came to a head when I got word that Susana and Bruno were getting married. I waited and waited to see when she would tell me. Finally I couldn't take it and I went down to the grocery store and confronted her.

"Susana got very embarrassed. She told me that Bruno had insisted on a family wedding and that friends wouldn't be there. Just like when she married Tony, she told me. She would be moving to Fall River where he had a floor in a two-family house and they could save up and buy a home. She promised to have some of her girlfriends over, eventually."

Flora stopped and all was silent.

"I'm guessing she never had you over?" said David, softly.

"There was no gathering. Even worse, there *were* friends at the wedding, just not *her* friends. Bruno had all of his Portuguese pals there, and Susana just a few of her family."

"Did you ever see her again, Aunt Flora?" asked David.

"Yes, from a distance some years later when she was in New Bedford. One time I saw her getting out of a car with two kids near her folks' home. She looked over and saw me, but then she looked away and pretended to have not seen me. Your Uncle kept sending Little Tony Christmas gifts and a gift on his birthday. Susana responded with a little note in the beginning, but after a while there was nothing."

"Well, Flora, not quite nothing," interrupted Al. "Remember, at a certain point Little Tony began sending me notes?"

Flora nodded her head. "Yes, Al, I'd forgotten. I don't even know whether Jack and Helena know about this."

"I think Little Tony was in his early teens. He sent me a letter after I'd sent him a present. His birthday, maybe, I can't remember. He said that his mother had told him about his actual father, Big Tony, and that he wanted to know about his dad. To say I was shocked would be mild. I couldn't believe it. I spoke with Flora about it and then wrote Little Tony a note about his father. For a few years, probably until he graduated from high school, he kept in touch. I don't know whether Susana or Bruno knew. He would ask me about his father, about World War II, about growing up in New Bedford."

Al looked at the pie, as yet untouched. "Isn't anyone going to have some pie?" Helena cut slices and gave them while Pamela refilled the coffee cups. "You know, Flora, he did write me after he left high school when he was in basic training, and I think one letter when he was in Vietnam. That last one was creepy. I don't remember the details, but I do remember feeling very uneasy after reading it. Something was bothering him."

David didn't know if he should feel lucky or cursed, his own family was a part of the murder investigation. Driving Pamela home, he told her, "I'm not sure I can cite my uncle and aunt in a story about the murder, it doesn't feel right." Pamela suggested he use the old 'anonymous sources'.

David worried how his boss at the paper would take the new twist in his investigation. For once he wished his sources really were anonymous.

26

The following Friday Gomes was sitting in Hank's store drinking a cup of coffee, filling Hank in on the story of Shepherd/Da Silva/Tavares. There was no one else in the store. Hank listened carefully, the fan humming in the background, for once, he wasn't pressing Gomes about his relationship with Pamela.

"David, the military was segregated during most of World War II. You knew that, didn't you?"

"Yeah, I guess so. What's your point?"

"Well, you're telling me that this guy who was actually Colored, or these days they would say 'Black,' went into the Army Air Corps and didn't go into an all-Black unit. Right?"

"Yeah, I guess that's what I'm saying. My uncle didn't go into a lot of detail about it."

"Hmm," said Hank, cracking his knuckles, a habit that irritated Gomes, though he never said so. "A black man would be crazy to try and pass on a white unit. Do you know the name of the plane he was on?"

"No, I don't. Just that it was a bomber."

Hank walked over to his desk, reached for a pad of paper and jotted down a few notes. "I have a few friends in the military. I'm going to ask a few questions, okay with you?"

"Of course, Hank, what are you thinking? What kind of friends?"

"You don't need to know. Besides, I'm not sure I'll find anything useful, I just have this itch that I can't scratch. There's something odd about a guy who passed for white all through the war and was a decorated hero. Anyway, let me do some checking and if you get additional info, give me a ring. Ok?"

"Will do. You know, they said that Tavares was very light-skinned. I hadn't thought much about the situation during World War II. By the time I got into the Army it was fully integrated."

Gomes sat for a moment reflecting on how much he didn't know about Hank. He was always a man of some mystery, a fact that Gomes had long accepted. The journalist in him wanted to ask questions, the friend in him knew it was better to let sleeping dogs lie.

<>

When Gomes got back to his office, Jacqueline walked over to his desk and had a seat as soon as he'd settled into his chair. "David, we need to talk."

Gomes kept quiet, unsure what to expect.

"David, you have spent a lot of time on the TJ Smith murder case. You have written some excellent articles. People on the Cape are talking about your work, but it feels to me that it is time to move on. I'm not sure what more you expect to uncover, but there are other stories that I need you to work on." Jacqueline had that serious 'I mean business' look in her eye that Gomes had learned to respect. .

"Listen, boss, I realize I've spent a lot of time on this, but I need your support. There's something very odd about this whole matter and I feel like I'm on the verge of putting two and two together."

"Meaning what, David?"

"Jacqueline, we have a situation where this otherwise well-respected contractor is assassinated with—as it turns out—a .270 caliber bolt action rifle. The rifle was almost certainly silenced. The police believe the assassin was a member of the victim's work crew who, it now turns out, had been reported dead in California. *He*, the suspect was originally from Fall River and was the child of a Cape Verdean war hero from World War II."

"That does have a lot of local connections, I admit," said Jacqueline.

"I don't have the missing link, other than both the war hero Tavares and the murder victim Smith served in World War II. And both, it appears, were in the Army Air Corps. The unanswered question is this: what would lead the suspect to want to kill TJ Smith in the first place?"

"Yes, this is most interesting, my David, but there are many unanswered questions. How will you ever answer them?"

"I feel like I can if you allow me to pursue this. Although my friend, Detective Amato, remains interested, the trail is getting cold and he has other cases to handle. I'm afraid that investigation will just die on the vine."

Jacqueline sat considering his request. The phone at her desk rang, but she ignored it. "So why, David, do you think that you can find out things that the police cannot? You are not a detective, and I don't want you pretending to be one."

"I've tapped into some things that the police haven't. And boss, there's one more thing. It's kind of delicate." Jacqueline waited, not liking 'delicate' issues, they usually caused the paper problems.

"This story is getting...personal. It appears that my family had a relationship with the suspect's father. Now I'm feeling that I have some responsibility to my family to uncover some answers. I know that may sound like gibberish, but it's the best that I can offer."

Jacqueline did not look happy. Or sympathetic. "David, you have been able to keep up with your other writing assignments so I have not closed the gate on this case. But you have spent a lot of time on this story and I am not sure that it is any longer worth it."

"I understand. I'm just asking for your patience."

Giving him one more week, and no longer, Jacqueline stood up, nodded, and returned to her desk. Gomes realized he did not have endless time to pursue this, and that he had a call to make.

27

Gomes pulled into the driveway of the home of the late TJ Smith, got out of his car and walked over to the door. He rang the bell, hearing the chimes play a melody. Before the tune was finished, he heard, "Welcome, David." Margie Smith, dressed in painter's pants and a man's work shirt, was in the open door smiling at him. "Please come in."

Mrs. Smith escorted Gomes to the living room, where she offered him something to drink. He accepted her offer of water and sat in the living room while she went into the kitchen to get it. Gomes was surprised when he heard footsteps, followed by Frank Smith's entry. Frank was looking very casual, wearing a faded T-shirt with the word "Provincetown" and a picture of a sand dune on it. He also wore a baseball cap backwards, looking the part of a catcher at a game.

"Frank, I thought you were going into the Coast Guard!" said Gomes.

"Yeah, Mister Gomes, I am. But when my father was killed I was able to get some more time from the Coast Guard so I could help Ma with a few things around here and with the business. I'm being inducted in two weeks."

"I'm glad you're able to help your Mom."

Margie entered the room with the water, handed the glass to Gomes, and sat down. "So, Mr. Gomes, you telephoned me. What can I do for you?"

Gomes took her through an update on the case. She leaned forward listening intently, clearly fascinated.

"Uh, Missus Smith, did your husband by ANY chance

know an Antonio Tavares? You mentioned he was in the Air Corps in Italy. I'm trying to figure out why Tavares's son would target your husband."

"Tavares, you say?" She sat a moment thinking. "I *think* my husband knew a Tavares...Let me check." She walked into the kitchen, bringing back her index card file box, the cards arranged alphabetically.

"Tavares...Tavares...Tavares...yes, Mister Gomes, he did know a Tavares. *Paul* Tavares from Wareham. I remember him. A nice young Portuguese man who was a contractor like TJ. They worked on some projects together. But, you said 'Antonio,' didn't you?"

"Yes, Antonio."

She closed the file box looking frustrated.

"Let's try this a different way. Are there any things that TJ brought back from the War that could give me a clue as to what it was like, who he knew...you know, things like that?"

Frank signaled to his mother that he would go and get something. He returned with a manila envelope on which was written "World War II." He pulled out a variety of items, including pictures, letters, and other odds and ends. Gomes looked over at Mrs. Smith who nodded that he should feel free to look through the material.

What immediately drew his attention were the photographs. There was a photograph of TJ as a young enlistee. Smith had aged well, looking at the time of his death not much different from the picture. There was a picture of a house on the back of which was the word, "Rome." There was a picture of TJ and another man with their arms around one another's shoulders.

"Who is this, Missus Smith?" Gomes pointed at the man in the picture with TJ.

"That's Al Gierek. I believe you spoke with him on the phone."

Gomes nodded in agreement, then continued looking at

the photos. There was a picture of a group of men standing in front of a bomber. Gomes could not tell what the plane was from the picture, he was not as good as Hank in identifying planes, especially bombers. But on the side of the bomber near the cockpit the name Lucky Legs was written. There was a drawing of a woman with her legs crossed, leaning against an invisible wall right above the name.

"'*Lucky Legs*'?" Gomes asked.

"Oh, Mister Gomes," Margie started, blushing, "the guys would name their planes all sorts of things. That was theirs!" Gomes smiled as he looked more steadily at the picture.

Margie pointed out her husband, who was standing slightly to the left of the person in the center, the pilot, Captain Jansen from Green Bay, Wisconsin. She also pointed out Gierek again, in case Gomes was unsure. "That one there to the right of the captain is the co-pilot, Mister DiUbaldo," said Margie. "I have only vague memories of the names of the other members of the crew."

Gomes put the photo down and looked at the other memorabilia. There were some letters that TJ had received while away, mainly from family. There was a Purple Heart, which Margie explained TJ had won after being shot and critically injured when a German fighter attacked his bomber. TJ shot down the fighter, she noted with great pride, though he was badly injured.

Though Gomes found all of this interesting, it did not get him any closer to the answers that he needed. Margie continued talking about TJ and World War II, about some of the difficulties he had seen among the Italian population, and some funny stories TJ had told her over the years. Gomes was only half listening. He kept asking himself: *What am I missing?*

Gomes closed his note pad, put it in his jacket pocket and got ready to leave. He stopped for a moment to look back at the photographs. There was something odd about the photo of the bomber's crew. He noticed that there was a crease along the photo that cut off part of the bomber and cut into the picture of the man standing to the far left of the pilot. Gomes picked up the picture again and looked at it.

The picture was somewhat distorted by the crease but the face caught Gomes's attention. He studied the picture, looking first at the person located near the crease and then at each other person in the photograph. He sat there for a moment, stunned. "Missus Smith, do you know this person here, near the crease in the photo?"

Margie examined it, a blank expression on her face. " I had forgotten all about him. My husband called him 'TeeTee.' That's all that I remember."

"Yeah, Mister Gomes, Tee-Tee. Ma, you must remember. That's the guy that I used to call 'The man who fell from the sky.'" Frank said it with a strange look on his face.

Gomes sat there looking at the photograph with the face of Antonio "Tony" Tavares staring at the camera: *the man who fell from the sky.*

28

Holding the old photograph up, Gomes said, "Missus Smith, this is *the* Antonio Tavares that I was mentioning. He's the war hero-father of the Teddy Shepherd the police are looking for.

Margie Smith seemed to have lost the color in her face. Frank spoke for her: "My father called him Tee-Tee, Mister Gomes. I remember when I was just a kid he told me the story of Tee-Tee and how he fell out of the plane. I never forgot that story and I would ask my father about it from time to time, but he never liked discussing it."

Still silent, Margie Smith seemed to be looking at Gomes but not seeing him. "Mister Gomes, my father told me that Tee-Tee saved their plane from exploding. There was a bomb stuck in the bomb-bay and he went back to deal with it. He and the bomb fell. He was a hero!"

"Tee-Tee," muttered Margie. "Tony Tavares. You know, in all the time that I had known TJ and been married to him, he never told me why they called him 'Tee-Tee.' I never put together that it was '*TT*' and not '*Tee-Tee*.' Stupid me. I thought that it had something to do with him being young and they were making fun of him or something."

"Mister Gomes," said Frank, "do you think that Da Silva or Tavares, whatever his name is holds or held *my* father responsible for the death of his father?"

"That's a good guess, Frank. Based on what you've told me and what my own family has said, I can't imagine why he would, unless Little Tony—as his mother calls him—somehow flipped out and needed someone to blame."

"That must be one hell of a 'flipping out,' said Frank. "I mean, after all this time, and to plot out a killing like that. That's not just holding my father responsible, that's some serious hatred."

Gomes could only nod in agreement. He looked over at Margie Smith who was shaking her head but saying nothing, tears welling up in her eyes.

Getting up to leave, Gomes thanked them for their time and asked them to get back with him if they thought of anything. He promised to keep them updated as well.

As he moved towards the door, Frank called out to him. "Mister Gomes, I remember something that may or may not be of importance." Gomes turned toward Frank.

"The last time that Mister and Missus Gierek visited us, in the early spring as my mom told you, Mister Gierek and my father spent a lot of time together. They seemed to be talking about something very important but they didn't let on. I asked father. All he said was that they were talking about old times. He tried to crack a smile but I could see in his eyes he was putting on an act.

"Well, my dad and Mister Gierek went out for a walk, and when they came back into the house I heard Mister Gierek say something like, 'it's just about scaring us…'"

"What was he talking about?"

"I have no idea. But I did see Mister Gierek show my dad something in an envelope. I couldn't see what it was. When my dad saw that I was looking at them, he stuffed the envelope into his pocket."

"Missus Smith, did you ask your husband about any of this after the Giereks left?"

"No. Frank mentioned it to me but I told him to stop being a busy-body. I told TJ that Frank was worried about him, but TJ just waved his hand and mumbled something, and that was it. You know, as Frank told you when we met, TJ was in a funny mood and I really didn't like pushing him. I wish...I wish that I had taken the whole thing more seriously." Margie shook her head, saying nothing more.

Gomes thanked them again, then headed back to his car. He was so distracted by his thoughts about the meeting that he didn't notice there was a car parked across from the Smith home. When Gomes pulled out, the car followed, the driver only turning on head lights once the two cars joined other traffic.

29

When Gomes walked into his house he was thinking about the face of Antonio Tavares in the photograph staring back at him. He decided his first task, despite his hunger, was to call Vincent Amato.

Amato never spoke much about his personal life, not even to Gomes. Gomes had met Amato's wife, Connie, a few times. When Gomes had visited their home for dinner a couple of times, his attempts to draw Connie into the conversation inevitably failed. Amato would sometimes engage her when Gomes was there, but other times he would act as if she was not there at all. This was not the sort of relationship that Gomes could ever imagine having.

Connie answered the phone. Before Gomes could ask her about how she was doing, she told him that Vinnie was there.

"I'm eating, Gomes. Can I call you later?" Amato didn't sound unfriendly, just distracted, as if he was chewing something.

"This will be quick, *Vincent*," responded Gomes. He only called Amato "Vincent" when he was being quite serious. "The connection between TJ Smith and the presumed killer—Da Silva—is definitely Da Silva's father, Antonio Tavares Senior. Tavares and Smith were crewmen of the same bomber during World War II, the *Lucky Legs*. Tavares was killed in an accident. Da Silva must have held Smith responsible for the death of his father."

There was silence on the other end of the phone. Amato must have walked out of the dining room since Gomes could no longer hear the television, which had been on when Connie picked up the phone.

"Alright, Gomes. Good work. But, let's say that's all true and Da Silva spent a lot of time putting this whole thing together. Why do that? Why not just come up to him and blow him away? He could have shot him any time. He had a high-powered silenced rifle. Why wait? Why the drama?"

"I don't have a good answer for that, but I think it ties in with that whole thing with the bank. Da Silva was not settling for killing Smith, he wanted to totally discredit him. That takes time. That's my best guess."

Amato was silent for a moment. "Listen, I'm glad you called. The FBI continues to ask questions about you. They're asking about things connected to the TJ Smith case, but they keep bringing up your connection with the Black Panther Party and the other militants in Boston."

"Yeah, the jerks came by my house the other day. I don't have a connection with the Panthers, Amato. I wrote a damned story about them, you know that. The guys in Boston are just friends, and not even close friends. What the hell is going on?" Gomes was frustrated and angry, his words becoming more forceful.

"Yeah, I know, Gomes," started Amato, "but don't kill the messenger." Gomes could hear the 'smile' in Amato's voice. "Listen, Gomes, they want to talk to you again, at least that's what they implied. I've been telling them there's nothing that you know that would help them, though this information about Da Silva's father might be valuable to them."

"Amato, let me be clear about something. I have nothing...I repeat, nothing more to say to them. If they want to speak with me, tell them *to contact my paper and our lawyer will arrange a meeting.* Tell them to get out of their tree and come back to earth. There's no connection between this case and the Panthers or any radical group."

"Alright, Gomes, have it your way. I'm just telling you."

"Vinnie, is that not good enough for you? Do you think that I should get on my knees for these guys?"

"Cool off, Gomes. I believe you. I just don't want to see you in any trouble with the effing FBI."

Hanging up with Amato, Gomes dialed Hank Matthews' line. "Hank, this is David. I'm sorry to bother you at home."

"No bother, David, what's going on?"

Gomes had never been to Hank's place. As far as Gomes could tell he lived by himself in Hyannis, not far from the Ocean Street docks. Gomes often thought of Hank's lifestyle as that of a monk, and he sometimes wondered whether Hank was doing penance for something.

"The plane, Hank," David continued with excitement. "Tavares and Smith were on the same bomber, Lucky Legs. A B-24. TJ's widow has a picture of the entire crew, and there on the edge was Antonio Tavares. TJ's kid called him 'the man who fell from the sky.'"

"David, this should be helpful. What else do the Smiths know about it?"

"Not much more. Does it mean anything to you?"

"Let me see what I can find out. I'll get back with you. No guarantees, my friend. I assume you don't have the serial number of the plane?"

"Sorry, all I have is the name, Lucky Legs."

"Not a problem. Let me look into this." Hank clicked off, another of his habits Gomes tolerated. Maybe that's how monks handle the telephone.

30

Labor Day weekend was a special time for the Gomes/Alves family. On the Sunday just before the holiday David's parents always hosted a large family gathering at their Mashpee home. From across New England family members from both the Gomes and as many of the Alves clans who were willing to socialize would converge on the family home, where Jack and Helena set up what looked like an encampment. Their large backyard had tents and barbecue grills, coolers with beer and soda, and tables with paper and plastic cups. Towards the end of the day, Helena would prepare strong coffee to ensure that all the family members and guests made it back home in one piece.

When he was younger, David looked forward to these family gatherings. Over the years, however, something seemed to have changed. He could never quite put his finger on it. He would almost always have a good time, but he felt less and less connected to these gatherings.

David promised he would drop by a little early to help with the set-up. Pamela rode with David to his parent's home. She enjoyed these Labor Day gatherings, feeling very much at home, which was not surprising given how much Jack and Helena adored her. And who they approved meant an automatic pass in all family gatherings, a fact that David was reflecting upon while making the quick drive to his parent's home.

Pamela, dressed for the cookout wearing sandals, jeans and a sleeveless white blouse, was in her own thoughts as

Gomes briefly looked over at her while stopped at a traffic light. As the light changed he moved the car forward, thinking about the "protocols" that operated at the Gomes/Alves family gatherings.

Family gatherings were not particularly inclusive. You had to be 'cleared' by David's parents or by his Aunt Denise.

As the car approached the Gomes/Alves home, David thought about his conversation with Jacqueline and then reflected on the experiences of those who were not given a 'pass' by either his parents or Aunt Denise.

If you were not given a 'pass', but invited by another family member, irrespective of being distant family or friend, there was something that was akin to a gauntlet, though it was not run all at once. You would be introduced and everyone would be both polite and friendly. Later, when you were relaxed, several family members, usually the women, would approach you and begin what was lovingly known as 'the interrogation.' A series of questions would be posed ranging from whether you were a relative or not. If a friend, were you Cape Verdean, Portuguese or something else? What type of job you had or what school you attended, what ability you had—especially if you were a woman—to cook and, if so, Krioulo food or not. If a male, one could expect the interrogation to involve, first, women family members and, later, an extensive round of drinks with the men, where some of the same and different questions were posed. While no one was ever expelled from a family gathering, if some key family members were not pleased with the answers from the 'interrogation', the guest would find themselves distanced by the family. They wouldn't appear at future family gatherings.

Pamela had never been subjected to the 'interrogation,' though as an outsider she received various comments, most flattering, but some not. Some relatives would make a point—usually in jokes—that she was not Cape Verdean. Other comments complimented her hair and by implication, did not complement her black skin. But Pamela was a trooper and got past it.

"Pamela!" yelled Helena as they entered the house. "If you hadn't brought David, I don't know what we would've done. Lord, do we need some help today!" Everyone smiled at Helena's joking. David could always tell that she wanted Pamela and him to tie the knot.

Jack was heating up a grill, as well as cooking *jag*. He waved to David and Pamela and pointed outside to where they needed help setting up. It was nearly noon and a couple of family members were already in attendance, sitting in some shade drinking beer.

Shortly after noon more family members arrived, some with friends. David watched carefully to check out the pecking order. He never participated in the gauntlet, making a point of welcoming everyone to his family's home. Jack and Helena were equally polite, though if they were not familiar with someone they tended to keep some distance.

Aunt Denise arrived bringing with her *gufongs*—a cornmeal donut—which was very popular. Everyone looked forward to them. Uncle Al and Aunt Flora arrived a few minutes later bringing plenty of beer—a mix of Narragansett and Budweiser—along with *linguica* sandwiches.

Suddenly what had been a relatively quiet family gathering became a festival. David took control of the stereo, after having repositioned the speakers, and it was party time. David was the principal "DJ" at family gatherings. He knew how to mix Cape Verdean music, particularly *morna* and *colodeira*, with African American jazz and soul music. His family loved it and he would always receive accolades for his choices of music, even from the younger family members who were more interested in soul and rock, less attracted to music from the homeland.

David felt relaxed. The food was good, Pamela looked amazing, and David loved her long earrings. She was obviously having a great time, with no interrogations. His parents were hugging each other, cooking and serving, always with smiles on their faces. It just felt right.

Which was why David realized that it could not last all night without some sort of incident.

It started in connection with a bottle of *Mateus* wine, though it could have been ignited by any number of things. It was slowly getting dark. Everyone was sharing insect repellent to keep the bugs away. Slowly, over the afternoon, the family and friends had segmented into groups, periodically coming back together and then retreating into their 'corners' to have more intimate discussions. Some of the younger folks had insisted that David play some soul dance music. David obliged with everything from James Brown to the Jackson 5 to the Temptations. With pride he played the music of the Tavares brothers from New Bedford, who performed as the band Chubby & the Turnpikes. Gomes thought they had potential to become nationally known.

While the music played, several relatives asked David about the story he had written on the Osterville murder. Uncle Al stood with David during much of this, filling in family and friends on some of the historical background on World War II and the other Tavares family. David tried to be respectful of his uncle, though having had some whiskey and a couple of beers, Uncle Al was ready to tell stories. As time went on he inserted himself more and more into the conversation as if he were the one writing the story.

David knew how alcohol enhanced Uncle Al's storytelling capacities: he became loud and playful. At that point Aunt Flora would rescue her husband, escorting him to the location of the hottest and strongest coffee.

David was in the middle of a discussion with his cousin's friend from Boston, explaining the steps that he had taken to find the apparent murderer when he noticed Uncle Al was no longer sitting near him. David sighed with relief, though he was uneasy about this gorgeous woman standing in front of him with dark, inquisitive eyes. Her name was Carmen and she was a close friend of his cousin Angelita. He could not tell whether she was Cape Verdean; he had not gotten her last name. She was very light-skinned, with straight hair and dark eyebrows, but she could have been Puerto Rican, Portuguese or a Black American., It didn't matter, what mattered was that he was engrossed in this conversation, she was beautiful, Pamela was not there and this could get uncomfortable.

He had just put on "Evil Ways" by Santana and was trying to figure out how to get out of this exchange with Carmen before his attraction to her and her apparent attraction to him became evident to all around. That's when he heard Uncle Al yell, "What the hell is this bottle of *Mateus* doing here!?"

Other voices quieted down in the backyard for a moment and then resumed their volume. Almost. David looked away from Carmen wondering what was happening. To his left, under one of the tents but near some trees, David saw some of his older relatives. Uncle Al was standing, saying something which David could not quite make out. Aunt Flora was on the move from the house over to Uncle Al, making David think of a fire engine rushing to a fire.

There was something about Uncle Al's voice and his animation that concerned David. He signaled to his cousin Joe, an 18 year old from Wareham who had served as a family DJ on several occasions.

"Hey, Joe, would you take over for me for a second? I need to check on something."

"Yeah, no problem. I heard it, too," Joe responded with a wink, looking over in the direction of Uncle Al.

David excused himself from the discussion with Carmen, who looked a bit confused by all that was unfolding. She mumbled something politely to David and touched his hand lightly as he turned over the stereo to Joe and headed toward Uncle Al.

As David got closer to the group of 6 family members he noticed they were seated or standing in a circle. One of David's uncles, Marcelino, his mother's brother, was in the middle of making an argument, pointing his right index finger at Uncle Al. Al never appreciated anyone pointing a finger at him, it had something to do with when he was in the Army.

"Listen, Al!" David heard his Uncle Marcelino yell. "Every time we get together you get on your high horse and start telling the rest of us what to think about Cape Verde, Portugal, Blacks in America, Vietnam, you name it. You keep 'talking about Cabral. Cabral, Cabral, Cabral. Give it a rest! Listen, we're Portuguese. Yeah, our families are from Cape Verde, but we're Portuguese. I'm sick of you calling me 'black.' Our ancestors were never slaves!"

The irony of Uncle Marcelino's statement was not lost on Uncle Al or David. Despite the fact that his and Helena's mother was Portuguese from the Azores, Uncle Marcelino was born looking darker, like his father, someone who would be identified as "Black" on any street in the United States. But in his own mind, that was a different story.

"Marcelino, you are so full of shit it's coming out your ears," Al responded, pushing Marcelino's finger away and slurring the 'your' in an even more exaggerated southeastern New England way. "We gather together as family and we should be able to talk bluntly. We're Cape Verdeans, and sitting here in the middle of our party is this damn bottle of *Mateus* to remind us that our people are subjects of fascist Portugal. Did you send flowers to Salazar's funeral, too?" Al was clearly trying to provoke Marcelino with his reference to the long-time Portuguese dictator Antonio Salazar.

Aunt Flora maneuvered over to Uncle Al's side and grabbed his arm. She whispered something to him.

"Yeah, Flora, get him the hell out of here before he hurts himself," said Marcelino in a dismissive manner, grabbing a bottle of beer he had been nursing.

Al looked at him with contempt. "You son of a—"

David jumped into the middle of the group just as Al stepped toward Marcelino, his hands balled into fists. "Okay, family, my mom is fixing some great coffee and I want to encourage you all to get some and take a break. Always glad we can have a healthy debate here at the house, but let's take it easy."

David could see that the argument had gone WAY beyond differences of views this time. As Aunt Flora pulled him, Al yelled, "You, Marcelino, thinking that you're actually Azorean or something...that's the kind of shit that got Tony Tavares in trouble!"

"You don't get it, Al. You keep talking this black shit. We're not *black*. Tony wanted to be accepted for what he *was* and not get treated second class. He didn't have a god damn thing in common with Negroes! Or should I say 'Blacks'?" Marcelino said the word with a sneer.

"I don't believe—" Al started, but Flora pulled him away, cutting him off in mid-sentence. Just as she pulled him up to the house, cousin Joe put on a Jackson 5 song and pumped up the volume loud enough to drown out the rest of the conversation. The younger folks jumped up and started to dance. David smiled at Joe as he moved away from the group and back towards the stereo.

As David resumed his DJ role, Joe grabbed a soda and sat by the stereo system looking around the backyard at everyone partying. David barely noticed when Uncle Al sat down next to him. Aunt Flora kissed Al on the forehead and headed into the house shouting something to Helena.

Uncle Al had a cup of coffee in his hand. He kept his face focused on the coffee, his head shaking sadly. David said nothing.

"You see, nephew," Al started as if he was continuing a conversation that had started earlier, "you see, that's what I was talking about."

"What's that, Uncle Al?" David asked.

"When I was telling you about Big Tony. What you just saw in Marcelino is the same shit that I heard from Big Tony. There was no more point in trying to talk sense into Marcelino than there was trying to talk sense into Tony. They're both in another world. It's pathetic!" Al shook his head again as he looked at the coffee.

"That poor, dumb bastard," Al continued, though it wasn't clear whether he was talking about Tony Tavares, Marcelino or someone else. He just kept looking into his coffee repeating the same words. In the distance David could hear Marcelino laughing and carrying on as if nothing had ever happened.

David thought it was definitely time for the party to come to an end.

31

The mass exodus of tourists at the end of the summer always brought a complicated mix of emotions to people on the Cape. It was an eternal subject of discussion between Gomes and other permanent Cape residents. The tourists would leave immediately after Labor Day—if not ON Labor Day—and the businesses that had opened for them shut down almost overnight. The Cape became a different place.

Things remained slow on the Osterville/Tavares story. The FBI seemed to vanish. Gomes had called Gierek again, but got nothing new. When Gomes told him the story about Tavares, Gierek repeated that there had been an accident in the bomber that killed Big Tony. Gierek closed off by referencing Big Tony as a "hero" and how tragic the whole situation had been.

September 19th hit Gomes like compressed air. The heat of the summer had dissipated and it was getting cooler but remained comfortable. With no plans for this particular Saturday, Gomes sat in his apartment drinking coffee and listening to the news when the phone rang. "Hello," Gomes answered.

"David, did you hear the news? Did you hear about Jimi Hendrix?" said Pamela in a frantic voice.

"Yeah, I heard. I can't believe it. I mean, we just saw that Woodstock film. I can't believe he would kill himself. Maybe drugs, but I don't want to believe that either. What a loss… What a disaster!"

Gomes had not always been a Hendrix fan, but the

flamboyant guitar player had grown on him. Watching and listening to Hendrix play his rendition of the "Star Spangled Banner" at the 1969 Woodstock Festival really shook Gomes. For the most part he was not into rock music, having been raised mainly on jazz by his parents, but Hendrix was something special, and that tune, with its sound of bombs falling and exploding resonated throughout his body and soul.

"David, let's get together today," said Pamela. "We shouldn't be home sitting by ourselves."

"Yeah, you're right. I'll pick you up later. Let's drive up to P-town and hang out. Nothing special. Get some clams or something." He was trying to build his spirits. Going to Provincetown, depending on the traffic, was always a pleasure for David, and with the tourists gone, traffic shouldn't be a problem. Gomes finished his coffee, grabbed his keys and a jacket and headed to the car.

When he drove up to her house, Pamela was outside waiting. She was wearing bell-bottom jeans, a nicely fitting long-sleeve blouse and a New York Mets baseball cap. The Mets cap was something she would do just to taunt Gomes, who was a Red Sox fan. The Mets victory in the 1969 World Series had brought ecstasy to her and millions of Mets fans. While in 1970 it didn't look like the Mets would end up in the Series, she was still proud of her team.

"You know Pam, we haven't spoken much about what happened at the family Labor Day party."

Pamela looked at him curiously from the passenger seat as they drove toward Route 6 to head to Provincetown. "You mean, what your Mother said?"

It took Gomes a minute to adjust. He had been thinking about the exchange between his uncles and had nearly forgotten his Mother's comment. Wow, was this Freudian??!!

"Ah, yeah, that was one of the things I figured we should talk about. I was thinking about the argument between my uncles."

As Pam focused her eyes on him, David flashed back to the Labor Day party. After the exchange between Uncle Marcelino and Uncle Al, and the discussion that he had with his uncle, Gomes had gone around to the front of the house for a few moments of peace. Pamela came up behind him and put her arms around his chest, holding him tight. He pulled her around and gave her a passionate kiss, surprising and pleasing her.

"When are you two going to do what everyone knows you should do?"

Pamela and David turned around in surprise. Standing there was his mother, arms folded with a mischievous smile on her face. "I needed some air, too. I didn't expect to find the two of you here making out."

Almost as if they were teenagers, Pamela and David hung their heads in embarrassment. Helena stepped forward. "The two of you are obviously in love. Pam, I have never seen my son taken with someone the way he is with you. So, children, what are you waiting for?"

Pamela turned her head toward David, who said, "Well, Mom, I don't think that Pam or I are quite ready for the big jump. Pam has a lot of things to do and, well, you know..."

Helena shook her head in disbelief and turned back to the house. David turned toward Pam, but she was no longer looking at him, having heard the sounds of children running around the side of the house in their direction, chasing each other in a game of Tag. As Gomes shifted gears, Pam poked him in the side. "Tag, you're it." When he didn't respond Pam added, "You answered your mother for the two of us, I'd like to know what you want to do."

There was a moment of silence as they turned onto Route 6 toward Provincetown. There was little traffic on the road, but a Chevy Impala went speeding down the right lane, making it difficult for David to merge onto the highway. Once on Route 6, Gomes shifted in his seat and cleared his throat.

"Pam, listen, you and I have discussed this. You have all these plans as a photojournalist. That's great and I want to support you. It just feels like I'd get in your way. You know how I feel about you, but you also know how I feel about my work at the paper. I can't just walk away."

"I'm not asking you to walk away from anything, David. My feelings towards you are clear. You know it, I know it, your folks know it, the whole damn world knows it. Of course I want to develop my photography, but so what?

Pamela shifted in the seat, turning toward him. "Is the real issue that *you* really don't want to make a commitment? You know that I'm not the jealous type, but I saw the way you and that woman were looking at each other at your parents' place. You may have thought I wasn't around, but I caught a glimpse."

David was shaken for a moment. Yes, he had been attracted to that woman—Carmen—but so what? He wasn't dead! But he had no plans to leave Pamela.

"Pam, I confess the woman was very attractive, but I'm not interested in exploring other relationships. I'm in love with you, pure and simple. Please, don't *ever* think that I'm looking to play the field."

He thought to himself *'This is where this discussion always ends.'* And it was true. They had discussed where their relationship was going several times. Gomes was not sure whether he was scared of commitment or of the likelihood that Pam's future would take her far away from the Cape. The one thing he knew for sure was that he was not interested in *another* relationship. Well, maybe that was not entirely clear, either. Not interested in the sense that he was not prepared to *act* on any other interest, but what was the harm in looking?

"Pam, what am I to do if you get a job away from the Cape? You know that's not only possible but quite realistic. If you go deeper into photography and photojournalism there is an odd's on chance that someone from a big city will want you to relocate. Then what?"

Pamela was silent, looking out the window. David chose that moment to pass a station wagon full of people. As they passed, Pamela looked into the station wagon at a large white family.

"Suppose a tsunami hit the Cape? Suppose the economy collapsed? You get my point, David? You can't prepare for every possibility. You figure it out and, in this case, WE figure it out as a couple."

"That's easy to say, Pam, until the moment of truth. Until I have to say good-bye to the Gazette."

"So, let's just be clear, David, the issue is not you getting in the way of my career, but my getting in the way of yours. Let's just be honest about this." She turned away from him, adjusted her sun glasses and leaned back into the seat, shifting so that she had greater leg room.

David said nothing as he increased the speed of the car, hoping to get to Provincetown in one piece before they actually had a fight.

"Pam, let's do this, alright? We're in the middle of September. Give me 'til January. I feel like I've been really distracted by this story. Let me wrap this up and then do some thinking. I want to be fair to you and to myself. I do need to figure out where I'm going in life and, frankly, I think that you need to figure that out as well. We need to have a real heart-to-heart about what we want to do and where we want to do it. Can we take that time?"

Gomes looked back and forth between the road ahead and Pamela. She nodded her head and said, "Yes."

Gomes took a deep breath, driving in silence and hoping the day would get better, it had started on one rocky road.

32

The passing weeks brought colder weather to the Cape. The days remained largely pleasant but the evenings were cut by a stiff wind from Canada. Gomes found himself looking into a story that had circulated for years as a rumor about a couple of supposed infiltrators from a German U-boat during World War II who, according to the story, landed on the Cape and hid a large cache of counterfeit dollars as part of a larger Nazi plot. Because the story had been around for so long, Jacqueline agreed to have Gomes do an investigation, though she did not want him to spend too much time on it. She thought it might interest people who had not paid much attention to *C&IG* in the past.

On Tuesday, Gomes was sitting at his typewriter putting the final touches on part I of the U-boat story when the phone rang.

"Gomes, it's Hank."

"Hank, what's up? You almost never call."

"You're right about that, Dave, but every so often I have a few surprises. Listen, can you drop by the shop today? I have something I want to go over with you. No emergency."

"Sure, man. How about..." Gomes looked at his watch. "How about I drop by around 3 this afternoon? I can stop and get us both coffee."

"Sounds good, I'll see you then."

They hung up, leaving Gomes wondering what would spark that sort of call.

At 3pm, Gomes opened the door to Hank's shop carrying

a bag with two cups of coffee. As was common in the off-season, things were quiet. Gomes walked in and saw Hank stick his head out from one of the rows.

"Mister Gomes, I presume?" said Hank with a friendly grin.

"Tis I, and no one else," Gomes replied with a chuckle. "Here's your coffee, Hank. So, what's going on?"

Hank signaled Gomes to head over to his work area where they could sit down. Hank pulled out a large, padded envelope that was stamped "United States Air Force." It was sealed, but Hank opened it, pulled out a folder and passed it over to Gomes.

The folder was marked "Confidential." A tab indicated *"'Lucky Legs' Investigation, March 1945 plus appendix"*. Gomes opened the folder. The pages were clipped together so that they could not be removed from the folder without opening the clip. At the top of the first page in bold capital letters it read: "INVESTIGATION INTO THE CAUSES OF THE DEATH OF SARGEANT ANTONIO TAVARES, BOMBARDIER ON B-24 KNOWN AS 'LUCKY LEGS,' MARCH 21, 1945." There was a long number that Gomes assumed to have been the serial number for the plane.

Hank turned to do some work in the store. Gomes heard in the background the chimes on the door ring as it was opened, followed by the sound of several voices, but immersed in reading the report, he did not look up to see who was entering.

The report did not seem to diverge from the stories that Gomes had already heard, but there was a great deal more detail. According to the report, Tavares agreed to look in the bomb bay after Lt. DiUbaldo reported that not all of the bombs had been released over their target. No one on the flight deck knew exactly what Tavares was going to attempt. Captain Jansen testified that he believed Tavares would examine the bomb bay and provide him with additional information.

Jansen assumed that the bomb bay door had opened, but

with the intensity of the wind nothing could really be heard. Radioman TJ Smith went to check on Tavares's progress and, according to Jansen, came running back saying that neither Tavares nor the bomb were any longer in the bomb bay.

Other members of the crew were interviewed, but no one had seen or heard anything. They were returning from their mission over northern Italy and Jansen had told the gunners to keep their eyes open for German planes because he and DiUbaldo had seen at least one Me-109—a common German interceptor/fighter plane—since leaving the target area.

Gomes kept reading the report, ignoring the background noise in the shop. The report indicated that no one in the rest of the bomber squadron saw the bomb or Tavares fall. Two planes had noticed the bomb bay doors open on the *Lucky Legs* and had radioed over to check on the problem. Jansen informed the other planes that they were trying to address the problem.

The report referenced a report by the crew's ground-based engineer, Sargeant Oscar Crane that was supposed to be an appendix #1 to the report. There was no such appendix in the file, though there was a document labelled *"Appendix #2,"* a report on the visit by a team to New Bedford to the home of Mrs. Susana Tavares where the medal was presented.

In the section entitled *"Conclusions"* the investigating committee determined that due to an unknown mechanical failure, an armed bomb had been lodged in the bomb bay. When this had come to the attention of the co-pilot, Tavares was asked to investigate. Though no one knew for sure, it appeared that Tavares worked to dislodge the bomb and, without any sort of security chord or parachute, lost his balance when releasing the bomb and fell to his death.

The report noted almost in passing that the ground-based engineer, after inspecting the plane, had been unable to identify the source of the apparent malfunction. Nevertheless, the investigating committee was satisfied that Tavares had courageously taken steps to save the plane, paying the ultimate price. The report noted that Tavares was nominated for a Silver Star.

The appendix, entitled *"Appendix #2: Report on Journey to the family of Sargeant Tavares,"* was a brief, one page report on the visit of officers to deliver the Silver Star to the family of Antonio Tavares. Although there was nothing particularly noteworthy in this appendix, one sentence caught Gomes' eye. It read, in part, "...Sargeant Tavares was surprisingly popular in the Colored community of New Bedford." There was no elaboration on this point.

Gomes closed the folder and sat there for a moment thinking. Only then he noticed there were no further sounds in the store and that Hank was staring at him.

"Hank, where the hell did you get this report?" Gomes asked, downing what was left of his now lukewarm coffee.

"You don't want to know the answer to that, David. Let's just say I have friends in the Defense Department who owe me big time. I just needed one of them to do some digging for me. They were actually happy to oblige." Hank smiled ironically, then wandered through the store.

"Well, what do you make of the report?"

"I was going to ask you the same thing. It looks pretty straightforward, doesn't it?"

Gomes looked down at the report again. "Well, yeah, I guess that it does, except it looks like the engineer had another opinion."

"Yeah, Dave, I noticed that, too."

Hank walked back to his work area and looked at the rack. He pulled out a smaller, business envelope, opened it and pulled out an 8 ½" x 11" paper that he handed over to Gomes.

The print was blurred in the way that type looks when it is a copy produced through carbon paper, but readable. On it were a list of names, addresses, phone numbers, along with brief notations. Gomes immediately recognized that the list must be that of the crew of the *Lucky Legs* since he saw familiar names, with Jansen's at the top.

"Another Christmas present in advance, my friend," Hank said with another ironic smile.

Gomes saw that two names on the list had the notation "Deceased" next to them. Jansen was listed as deceased, and in parenthesis it noted "KIA in Vietnam." Killed In Action. The other name was Patrick Rawlings, a gunner, listed as deceased in 1962 with a last reported address in Des Moines, Iowa.

"As far as I know, Dave, that list is up to date. I hope that it helps. You can keep that list, by the way, but the folder I need to get that out of circulation."

Gomes looked up from the list, a look of wonder on his face. "Hank, I owe you! My thanks to you and your friends in the Defense Department. There is no way in hell I could've gotten this information. Thank 'em for me, alright?"

Hank gave Gomes a crisp salute as Gomes headed out of the store. He had a lot of work to do.

33

Returning to the office, Gomes sat at his desk looking at the list of names from the *Lucky Legs*. He assumed that each of these individuals had been interviewed in the investigation. The names were all over the country, though he noticed that there were three in the northeast: DiUbaldo in Boston, Gierek in Woodbridge, Connecticut (wherever that was), and a Jacob Schlein in New Rochelle, New York, which Gomes knew was a suburb of New York City. The engineer was last listed as being in Pittsburgh.

An idea came to Gomes. He needed to call Susana Da Silva. Looking at his watch, he suspected she was probably not yet home from work, so he made a note to call her after hours. He then returned to the story that the FBI agents had seemed interested in, the reports of a network of anti-war activists on the Cape who were helping draft resisters get to Canada. Gomes knew that it was true but he was having a lot of trouble writing the story because of the potential implications for those involved. He decided to put the story aside until he could decide between his politics, his ethics and his responsibility.

Gomes returned to the work he had done on the alleged U-boat and the counterfeit money. Since was no substantiation to the story, Gomes decided to explore why the story had remained a part of Cape Cod folklore.

Gomes lost track of the time. It had become dark outside, the days were growing shorter. When he looked at his watch he realized that he had been working steadily and it was now 6:30pm.

Jacqueline was still at her desk, but everyone else was gone as best he could tell. He picked up the phone to dial Susana Da Silva. On the third ring Bruno answered.

"Mister Da Silva, this is David Gomes from the *Cape & Islands Gazette*. You might remember I interviewed you and your wife a while back."

"Yeah, I remember you, Gomes. What ya' want?" Bruno was not particularly warm and fuzzy this evening.

"Sir, if you don't mind, may I speak with Missus Da Silva? I have a follow up question on the story that I've been doing about...you know, your son's alleged involvement in TJ Smith's death."

Bruno didn't say anything. Gomes could hear muffled sounds in the background on the line, sounding like people speaking.

"Hello, Mister Gomes? I hope that you are well. What can I do for you?" Susana Da Silva sounded relaxed and friendly.

"Missus Da Silva, I'm well. Thank you for taking my call. I hope that you're well also?"

"Yes, I am. I haven't heard anything more from my son, if that's the reason for your call."

"No, that wasn't why I was calling. I've been doing some research on the plane that your late husband flew in. I got curious. Did you ever hear from any of the crew of the plane after your husband's death?"

"No, I don't think so...Well, actually, there was one person. Mr. Schlein...What was his first name?? I can't remember his first name."

"*Jacob* Schlein?" Gomes asked, though he already knew the answer.

"Yes, of course, that's it: 'Jacob.' He came by to visit me in 1946 after he returned from Europe. I think that he stayed with some friends outside of New Bedford. He told me stories about my Tony. He also told me about what happened when Tony...died. By that time Little Tony had been born. "

"When was the last time that you saw Jacob Schlein, Missus Da Silva?"

"Oh, a while ago. Let me see. This is 1970. It must have been, what, 1959 or 1960. Little Tony was in his teen years. Mr. Schlein was on his way to Boston, so he decided to stop by on his way. He didn't stay very long. A few hours. We had a nice lunch. He had time to spend with Little Tony. And then he went on his way to Boston. I haven't seen him since, but he kept sending Little Tony birthday cards and a few dollars until my son turned 18."

"What happened when Little Tony turned 18?"

"Oh, nothing. It was just that he was 18. Mr. Schlein sent him a nice note telling him that he was now a 'man' and that he had some important decisions to make. He may have continued to send him cards, but I don't know. As I told you, as soon as Tony could, he joined the Air Force."

Gomes could hear in her voice a combination of emotions, especially a deep sadness.

"Missus Da Silva, I won't keep you any longer. Let me ask you one more thing, though. Do you have a good number for Mister Schlein?"

"Well, I think that I have a couple of numbers. He owns, or at least he *owned* a hardware store in New Rochelle, New York. I think I have the number for the store and his home number. Can you hold on for a minute so that I can check?"

Gomes thanked her and waited while she stepped away from the phone. Gomes could not hear anything. A few minutes later she returned and read him the two numbers she had. The home number corresponded to the number that Hank had provided Gomes. Gomes thanked her for her time and got ready to hang up when he stopped.

"Missus Da Silva, my uncle and aunt, Al and Flora Gomes, told me that they knew you a long time ago."

There was complete silence on the phone. It was so silent that Gomes wondered whether Mrs. Da Silva had hung up.

"You're Al and Flora's nephew?" she finally asked quietly and cautiously. "I wondered about that but didn't want to pry."

"Yes, I'm Jack and Helena's son."

"Well, well. Those are names I haven't heard in a long time."

The silence returned. Uncomfortable, Gomes was again getting ready to say good-bye when Mrs. Da Silva broke the silence. "Mister Gomes, I'm sure that your uncle and aunt, and maybe your parents, had nothing good to say about me. I wasn't...I wasn't a good friend to them. I've never had friends as good as your uncle and aunt. They were there when I needed them and I...well, I just..." She did not complete her sentence.

"Well, I just wanted you to know."

"Mister Gomes, it was a long time ago. I was a young and desperate girl. Please tell your uncle and aunt I know they can never forgive me, but please tell them...tell them that I can't forgive myself."

Susana admitted she had made some big mistakes marrying Bruno. She kept thinking that his family would accept her friends, and ALL of her family. "I'm sorry for getting into this with you. I lost so much, Mister Gomes. So much."

Gomes felt an impulse to try and smooth over everything. But he had seen the hurt on the faces of his uncle and aunt that flowed from a sense of utter betrayal. Susana Da Silva had never offered his uncle and aunt an apology and never tried to make amends. While Gomes believed she was sincere, it struck him how she identified the problem as Bruno and his family and how they viewed *her* friends and family. He thought, *for God's sake, you're Cape Verdean too! How do you think they regarded you, never mind your friends?"*

Gomes thanked her for her help and they hung up at the same time. He looked at his watch and decided there was no particular reason to wait, so he decided to call Jacob Schlein. Before his hand reached the phone the nightline rang.

When Susan O'Hara would leave the office the phones

were switched to a nightline. This meant anyone in the office could pick up any incoming call. If the phone rang more than six times an answering service took the call. But the general practice was that if you were working late you took the call.

Gomes looked over at Jacqueline as he picked up the phone.

"Mister Gomes? Oh, I'm glad that you're still in the office."

"Yes, Missus Smith, this is me. You're calling pretty late," said, Gomes, curious why Margie Smith would be calling at this hour.

"Mister Gomes. Al Gierek...Al Gierek is dead!"

"Dead??"

"Yes, dead. He fell off of a building in New Haven."

34

When Jacqueline overheard Gomes say "Dead," she stopped working and turned her attention toward him. The young reporter was scribbling notes as he listened carefully to Margie Smith.

Margie Smith explained that Jennifer Gierek had just called her. Al's body was found near a dumpster in back of the Lafayette Building on Temple and George Street in downtown New Haven where he had either jumped or been thrown from the top floor of the Lafayette Office building. The police were investigating, but they were telling Jennifer that their assumption was a suicide. Jennifer could not, in fact, *would not* believe that. Jacqueline saw Gomes write "Suicide? Pushed?" and underline the notes.

Mrs. Smith was crying on the phone and kept asking Gomes whether there was any connection between Gierek's death and TJ's. Gomes could not give an answer, but he kept trying to assure her the police would thoroughly investigate the crime.

"Missus Smith, I can't make any promises, but IF I can get to New Haven, that is, if I can get permission to go to New Haven, I'd like to speak with Missus Gierek. Do you think you could call her and put in a good word for me? It may not make a difference but it might help."

Between sobs, Mrs. Smith said, "Of course, Mister Gomes. If you think that it would help to get to the bottom of this craziness, of course I'll call her for you. I'm sure that she'll speak with you."

Gomes thanked Mrs. Smith and hung up. Jacqueline was looking at Gomes with concern and questions as he hung up the phone. Gomes stood up and walked over to her desk.

"Jacqueline," he started, "can I grab a minute of your time?"

"*Bien sur,*" responded Jacqueline, pointing to the chair in front of her desk.

"Jacqueline, I have a favor to ask of you. Well, let me start with this. TJ Smith's war buddy and good friend, Al Gierek, was just killed. Not clear whether it was a suicide or homicide, but something VERY eerie is going on here. I want to go to New Haven and speak with his widow and with the cops. There's also someone else that was in the same plane—the bomber, *Lucky Legs*—a guy named Jacob Schlein who lives in New Rochelle, New York who, it turns out, stayed in contact with the Da Silva family. Jacqueline, I'd like to go and talk with these folks, and I could get it done in one quick trip."

Jacqueline looked at him steadily while he was speaking. "David...*cher* David I have given you...what's the expression...a long leash on this one. You have written some interesting stories about this case. But I feel that this whole 'TJ Smith' matter is preoccupying you. I need for you to come up with new stories and new ideas for stories. I need for you to pursue some of the ideas that you and I have explored. I feel like you are being drawn deeper into this, almost as if it is a 1940s detective film. You know, a *film noir.*"

Jacqueline's Quebecois accent was always pleasant to hear, even when Gomes was being chastised. She never humiliated anyone, even when she was angry, which she didn't seem to be at this moment. But it was always clear when she was serious about something and, at this moment, she was as serious as a hand grenade.

Gomes glanced at his notes hastily scribbled on a pad. "Jacqueline, I'm on to something. This won't involve more than a couple of days on the road. And, no, this is not about me trying to act like a detective. This story is taking on a life of its own."

"What you do on your own time is up to you. What you do on my time is up to me. I regret having to put it that way, but that is the reality. You have started researching and investigating the underground organization smuggling deserters and draft dodgers to Canada, yet you don't seem to have the time to follow through on it. It's not like I have 50 reporters around that I can assign to pick up where you leave off. There are three of us here plus several stringers. We're barely making ends meet. We're a small-town paper! How can I afford for you to go off on endless stories?"

"I'm trying to figure out how to write that story on the underground organization, and I'm still working on that U-boat story, but..." Gomes looked at Jacqueline, whose visage indicated that she was not 'buying' what he was 'selling.' He realized that there was no point in continuing the discussion. He did not take this personally. She was not being cruel, he knew. She was under a lot of pressure. But that did not make it easier.

He thanked Jacqueline, and left the office, asking himself what the hell was he going to do next?

35

Gomes had not driven more than two blocks from his office when he pulled over at a gas station and went to the pay phone. He called Pamela to see if she had eaten dinner yet and if she had time to talk. She was free for the evening, so Gomes promised to pick up some Chinese food and be over there as soon as he could.

Pamela lived in a small, grey, single family home off of West Main Street in Hyannis that was owned by one of her relatives that Gomes had met only in passing.

As the door opened, Gomes heard an Earth, Wind & Fire song playing in the background. Pamela, wearing sandals, jeans and a sleeveless low-neck sweater, welcomed Gomes with a long, full kiss. She had the best lips he had ever kissed, and each time that she kissed him he could feel her love. After her kisses he always—always heard a voice in his head saying to him, "Hey, idiot, if you lose this relationship you will NEVER find anyone like her again." Yet, after the discussion that they had while driving up to P-town, he was still unsure how he wanted the relationship to play out.

Entering Pamela's home was akin to entering a photographic exhibit at a museum. Pamela had not only several of her own photographs, but photographs and prints from other artists. Each was well placed throughout the house. The furniture was simple, attractive, and complemented the photographs.

Gomes walked into the kitchen with the Chinese food, where Pamela had already set the table. Pamela opened the refrigerator and pulled out two beers.

"A beer kind of evening, huh?" Gomes asked with a smile.

"There was something in your voice when you called that made me think this was going to be an evening for a discussion. Since I don't see a ring in your hand, I assume that this is something un-romantic."

Though Pamela said it with a smile, Gomes knew Pamela was still unhappy with his unwillingness to commit. "My love for you, Pamela dear is eternal. But at the moment I need you to put on your 'counselor' hat. My decision could determine whether I have a job or not."

Pamela and Gomes dished out the food and sat down, Gomes giving Pamela a kiss on her shoulder. The food was good and they went through it quickly, leaving no leftovers. While eating, they found themselves laughing about an affair that had just been made public involving a major restaurant owner in Yarmouth. The owner of the restaurant was a flamboyant middle-aged, nicely shaped white woman who for many years had apparently sustained a special interest in several twenty-something black men. Recently, one of the young men fell in love with the owner, made his feelings known, and somehow it went public.

Gomes cleared off the table and started to wash the dishes. "Pamela, I need your advice about whether to go forward with the 'TJ Smith' story. I feel like I've reached the fork in the road." Gomes described where things were in the investigation. He ended by describing his earlier discussion with Jacqueline.

"So, my love, what do I do? Should I drop this for now? Should I continue? Jacqueline is right that this case could go on forever. *C&IG* is not a detective agency and my name isn't 'Joe Mannix.' I get that. But, damn, Pam, there's something about this case! Something that doesn't add up. But worse, Pam, my guess is that we shall see other victims."

"You think the death of this guy in New Haven,

what's-his-name, was murder? It wasn't suicide?"

"It's too early to know, babe, but my guess is that it was murder. Either that or it was a suicide that was related to the circumstances of TJ's death. Either way, the death is definitely connected. I'm sure of it."

Pamela dried off the dishes and put them away, saying nothing. Hanging up the dish towel, she retrieved two more beers from the fridge, saying "Did it ever occur to you that Jacqueline may be worried about *you*?"

"Worried about *me*? You think she's afraid that I've lost my mind? That I've become obsessed with this case!"

Pamela gave him her deadliest look. "That's not what I meant. I think that Jacqueline may be worried that in your pursuit of Da Silva/Tavares or whatever his name is you're entering a really really dangerous world."

"I'm not pursuing Da Silva, I'm just trying to get the story."

"You know, David, sometimes you miss the forest for the trees. It does *NOT* matter what your intent is. For Da Silva it might appear that you're pursuing *him*, and he may not appreciate that. I think Jacqueline is concerned that Da Silva could turn his gun on *you*, and I'm not using that as some sort of metaphor."

Gomes confessed that Hank had warned him of the same possibility: that Shepherd/DaSilva might want to eliminate a pesky reporter if he thought the newspaper was getting too close to the truth.

"David, you have written some good stories about this case and you've opened it up. But this guy is a well-trained killer. He pulled off at least one murder and then vanished. Then, despite the fact that the cops know who he is, he may have pulled off another killing. Jacqueline and I are both worried about you. She wants to protect you, and I don't want you killed!"

"I can't give up on this case, now, I've invested too much time. Too much of myself!"

The couple nursed their beers and their fears, with Gomes afraid he hadn't convinced Pamela, and Pamela not able to tell him she wondered if he wasn't chasing some kind of journalist fame. Like a Pulitzer Prize.

"David my love, I can see that you need to pursue this story. But you need to start acting like you're pursuing a killer. You need to take this *seriously*. You need to realize that this guy may, much like a pursued animal, turn around and lash out at you."

"I'm hip to what you're saying. I get it. And okay, maybe I've been naïve. But I appreciate that you understand that I have to finish this story. Maybe I should get a gun permit?"

Pamela grabbed his arm and squeezed, hard. "This killer has more training than you'll ever have, a hand gun will *not* help you. Remember he was an Air Commando, we're not dealing with a wronged lover who happened to have a .38 around the house."

David nodded in agreement, knowing she was right. "Then I'll have to keep my eyes open much wider than they've ever been."

"Yes, and you'll need to keep others—especially yours truly—informed of your moves. You don't need to be slick."

The two of them sat in silence. Occasionally one could hear a vehicle driving in the distance. David thought that maybe it was time to go. It wasn't.

"David, I understand that this story is important to you, but to be honest, I'm not entirely sure why? You know, why take these risks? Are you looking for some kind of break-out story that'll make your career? Is that it?"

"Yeah, this is the most important story I've worked on as a journalist. But that's not why I need to keep on it." Gomes took her hand, gently. The touch of her skin was always comforting.

"Until that dinner with my uncle and aunt, I could have walked away from this story. Yeah, it was an interesting one.

But you saw that look on the faces of my uncle and aunt. When Al came out of the kitchen and wanted to confirm that I was talking about Tony Tavares Senior, well, there was something in his voice and in his eyes that I won't ever forget.

"Like what?"

"There's something in this story that's 'family,' and I mean that in two ways. It's about the Gomes/Alves family. It's also about us, Cape Verdeans. I haven't put all the pieces together yet, but this Tavares was a hero for our people. Something upset his son, and I have got to figure it out. Maybe the guy was just nuts and *so* idolized his father that he just went over the top. I don't know. But I do know that if I don't find out the answer, I'm going to be very restless, Pam. Very restless.

"You feel like you owe your uncle and aunt the answers, don't you?"

"They lost two friends: one to death and the other to, I don't know what to call it other than self-imposed exile or something? Da Silva/Tavares, whatever his name is, he's something of a loose end, and you know what happens with loose ends? They can lead to a whole garment unraveling."

Pam squeezed his hand and leaned closer to him. "Just keep in mind, my dear, this may not end well. You may not get the answers you are looking for. You may not get answers at all. My concern is that you're not hurt as a result."

Pamela hugged Gomes, who held her tightly. Tears ran down Gomes' face, surprising him. He wiped them away. At exactly the same time—as seemed common for them—Gomes and Pamela said to each other, "I love you."

36

The next morning Gomes walked into Emily's in Hyannis. Amato was already there. "Thanks for meeting me, Amato," offered Gomes as he sat down at the booth.

"Not a problem, Gomes. I had to eat."

The two of them ordered coffee and breakfast. Amato folded up the paper he had been reading and moved it onto the bench. "I guess that she called you?"

'She'?" David replied.

"Yeah, Missus Smith. TJ's widow. I figured you heard about the jumper in New Haven from her." Amato turned to thank their favorite waitress who was delivering their coffee, then turned back toward Gomes.

"Yeah, she called me. I spoke with my boss about pursuing the case and she tells me that I have too much to do."

Amato looked over the rim of the coffee cup. "Gomes, let me tell you something. This case is becoming even more... mysterious. I made some calls as soon as I heard about it. The New Haven Police think that it was a suicide. Gierek was, apparently, having a meeting with someone in the restaurant on the first floor. The meeting ended, Gierek went upstairs and then, oops, out the window."

"Amato, you cannot possibly believe that it was that easy, can you? I mean, come on, man."

"I'm not sure what I believe any more. Gierek didn't seem to be especially forthcoming when he was interviewed after TJ's death. TJ's widow and son both said that something seemed to be bothering both TJ and Gierek. Gomes, I think that it is very possible, if not probable, that Gierek became depressed about TJ's death."

"Or scared. He could have been scared out of his wit, Amato."

"You know, Gomes, last night when you called me you said your boss and Pamela are worried about you. I think that you should listen to them. Da Silva sounds like the sort of person to take you out and not think twice about it. This is getting way over your head, buddy, you should leave this matter with those of us in law enforcement to settle."

The food arrived at just that moment. Amato took a second to season his breakfast and then dug in. Gomes never had to season the food at Emily's.

"Amato, I can't give this up! I agree I have to take my own security more seriously, but I think that you may not have assessed Da Silva the right way. He's given no indication of killing just anybody. Think about it. Why didn't he eliminate his landlady in Mashpee so that there could be no possible identification? This guy is skilled. He could have made it look like an accident and no one would've been the wiser. No, this guy is on a mission and we have to figure out why."

Amato picked up the coffee for a sip. "Alright, Gomes, you've made a good point. I'm operating on the assumption that Da Silva either flipped out or holds the crew responsible for letting his father die. In either case, he's a little nuts. I mean, war is war and accidents happen."

"Friendly fire."

"Exactly. But more importantly, his father was a hero and everyone's acknowledged that. To hold the crew responsible for an accident is *way* over the top. That leads me to think that when he was over in Vietnam something happened to him."

Amato looked at his watch and grimaced. Grabbing a last bite of his food, he said, "I have to run, let's talk later. But let me say one thing before I skidoo. This case has become WAY bigger than both you and me. Neither of us has the resources to really pursue this. On top of that, my bosses have been telling me that *I* need to shift gears and leave this to the FBI and the State Police. I think, my good friend, that YOU should take *your* boss's advice and start focusing on other stories. I can keep you posted from what I hear from the FBI but you need to be careful."

"I will, but— "

"Look, I don't need to remind you that the FBI doesn't think of you as a friend. You might get caught up in something. You know, the way that those dolphins get caught in fishermen's nets even though the fishermen are looking for fish? Not a nice end for the dolphin, you know."

Amato went through his wallet and pulled out some money for his share of what he knew the bill was and stood up to leave. Gomes sat in the booth finishing his coffee, half his food still on his plate, but he'd lost his appetite. If he was losing Amato's support he didn't see how he could carry on with the case.

Fricking FBI.

37

There was something about early morning drives that Gomes always liked, particularly early Saturday mornings. He would have preferred to have Pamela with him, but this wasn't the sort of trip to share with her.

The roads were fairly clear, though there was a light snow coming down. The meteorologists had said it was not supposed to amount to much. Gomes figured that in leaving home early he could make good time. He switched channels on the radio looking for the music he liked.

Gomes pulled over at a rest stop on Route 95, southwest of Providence on the Connecticut side of the border. He opened the thermos that Pamela had prepared for him with some tasty coffee. He needed some time to think about the questions that he was going to be asking at each stop. He also needed to make sure he could squeeze meetings with the New Haven Police, Mrs. Gierek, and Mr. Schlein in New Rochelle. into one day.

At 9:30 am Gomes exited Route 95 and headed into downtown New Haven to meet with a Detective Paul Collins. Amato had arranged the meeting. Collins was not a personal friend of Amato's, but he had agreed to speak with Gomes. The directions to the police station were fairly straight forward. At the police parking lot he saw a small area for Visitor Parking that was completely full, so he parked on the street at the metered parking.

Gomes walked into the police station behind two officers. To Gomes's surprise, they held the door open for him, for which he immediately thanked them. He looked around and saw what appeared to be the information desk. The name plate identified the person at the desk as *"Sergeant Frank McGraw."*

"Excuse me, Sargeant McGraw," he started. "My name is David Gomes. I have an appointment with a Detective Paul Collins."

McGraw, 40ish, with a thick mustache and a chunky build, looked up from some paper work, put the pen down and looked at Gomes in an unfriendly manner.

"Take a seat over there," McGraw said, pointing in the direction of a waiting area. There were two benches, though they did not look particularly comfortable. There were two other people sitting in that area, though it did not appear that they knew one another. One was an older, disheveled look-ing white woman, probably in her 60s, holding some worry beads in her hands. The other person was a brown-skinned Latino man probably in his late 20s who kept crossing and uncrossing his legs, looking very impatient. He looked at his watch and looked up at Gomes with an expression of disgust and frustration on his face.

Taking a seat on the bench giving himself space from the other two people, Gomes noticed that McGraw had picked up the phone and dialed a number. Gomes could not hear the conversation.

Gomes took a paperback book out from his small brief-case. He sat back to read the science fiction that he loved but rarely had time to enjoy. In the background the comings and goings of personnel, ringing telephones, civilian inquiries and prisoners all made for a constant hum. That said, Gomes was glad to be sitting down in a chair and not driving.

Gomes looked up when he heard a door close and saw a well-dressed man coming toward the waiting area. In a suit, probably in his 30s with sandy hair and a deep tan, looking like he spent a lot of time at the beach. In fact, the man looked a lot like the actor Steve McQueen. The man looked around the waiting area, but not specifically at Gomes. He walked back over to McGraw, leaned against the desk and said something to him. McGraw pointed at Gomes. With a nod "Steve McQueen" walked back over to the waiting area.

"David Gomes?" he asked, pronouncing it, *"Gomez."*

"Yeah, that's me." Gomes replied as he stood up.

Gomes followed 'Steve McQueen,' as he had started to think of him, to an office with the name *"Detective Paul Collins"* written on the glass door. Collins sat at his desk and pointed to a chair where Gomes could sit. Gomes looked around the small modest office and noticed various pictures and awards on his wall.

"In case you've not guessed, I'm Detective Collins. Detective Amato called me about you but I was expecting someone... Spanish based on your name." Collins finished his semi-question with a peculiar facial expression that seemed to be a cross between a frown and a smile. He spoke with an accent that sounded less New England and more New York or New Jersey, Gomes couldn't tell.

"Yes, Detective, my name is Gomes, spelled G-O-M-E-S. It is not Gomez. My grandparents came from a Portuguese *colony* called Cape Verde, off the coast of Senegal. Have you ever heard of it?" Gomes tried to display as little emotion as possible, though he surprised himself at the force of his words.

"No, never heard of it," replied Collins.

Gomes decided to get right down to business. "In any case, Detective, I appreciate your time. I know that you're a busy person. I'm interested in the death of Mister Al Gierek. As Detective Amato may have told you, I've been doing a story about the death—actually the murder—of a man named TJ Smith, who was a close friend of Mister Gierek's. When I heard about Gierek's death I immediately thought there might be a connection."

Collins shook his head. "Gierek was a jumper, Mister

Gomes, as best as I can tell." The detective took out a cigarette, lit it, and took a puff. "Gierek's widow said that he had been very distressed by and depressed about the murder of his friend from Cape Cod. On the day of his death he had a lunch meeting with a Mister Todd Nadeau. Gierek was an insurance salesman. He was meeting with Nadeau to sell him a policy. The meeting went on for about an hour. After the meeting ended Nadeau left and a few minutes later Gierek picked up his things and also left. That was the last that anyone saw him. As best as we can tell, he went up to a vacant office on the top floor. The door was open or Gierek had a key, we're not sure. He sat there for a while and drank a considerable amount of rum. He then threw a chair through the window and jumped. End of story."

Collins sat back in his chair and exhaled some smoke, looking satisfied with his report and conclusion.

"Detective Collins, was there any suggestion that Gierek was suicidal?"

"Ah, no, but his wife and son said that he was very upset."

"A lot of people get upset, particularly when their best friend dies, but they don't throw themselves out of a building."

"Yeah, I know that, but it all fits together." Collins was starting to look irritated.

Gomes looked down at his pad where he had been writing notes. "Who is this 'Nadeau' that you mentioned?"

Collins cleared his throat. "We don't know. There was a notation of the meeting in Gierek's datebook. There was also some material that Gierek had in his bag—he left it in the vacant room before he jumped—about the guy. It indicated that the guy was 30 years old, worked as a welder at the Groton shipyard, was single, and lived in East Haven. There was a telephone number but Gierek must've written it down wrong because it was a number for a phone booth in East Haven. Anyway, that's all that we have. We haven't been able to find the guy. Yet."

Gomes was unconvinced. "Have you closed the investigation?"

"Not officially, but this case is going nowhere fast." Collins looked at his watch. "Look, I know that we don't have anything on this guy Nadeau, but the man might've just not been straight with Gierek. Maybe he was trying to pull a fast one. In any case, we're convinced Gierek was a jumper."

Gomes understood that as far as Collins was concerned, the investigation and the interview was over. He packed up, thanked Collins and exited. When he got outside the police station he realized that he had extra time prior to going to the Gierek home. He looked around and asked a nearby officer, who was on his way to a patrol car, for directions to the Lafayette Building. Gomes went to his car, put more time on the meter, then started walking to the scene of the crime.

38

It was a cold twenty minute walk to the Lafayette Building. The building had been built in the late 1930s and had some connection to Yale University. In the lobby Gomes was reading through a directory of various companies when a deep voice said, "May I help you, sir?"

Gomes was startled by the voice, it sounded almost Shakespearean, along the lines of the actor Ossie Davis. He turned quickly to see standing in front of him a man, probably in his late 50s or early 60s, with grey hair, grey mustache and a rich brown skin. The name badge on his dark uniform read "Lou."

"No, thank you, Mister...Lou," Gomes replied. "Just looking."

Lou gave Gomes a slight smile and a nod of the head. "If you have any questions, I'm usually seated over there." Lou pointed to a station in the lobby near the elevators.

Gomes thanked him. Spotting the entrance to the restaurant where Gierek had reportedly eaten his last meal, Gomes walked toward the entry to the restaurant. The *Game Room* was more of a bar & grill. Gomes was sure a lot of business transpired at this establishment, it had that look.

Gomes entered and walked over to the maître d's station. A young Asian woman with long black hair and light-brown skin stood there. She had the look of a college student, though, in her dark blue dress, she appeared very professional. She also conveyed being ready to be of help. Something about the way she carried herself impressed Gomes.

"Good morning, sir. Can I seat you at a table?" she asked

with a voice like a song.

Gomes was famished, but he decided that that would need to wait, at least for now.

"Thank you, but I wanted to ask a question." The young woman looked at Gomes suspiciously, not sure what to expect next. "I'm looking for the manager. I have a question that he might be able to help me with."

"Certainly, sir. Give me a moment," she offered with a smile, and then walked back toward the bar. Gomes looked around. There weren't many people in the establishment, but he could imagine during the work week it was quite busy.

He was lost in thought when he saw the young woman returning with another woman, this one white, in her 30s, blondish hair, and well dressed in a dark blue skirt and jacket. To borrow from an expression long associated with Duke Ellington, she made her outfit look outstanding.

The older woman had a polite smile on her face as she walked over and offered her hand to shake. "Good morning, sir. My name is Stephanie Heinrich. I'm the owner of this establishment. Miss Carrera indicated that you wanted to speak with the manager. What can I do for you?" Heinrich was polite, but no-nonsense.

Heinrich suggested that they sit down. They sat in one of the open booths not far from the second door opening to the street. Heinrich signaled someone that Gomes could not see and then refocused her attention on Gomes.

"Miss Heinrich—"

"It's Missus Heinrich," she noted before Gomes had gone far.

"Missus Heinrich, my apologies. My name is David Gomes. I'm a reporter with the Cape & Islands Gazette in Hyannis, on Cape Cod. I'm here doing a story about the death of Mister Gierek who fell from this building early this week."

Before she had a chance to respond, a waiter came over to the table with two glasses of water. Gomes thanked the young man.

"Would you care for anything else, Muster Gomes? Perhaps some coffee or tea?"

"I could do with some strong coffee if it's available."

"Of course." She offered the waiter a nod. He quietly moved away. "Mister Gomes, you're a bit of a distance from home, aren't you?" She asked it with a charming smile.

"Yes, you noticed that." Gomes flashed an equally charming smile. "I've been working on a story that starts on the Cape and may be related to the death of Mister Gierek."

Heinrich took on a more serious look. The waiter returned with two coffees and cream and sugar. Heinrich picked up her cup and took a sip. Gomes put a spoon of sugar plus a touch of cream into his coffee.

"I wasn't trying to make light of the man's death, Mister Gomes," Heinrich said with a look of concern and sympathy. "I think that it unsettled all of us. You know how people sometimes start acting after a tragedy?"

"I was told by the police that Mister Gierek had a meeting here shortly before his death. I was wondering whether I could speak with whoever might have seen him or waited on him? I won't take a lot of their time."

Heinrich paused to consider her reply. "Well, here's the good news *and* the bad news. I was here the day that Mister Gierek…died. I remember him coming into our establishment and I remember that he met with someone. But truth be told, I was quite busy and didn't notice who he met with. In fact, Mister Gierek and I only nodded at one another. The person who took care of him that day was Claudia Kristofferson."

Gomes adjusted himself in his seat and made note of the name. "Is Miss Kristofferson here today?"

"That's where the bad news starts. The day after Mister Gierek was killed, Claudia quit. She didn't even report in for her shift. She called and said that she was out and would not be returning."

Gomes looked puzzled.

"I think she was traumatized by the news. I don't know. She was crying when she called. She said she kept thinking how she had seen Mister Gierek before his death. I tried to calm her down. I told her that we needed her back and that there was nothing that any of us could have done to prevent this." With a sad smile she added, "None of what I said seemed to matter."

"Do you have a way of reaching her?"

Heinrich looked around the restaurant until she got the attention of Miss Carrera, who came over to the table. "Lisa, would you get me Claudia's phone number?"

Carrera nodded her head and hurried away.

"Missus Heinrich, you seem to have known Mister Gierek. I was wondering what you could tell me about him."

"Well, I wouldn't say that I 'knew' him. I can say that he regularly came into our restaurant, sometimes by himself, sometimes with another person. Our restaurant was something of an office for him."

"What would you say about him?"

"Mister Gierek was sort of three different people. The 'first' was insurance salesman. From what I could tell, he was quite successful. I've heard he had a nice house in Woodbridge—that's a suburb of New Haven in case you didn't know—and he seemed to regularly have clients here to meet with him. The 'second' Gierek was a...comedian. He could deliver jokes like a professional. He would have people rolling on the floor. I mean, he really should have gone on the stage. He could be bitterly sarcastic, like the comedian Don Rickles, while at the same time take an everyday experience and just make it hilarious. He had this great laugh, but here is where it gets odd. His eyes rarely smiled."

Heinrich stopped for a moment and finished her coffee while she was thinking.

"I guess that takes us to the 'third' Gierek. There was a deep sadness in the man that he would never explain."

Gomes was impressed at her power of observation. She would make a great therapist. "Was his sadness enough to lead to suicide?"

"I can't say, I'm no psychiatrist. But it didn't *feel* like that. It was different. I know people who are really depressed. In some cases they aren't even able to move. That wasn't the case with Mister Gierek. This was different. There was something in his eyes, or maybe something *missing* from his eyes. Yes, something missing."

"Like what?"

Heinrich shrugged her shoulders. "Joy? Contentment? Peace? Maybe that was it: peace."

She added that Gierek had come on to her once. He knew that she was married, but he came on anyway. It surprised Heinrich.

"Was he a little intoxicated?"

"What are you saying, that someone has to be intoxicated before they'd come onto me?" Her eyes flashed with anger.

Embarrassed, Gomes fumbled around for words. "No, no, that's not what I meant. I meant..."

Heinrich started to laugh, and this laugh was definitely in her eyes. It was also quite infectious and a bit alluring.

"I know what you meant! I just couldn't resist throwing that dart." She gave him a mischievous smile. Gomes was still flustered, but he started to chuckle himself.

"No, Mister Gierek was not intoxicated. That's what made the whole situation weird. A client of his had just left and he was sitting in a booth. That booth over near the door." She pointed towards the booth. "He eventually started talking with me about a certain kind of unhappiness. He said that he often felt like taking off. There's this Caribbean island, Antigua, that he visited once on vacation. He kept talking about moving there and running a charter boat or something. Then he asked me to run away with him. Well, I knew he was joking, so I joked along. My husband and I were not getting along too well at the time, anyway, so it was an interesting fantasy, I guess you'd say. The conversation then started to get serious. He said he wanted to start seeing me. I was surprised. I was flattered, but I had to cool him out. So, I did. Nicely."

"He never brought up Antigua and you again?"

"No, never. He continued to be friendly. In fact, he acted as if it had never happened! But I could tell that he had *not* been joking. I don't know whether it was me he wanted or whether he just wanted...out. But, no, Mister Gomes, he never struck me as suicidal."

Heinrich saw Carrera returning. "Well, Mister Gomes, Miss Carrera has your information. I will bid you fare well, and hope to see you again some time." She offered a flirtatious smile as she stood up from the booth.

Gomes smiled in return, trying to be friendly and professional, hoping not to convey his own attraction to her. He stood up as Heinrich shook his hand and walked away. Carrera handed him a piece of paper. He saw two numbers. He looked up at Carrera for an explanation.

"The first number is Claudia's home number. The second number is where she's now working. She's on the evening shift at a place called "Doc's," over near the Yale campus. "

Gomes thought he could get to the Gierek home soon enough and then drive to New Rochelle to see Jacob Schlein, the other former crew member of the *Lucky Legs*. Though he knew he would be exhausted, he decided he would return to New Haven that evening, it was on his way back to the Cape, and try to catch up with Claudia Kristofferson.

When he stepped into the lobby of the Lafayette building, Gomes saw the security guard sitting at his desk reading a newspaper. He decided the visit to the Gierek home would have to wait, there was one more lead he had to follow up

39

"Mister *Lou*," Gomes said, approaching the security guard's desk, "would you have a few minutes for me to ask you something?"

Mr. Lou looked up and smiled, closing the newspaper. "Of course. How may I help you?" The security guard sounded as if he were a professional actor. Each word was pronounced clearly and neatly. Gomes introduced himself and explained his visit.

"So, Mister Lou…"

"Mister Gomes, thank you for respecting me by calling me 'Mister' but my full name is Louis Randolph. Management wanted us to have our first names on these tags."

"Okay. *Mister Randolph*, are you here every day?"

Randolph's face was friendly but guarded. "I'm normally here Monday through Friday. I know, today is Saturday, but our union contract gets us overtime on the weekend. One of the guys couldn't make it in and I'm substituting for him."

"Were you here the day that Mister Gierek fell to his death?"

"Yes, sir, I was here."

"Did you notice anything with him that led you to believe he might kill himself?"

"I don't really think he *did* kill himself. Mister Gierek would speak with me every day when he came through these halls. We didn't talk much, but we would chat about this and that. On that day he didn't say anything that would've led me to believe that he was going to end his own life."

Randolph was standing still, almost at attention, very military.

"Well, Mister Randolph, what do you think happened?"

"I can't say that I know, exactly."

Something about the way that Randolph said it got Gomes' antenna up. "Did you see him right before his death?"

"Indeed I did. He'd been in that restaurant and left. Then he then came back."

"He came *back*?" Gomes asked, his eyebrows raised.

"Yes, sir, he came back. He ran into the man he was meeting at the restaurant."

"Let me get this straight. The man that Mister Gierek was meeting in the restaurant left the building. Gierek then left the building but ran into the man and returned. That's what you're saying?"

Randolph looked Gomes straight in the eyes. "Yes, that's what I am saying. They both came back. The other man put his arm around Mister Gierek, he was speaking with him softly. And seriously."

"Did they just stand here and talk?"

"Oh, no. They walked over to the elevator. That was the last I saw of poor Mister Gierek."

"Then what happened?"

"The gentleman that met with Mister Gierek walked by me some time later and went toward the restrooms over there." Randolph pointed down the hallway towards the restrooms.

"This is getting complicated," said Gomes. "Let me get this right. Mister Gierek and Mister X walked past you and then Mister X came back without Gierek. The next thing that we know, Mister Gierek is found dead. Did I get that right?"

"Yes, sir, that's about it," responded Randolph with no expression on his face.

"What did this other man look like?"

"Hard to say. He was wearing a heavy dark coat, had a hat and sunglasses. About 6 foot. Couldn't tell the color of his hair. Just another white guy, though well built."

"Uh, did you tell the police about any of this?"

"No. They never asked me anything."

Surprised, Gomes asked Lou, "But Mister Randolph, with all respect, how could you not tell them what you told me?"

Randolph had a strange expression on his face: a combination of fatalism, anger, resentment and something else. Resignation, perhaps.

"You know, I've worked here since I got out of the Army in '54. I was in Korea 'til after the war ended. There are people I've seen in this building year after year, going back a long while. Many of them will speak when they see me, but if you ever asked one of them about me, they wouldn't even know my last name." Randolph had that look of resignation again. "The police never asked me *one thing*. They just walked by, went upstairs, went outside and came to their own conclusions."

It started to sink in. Gomes stuck out his hand to shake Randolph's. He thanked him for his time and then headed to his car, while Randolph returned to his desk, sat down, and returned to his newspaper.

<u>40</u>

After leaving security guard Louis Randolph, Gomes stopped for a couple of slices of pizza on his way back to his car. He ate the pizza while driving out of town, setting the pizza box on the passenger seat when he had to shift the Volkswagen.

He had no idea how to get to the Gierek's, but Paolo, the pizza shop owner, was friendly and helpful. A short Italian guy with a balding head, he would have made a great bartender, or a great therapist, because he knew how to strike up a conversation, and listen. Paolo drew a little map on the back of a pizza box.

As he drove and ate, Gomes reflected on the discussion with Randolph. The security guard had confirmed Gomes's gut feeling that Gierek's death was murder, not suicide. Randolph's description of the other man was too vague to tell whether it was Da Silva, but it was similar enough that he remained suspect number one.

Gomes was struck by Randolph's attitude. At first, Gomes had not understood why Randolph didn't seek out the police to tell them what he had seen. But there was something in Randolph's look that contained so much pain and resentment. Randolph clearly felt invisible and, perhaps, in this case he just accepted his invisibility.

Following the map, Gomes soon found himself looking at beautiful neighborhoods with large homes and plenty of trees. A moment later he found himself in front of a white, two- story home with an attached two-car garage.

Gomes parked in front of the house and walked up the

driveway toward the main entrance. The neighborhood was quiet. Looking around, Gomes saw only one person, an older white man across the street raking his yard. The man looked up and kept his eyes focused on Gomes as the reporter walked to the front door and rang the bell.

The door was opened by a white woman, probably in her 40s, about 5' 3", wearing a non-descript black dress. Gomes noted that upon opening the house door she locked the storm door.

Gomes introduced himself in a loud voice, since the storm door muffled sound. He informed her that Margie Smith had called about him. The woman, who he assumed was Jennifer Gierek, looked puzzled by his appearance. She asked for identification, still speaking through the storm door. Even after examining Gomes' press badge, she asked was he was *really* David Gomes. Finally she unlocked the storm door and let Gomes in.

"So, you are the David Gomez who Margie told me so much about," she said, mispronouncing his name while trying to construct a smile on her face.

"Yes, ma'am. I assume that you are Missus Gierek. I'm deeply sorry about the loss of your husband. Thank you so much for taking the time to meet with me."

"Yes, Mister Gomez. Please come in and have a seat. I'm sorry if I was rude, but you looked a little different than I expected."

"It's *Gomes*, Missus Gierek. G-O-M-E-S. It is a Portuguese name. But thank you for seeing me. This is a very beautiful house, by the way."

"Yes, we love this house. Can I get you anything to drink, Mister *Gomes*?"

He took a seat in the living room. "No, thank you, I don't want to take up a lot of your time, I just have a few questions." As Gomes took out his notebook, Mrs. Gierek had her fingers locked in an embrace, looking uncomfortable. "The police said they believe your late husband took his own life. Do you think that's possible?" Gomes asked his question quietly and sympathetically.

"No, Mister Gomes, I can't accept that idea. Yes, my husband had been sad for a while, you know, after TJ was murdered. He was deeply shaken by that. But my husband was *not* the suicide type. He said to me on several occasions that having gone through World War II he'd seen enough death. He had no interest in bringing it on any faster."

Mrs. Gierek looked out the window as if seeking the horizon. Gomes decided to shift gears. "Ma'am, how did you and your husband come to Woodbridge?"

Before she could answer they heard the storm door opening followed by keys unlocking the front door. When the door opened, a pale young man with close-cropped hair and a little peach fuzz on his chin stepped inside. He looked from Gomes to Mrs. Gierek and back again.

"Who the hell are you?" the man asked, his mouth drawn in a sneer of hostility. Gomes stood up to introduce himself, but before he could speak the man came forward and asked again: "I said, who the hell are you?"

Gomes put his hand out to shake the young man's hand, but the newcomer ignored the overture.

"Michael, this is Mister Gomes, the reporter that I mentioned to you." Missus Gierek spoke in a weak voice tinged with regret.

"What's a nigger reporter doing here looking into Dad's death? We don't need a nigger reporter, we need someone who knows what they're doing. These nigger reporters have been creating all sorts of problems and now I can't believe that one is here in *my own* living room!"

Gomes stood there in silence. Jennifer Gierek's son looked like an out of shape football player. He was dressed casually and carried a gym bag.

"Michael, I've told you how you are and are not to speak

when you're in my house. Mister Gomes is a guest."

Jennifer's words were direct and a little more forceful than her first words to her son. Michael looked at Gomes and snarled. Gomes was afraid the young man was going to throw a punch. He was relieved when the fellow abruptly walked up the stairs and vanished.

"My apologies, Mister Gomes. Michael is a very emotional young man. He's been terribly upset about his father's death. He sometimes...well, he sometimes..." She left the sentence unfinished, folding her hands and looked down at them.

Gomes found it interesting that Michael's remorse about the death of his father would lead to such a racist assault, but *welcome to the USA*, he thought. He gave Mrs. Gierek a moment before proceeding.

"Before Michael came in I was asking you about how you and your husband got to Woodbridge."

"Oh, yes. Well, it was after the War. That's when Al and I met and married. Al was from New York City and I was from this small town in southern New Jersey. You've never heard of it. Well, Al LOVED New York. I met him through a cousin of mine and the next thing that I knew I was going out with Al dancing all over the place. He introduced me to TJ and Margie and we became fast friends.

"Those were good times. Al wanted to stay in New York but I didn't. I don't like the big city. Never have. I went there to work but didn't like living there. Every time that I could I would go back to Jersey." She pronounced her home state with the common accent 'Jerz-zee'.

"Well, we decided to compromise. TJ and Margie wanted us to move to Massachusetts, but that was too far from New York and Jersey for me and Al, so we settled on New Haven, in part because of a job that Al got. After a few years Al got a break with the insurance company and turned out to be a great salesman.

"By that time we had two children: Michael, who you just

met, and Karen, who is away at school, we stumbled across this house and we've been here ever since."

Jennifer had on her face a smile of satisfaction or pride, Gomes couldn't be sure. He asked her more questions about the family, life in New Haven, and friends, then he shifted gears. "Missus Gierek, did your husband ever discuss his experiences in the War?"

"Every so often. Sometimes something or somebody would remind him of an experience he had. Serving on a bomber was a scary experience. He would say that it was not like what you saw in the movies or on television."

"Do you have anything, anything at all from your husband's time in the War? Any pictures? Letters?"

Jennifer looked at him curiously. "What are you thinking about?"

"I'm trying to figure out any connections between what happened to your husband and what happened to TJ Smith."

"You think that the same person who killed TJ killed my husband?"

"That crossed my mind. The description of the last person seen with your husband is vague, but it might have been the same person, I don't know for sure."

Jennifer Gierek got up from her chair, signaling that she would be right back. She first went into the kitchen, where Gomes could hear her filling a kettle with water. Then she went upstairs. Gomes could hear her talking with Michael. His voice became loud at a certain point, though Gomes could not make out what was being discussed, then silence.

Gomes picked up a copy of *Time* magazine from a table next to his chair and thumbed through it, looking at the pictures more than anything else. He heard the kettle whistle with boiling water. There were no sounds on the second floor. He decided to head to the kitchen, where he saw two cups sitting beside a box of teabags. Gomes turned the burner off, the sound of the whistling slowly dying. He returned to his seat, deciding it was best that he not serve up the tea.

A few minutes later Gomes heard Jennifer coming down the steps. She carried a canvas bag that she placed on the living room floor and went to the kitchen. "Would you like some tea?"

"Most certainly, thank you. On a day like this, tea is good for the soul."

"Isn't it red wine that's supposed to be good for the soul? Or is it good for the blood? I can never remember." Jennifer asked him what he wanted in his tea. She emerged carrying two cups of steaming tea, slices of lemon and sugar.

"Mister Gomes, I have this bag of memories. Much of what I remember Al having collected from that time is in that bag. You may look through it."

Gomes took a sip from the tea, then opened the bag and looked through it. It was a real hodge-podge. There were photos, some government documents from the end of his military service, some letters and an autographed baseball (though it was difficult to read the name).

Gomes separated the material into different piles. The documents were of little interest, but the photos were a fascinating mix of parties and touristy sites, all from the late 1940s. There were photos of a young TJ and Margie Smith, and a few photos of an older couple that were not identified.

Gomes came across photos from the War of Al and TJ, some women, a photo of a ship and one of the Lucky Legs bomber crew. In fact, it was the same photo that Margie Smith had shared with Gomes.

Gomes stared at the photo.

"You've seen the photo before, haven't you?" Jennifer asked.

"Yes. Margie Smith showed me this same photo. Except this one is a little different. It has a tear through the person standing on the far right of the group. I can only see his legs and shoes."

Gomes realized that if he hadn't seen the other photo he

would not have known that Antonio Tavares—'TeeTee'—had literally been cut out of the Gierek's picture.

"Missus Gierek, do you know the name of the person who was cut out of the photo?"

Jennifer looked over the photo, slowly shaking her head. "No, I never really noticed this. My God, I don't think that I've even looked at this photo in, what, twenty years!"

"Did your husband ever mention a fellow crewman of his named Antonio—Tony—Tavares? They called him 'TeeTee'."

Jennifer thought for a moment. "I was going to say 'no,' but I do remember Al mentioning that name once. I believe he died during the war, but I don't remember how."

"Missus Gierek, are there any people who might want to do harm to your husband?"

"You mean, besides my son. I'm only half joking. My son and Al were always fighting. Al was a true liberal. He was out there supporting labor unions, civil rights. He was even against the Vietnam War. Michael became increasingly supportive of George Wallace. He worked on his '68 campaign. He and Al were always at each other's throats."

She took a moment to finish her tea. "As far as I know, Al had no enemies. His clients loved him. He never told me about any threats. No, I can't think of anyone."

"One last question. "You mentioned that your husband was very broken up over the murder of TJ Smith. Take me back prior to this murder. Was there anything that you noticed? Even something small?"

Jennifer closed her eyes for a moment. Gomes was not sure whether she was crying or thinking, or perhaps both. "Something *was* bothering Al, but I never learned what. He said he needed to talk through some things with TJ, so, we went to visit him and Margie, but I don't know what they talked about.

"When TJ was murdered, well, he just came apart. He wouldn't go out of the house for days. He was beside himself in grief, they were very close."

As she escorted Gomes to the front door, she stood in the doorway and said, "You know how I'm sure Al didn't kill himself? *Rum.*"

"Rum, Missus Gierek?"

"Yes, rum. The police told me that Al had gone into a vacant office and drank a pint of rum before he jumped out of the window. My husband *hated* rum! He was a beer and whiskey man. Al would never have rum as his last drink, it would have been *Johnnie Walker Red!*"

41

As Gomes drove toward New Rochelle to see Jacob Schlein he recalled his confrontation with Michael. The young man had followed Gomes to the car, taunting him with racial epithets, saying that a 'nigger' was not welcome in his neighborhood. When Gomes tried to open the car door, Michael grabbed him by the arm, saying, "Stay out of my neighborhood, Mister Nigger reporter!"

While in the military Gomes had studied martial arts and he kept up his training after discharge. Gomes grabbed Michael's hand and twisted it hard, forcing the young man down to his knees. Michael yelled out, and Gomes kept twisting.

"Let me explain something to you, Michael. It's simple. There are no 'niggers.' Got that? You keep your fucking hands off of me and other black people. You hear me, asshole?"

In intense pain bringing tears to his eyes, Michael nodded his head. Gomes twisted harder. "Yeah, I got it," Michael said through gritted teeth, just this side of screaming. Gomes released him, got in the car and drove away. A part of Gomes that he rarely showed wished he had broken Michael's wrist. But he knew all too well that that step would have brought in the Woodbridge Police.

Gomes knew little about New Rochelle other than it was a suburb of New York City. He drove over to Rt. 95 and followed it south to New Rochelle, then followed the directions that Mr. Schlein had given him on the phone. As he drove into the city looking for a hardware store off of Main Street, it was clear that New Rochelle was racially segregated.

JS Hardware was exactly where Mr. Schlein had said that it would be. Gomes parked and walked over to the store. The shop was clean and well-ordered. Items were clearly marked so you didn't have to guess where to find something or their cost. Gomes noticed a young woman in coveralls and a work shirt that was initialed *JS Hardware* above the name "Barbara". Before Gomes could say anything, Barbara was standing right in front of him.

"May I help you, sir?" she asked smiling beneath a New York Mets baseball cap.

"Yes, thanks. My name is David Gomes. I have an appointment with Mister Schlein. Is he around?"

"He stepped out for a minute to get something from another store. He should be back in about 15 minutes if you don't mind waiting. There's a bench over there, if you want to get off of your feet. He really shouldn't be long."

Gomes thanked her and sat on the bench. He saw Barbara go to the counter, where she rang up a sale while an older woman wearing a *JS Hardware* apron straightened up a shelf behind her.

While he sat there he saw two men approach Barbara. One of them cracked a lewd joke while the other leaned closer and leered. Barbara told them if they needed any help to look for her and moved back to the counter.

The two men, white, overweight and in their 30s, began making comments about Barbara, saying she was a lesbian and that they could straighten her out. Neither of the men noticed the older woman approaching. She was maybe 5 feet tall and solidly built. And she had a hammer in her hand.

Whatever she said—and Gomes struggled to hear—put the fear of God into the men. They started backing out of the store, apologizing and saying they would come back when they were sure what they wanted to buy. As soon as the men left the store, the aproned woman returned the hammer to its place on a rack. Gomes thought this was one hell of a store.

A moment later a middle-aged man walked in carrying two boxes. He was close to 6 feet tall and quite fit, with unruly grey hair, a drooping grey mustache and a Mets baseball cap. His shirt had the store logo and the name "Jake" on it.

"Merle!" he yelled to the older woman, "as much business as I give Blake you'd think the guy could help me out when I need it. I mean, all he gave me were these two damn boxes!"

The older woman Gomes had seen with the hammer gave Jake a sympathetic look. As Jake took the boxes to the back of the store, Barbara walked over and whispered to him that the reporter was there. Jake put the boxes away and approached Gomes.

"You must be David Gomes."

"Yes, sir, and you must be Mister Schlein?"

"Call me Jake. Let's go somewhere we can talk," replied Jake in a gruff but friendly manner. Gomes hurried after him, thanking Barbara as they went out the door.

Jake zipped up his coat and turned toward Gomes. "Have you eaten anything?" He had a strong New York accent.

"No, I haven't and I'm hungry. I could use some coffee. I've had a long day already and I still have to drive home."

"You mean back to the Cape? You gotta be kidding. You need to get a room and go back tomorrow."

"Thanks for the suggestion, but I need to get back."

They walked to Main Street and entered a diner called Sally's, where Jake announced his presence. The wait-staff started joking around as if Jake were some sort of royalty. Jake walked to a corner booth, pulled a cigar out of his coat pocket, lit it, and sat back, Gomes settling in across from him.

"Well, your majesty, what can your humble servant do today?" said a shapely woman in a waitress outfit with platinum blonde hair, pale skin and pellucid blue eyes. In her late 40s or maybe 50s, she reminded Gomes of Lana Turner.

The waitress and Jake joked around, and then he ordered

a turkey sandwich and coffee, hot. "And be sure to pre-heat the mug." Gomes ordered the same, not requesting a heated cup. The waitress took the orders and walked away, quickly returning with two cups of steaming coffee.

"That's the owner, Sally Donaldson. When she was younger she was a dancer. A stripper, actually. Man, you can look at that body now and tell what it was like when she was young. Every man wanted her. To be honest, most men STILL want her! But back then she was stuck on this gangster. The guy was no good for her, but she stuck around.

"Well, did you ever see that movie with Abbott & Costello called Hold that Ghost? The guys go to this abandoned cabin that had been owned by a gangster and they come across all of this money."

Though familiar with the famous comedy team of Abbott & Costello, Gomes had never seen the film and just shook his head.

"No matter," said Schlein. "Well, Sally's boyfriend was killed by another gangster. Very ugly. Anyway, he had put away a lot of cash and no one knew where he hid it. No one except *Sally*. So, Sally gets the money and splits town and comes to New Rochelle. She uses the money to buy this place and has been running it ever since."

"So she's not from New Rochelle?"

"Not from New Rochelle and her name isn't Sally Donaldson. Don't ask me how I know any of this, but I know. I've looked out for Sally and she's looked out for me."

Jake took a puff from the cigar and sized up Gomes. A few more puffs and the food arrived.

"Well, Mister Gomes, you mind if I call you Dave? What can I do for you?"

"Yes, sure, Jake. Like I told you on the phone, I'm doing a story on the murder of TJ Smith, who you flew with during the War. So, now Al Gierek is dead and it looks to me like a homicide. I'm trying to get background because all the arrows seem to be pointing toward the son of another crew-man from your bomber, Antonio Tavares."

Jake listened, chewing on his sandwich and drinking his coffee. Gomes dug in, too, finding the turkey sandwich delicious with a fabulous sauce. Jake let the cigar go out.

"I'm not sure I can be of much help. Yeah, I served with TT—that's what we called him—and after the war I visited his widow and tried to be there for their son. But, look, if you're telling me that the son is behind these killings, that's damn hard to believe. I guess anything's possible, but still..."

"Mister Schlein...Jake. What can you tell me about TT? What sort of guy was he?"

Schlein held his coffee cup for a refill and smiled at Sally, then he turned back to Gomes and lost the smile. "He was a good kid, Dave. A straight-ahead kinda guy. Worked hard and was always there to help. Most of us had been together for a while and he came to the unit, when was it, late '44. He tried to get along with everyone and he worked hard. He didn't deserve to die that way." Jake relit his cigar and took a puff.

"So, what happened?"

Jake leaned back as Sally refilled his cup. Jake looked at her longingly as she walked away. Gomes thought there was more to their relationship than the man had admitted.

"Dave, we were returning from northern Italy. The bomb run had been pretty uneventful. We used to call them 'milk runs.' Even the flak had not been that bad. We had seen worse over the years. A LOT worse.

"Well, there weren't a lot of German planes up in the air in March 1945, but you never knew. So, the Captain, our pilot, Captain Jansen, came over the intercom telling us to keep our eyes out for German fighters. For some reason I even remember his words. He said: 'C'mon you clowns, look alive. DiUbaldo and I thought we saw a 109 a minute ago. We're not home-free yet.'"

"The next thing I knew I heard the bomb bay doors open. That was strange because we finished the bomb run. Then over the intercom the captain told us there was a problem that was being dealt with and he would keep us posted. Well, that got us all nervous, but then, a few minutes later, we heard the bomb bay doors close."

"What about Tavares?"

"I was looking for 109s when the captain came over the intercom again. There was something in his voice when he called us to attention. He said that there had been an accident. He said that TT had gone to shake loose a bomb that failed to release."

Schlein stopped for a second to compose himself. He went to light up his cigar, but Sally looked at him and shook her head 'no.' Schlein shrugged and put the cigar down.

"The Captain said that TT had fallen. That he didn't have a safety chord on. We knew that he wouldn't have had a parachute on either. Then the captain signed off.

"We were all in shock. When we landed, those of us in the rear of the plane wanted to know what happened. So did our engineer, who raced his Jeep over to the Lucky Legs as soon as we came to a stop after landing. The captain said that TT had shaken the unreleased bomb loose but that he must have lost his footing and fallen to his death." Schlein stopped there and drank what remained of his coffee. Gomes asked about the investigation. Schlein said the military ruled there was a malfunction with the bomb release and that TT had been courageous but maybe a little careless, not wearing his harness.

"I read the report," said Gomes, surprising Schlein. "There was some disagreement about the bomb bay. The engineer reported he couldn't find anyhing wrong with the bomb rack."

"Yeah, that's right. The captain accused our engineer of calling him a liar. The engineer backed down more or less, but he still said he couldn't find any mechanical problem. And that was that."

Gomes let the waitress remove their plates. "What do you think really happened, Jake?"

"How the hell do I know? I'm no engineer. I figure it's what they said. One hell of a way to die, though, falling, with no chute."

"Jake, after the war you stayed connected with the family. Why was that, besides the fact that you're a great guy?"

"I'm not sure about the 'great guy' stuff, but, look, I liked the kid, and, well, I think that I felt, you know, a little guilty about what happened."

Gomes waited for more.

"Like I said, most of the crew had been together for a while. TT was young and full of spit and vinegar. He was a hell of a good bombardier, too. But he was taking the place of a great guy—Paul Sanders—who was killed by flack on a bomb run. Some of the guys weren't ready for someone to replace Paul. It may not sound rational to you, but some of the guys gave him a rough time."

"Did TJ Smith and Al Gierek give him a 'hard time'?"

The look on Schlein's face abruptly changed. Gomes wasn't sure what it meant, but it seemed like Schlein was debating something in himself.

"I don't know. All I can say is, Captain and Lt. DiUbaldo were the ring-leaders, especially that *ass* DiUbaldo. Di was always riding the kid. He was a real son of a bitch. Maybe I felt like I had to make up for that. I don't know. It just felt like the right thing to do."

Schlein looked at his watch again and started to say something, but Gomes cut him off. "Jake, I won't take much more of your time. You've been very generous, but let me ask you two more questions. Okay?"

Schlein nodded as he signaled Sally for the check. She wrote something down and returned with the check. Schlein pulled out his wallet and put some money down on the check as Gomes said, "First question: have you seen any of the crew since the War?"

"No," Schlein said curtly, sounding like 'no efffing way.'

"Alright, last question: could you tell me about Little Tony?"

Sadness dwelled on Schlein's face. "They think Little Tony's the killer, don't they?"

"That's one theory. Tavares-Da Silva changed his name, got a job with TJ Smith and disappeared the day Smith was killed. Left no trace. He *may* also fit the description of the last person who was seen with Al Gierek."

Schlein put the cigar in his mouth. Gomes reached for his wallet, but his host stopped him.

"Little Tony—I guess he's not little anymore—was a good kid. I would send him a few dollars on his birthday with a note. When he became a teenager he started to write me! Real letters, not just 'thank you's' that his mother told him to write." Schlein had a smile of pride for Little Tony.

"Little Tony asked me about his father, about the Air Corps, about the War…things like that. But he was in a difficult situation, he and his stepfather didn't get along."

"What did you make of that?"

"Most guys I know don't like the idea of raising someone else's kid. Da Silva was alright, I guess. He worked hard, brought home a dollar, took care of the family. But it was clear he had no love for Little Tony. The boy felt left out. When his sister—half-sister—was born, *she* was the star of the show. Little Tony changed, and not for the better."

"Do you think that Little Tony murdered Smith?"

"I thought that you asked your last question, Dave." Schlein led Gomes out of the diner. "I haven't seen the kid in over ten years. He grew up, went into the Air Force, went to Vietnam…A lot of things can happen to a person."

Shaking hands good-bye, Gomes asked one last question: If Schlein was worried that Little Tony would come after him.

"Me? Nah, Tony's got no beef with me. I've got nothing to worry about. Nothing"

Gomes got in his car and headed back to New Haven. Though exhausted, he had to make this last stop.

42

It was dark by the time that Gomes reached New Haven, hoping that Claudia Kristofferson was on duty and would speak with him. Gomes found Doc's Bar, parked, and walked into the restaurant.

The outside of Doc's was non-descript. As soon as he opened the door to enter the joint he was hit by the volume and intensity of James Brown's *"Super Bad"*. After a moment he was able to adjust his hearing so he wasn't overwhelmed by the sound.

Doc's was pretty much as Carrera had described it. It was far from fancy and clearly aimed at college students. There were posters about concerts and one of Huey P. Newton and Bobby Seale, the iconic leaders of the Black Panther Party. Seale had been facing charges in New Haven in connection with the murder of another Panther who had come under suspicion for being a police informant.

The clientele of Doc's was virtually all white, though Gomes saw a couple of black faces and an East Asian face, with one of the black folks dressed like Jimi Hendrix.

Gomes walked over to the bar, ordered a ginger ale, and then asked the bartender if Claudia Kristofferson was around. The bartender, a white man in his 40s with long hair and dark moustache gave Gomes a serious inspection. He asked Gomes why he wanted to see Kristofferson and who was he anyway.

Gomes politely introduced himself and showed identification. He told the bartender he was working on a story for his newspaper and that Claudia might be able to provide some background. The bartender pointed toward a tall, brown-haired young woman in a waitress's apron who was serving a table of six young men, all looking like typical college 'jocks,' wearing heavy jackets with team logos on them. The bartender yelled to Claudia to come to the bar. She signaled that she would be there in a moment.

Gomes sat on the bar stool waiting. She finished with the table and walked over. She was certainly a sight for sore eyes. Though she knew that men were looking her up and down, she took it in stride, reminding him of the waitress at Bob's in Mashpee.

"Claudia," the barman said, "this guy Gomez here wants to talk with you for a few. He's some sort of reporter. I told him that it was okay with me if it's okay with you, you can take a quick break."

"Miss Kristofferson, my name is Dave Gomes—that is G-O-M-E-S. It's a Portuguese name. I'm with a paper called the Cape & Islands Gazette from up on Cape Cod. May I have a few minutes of your time?"

"Yes, Mister Gomes, Lisa Carrera said you might look me up. This is about Mister Gierek, isn't it?," The bartender shrugged his shoulders and went back to serving drinks.

"Yes, your friend, Miss Carrera gave me your number. Let's back up and begin at the beginning. I'm trying to find out a little about Mister Gierek, but it all starts with my working on a story about a murder that took place on Cape Cod. The person who was killed was a close friend of Al Gierek. So, when I heard about Gierek's death I wanted to come down and speak with a few people."

Kristofferson was quite obviously uncomfortable. When she first came over she had been quite 'cool,' but now she was agitated.

"I don't know what I can tell you," she started, speaking fast. "I didn't really know him. I mean, he came into the restaurant all the time but that was about it. A little chit-chat. That's all."

"I understand, Miss Kristofferson. Look, I can make this quick. If we can just sit down, maybe over at that booth, it might be a bit more relaxed."

Kristofferson looked at the corner booth, nodded and led the way to the booth. They both sat down.

"Miss Kristofferson, you were there on the day that Al Gierek died, correct?"

Kristofferson sighed, looked at the floor. "Yeah, I was working that day."

"You were serving the table where he and his companion were seated?"

"Yes."

"Did you notice anything about Mister Gierek or his companion?"

"What do you mean?"

"I mean, Mister Gierek regularly came to the restaurant. Was there anything different this time?"

Kristofferson sat there for a moment thinking. "No, nothing unusual."

"Had you ever seen the man that he was with before?"

"Look, I went through this with the police. No, I never saw the guy before. And before you ask, I can't give a good description. He had sunglasses, he was pretty tall, he wore a sort of businessman's hat but I think he was bald. The two of them looked busy, so I didn't bother them except to take their orders." Kristofferson looked down at her watch.

"When did you find out that the man had died?"

"I found out about an hour after he left the restaurant. Someone came running into the restaurant and told us that there was a body in the alley behind the building. They didn't know who it was, at least, at first. Then about 15-20 minutes later, word spread that it was Mister Gierek. We were...horrified."

"Thank you for taking this time, Miss Kristofferson—"

"Look, I appreciate the 'Miss' but you can call me 'Claudia.' Everyone does."

"Thanks, Claudia. You can call me 'Dave'. Let me just ask you, why did you quit after Mister Gierek's death?"

Claudia excused herself, saying she would be right back. She returned with a ginger ale.

"I wasn't being rude in not bringing you something to drink, I saw you were still nursing that ginger ale," she offered with a polite smile, taking a few sips. "Well, Dave, there were two reasons I left. The first was that I was shocked by the death. This was a man that I saw regularly and who had only been in the restaurant right before he died. I just couldn't get over it. I needed to get away from there."

Claudia drank some more of the soda and just sat there.

"You said that there were two reasons, Claudia."

"Yeah, I guess I did say. "Listen, are we talking on the record or off the record, as I guess you all say in the newspaper world?"

"Well, at least until this moment, it has been on the record. Why?"

"Dave, you look like a trustworthy guy, which is probably why Lisa gave you my number. So, I'm going to tell you something that I haven't told anyone else. But you absolutely CANNOT publish it. Understand? If you can't agree that's okay, I'll head back to work."

Gomes closed his pad and put his pen in his jacket. "Understood, Claudia."

"The guy who was with Mister Gierek left first. You probably know that. He put on his coat and left. He seemed to be in a good mood and Mister Gierek said he would pay the check. *Then he* put on his coat and scarf, thanked everyone, and headed out.

"About 45 minutes later, before we got news that Mister Gierek had died, I took my break. I walked out to the lobby and headed over to the elevator to get some cigarettes. You know, they have a machine over near the elevators but close to the lobby.

"Well, I put my money in the machine and got a pack of cigarettes when one of the elevator doors opens. Out walks this man. You know, the same guy that was meeting with Mister Gierek. I was surprised to see him. I mean, when he left the restaurant I saw him put on his coat and he buttoned it up, like he was going outside. But all of a sudden, here he is standing in front of me with an open coat."

"What did you do?"

"I sort of nodded hello, but he gave me this look. I mean, the guy was wearing sunglasses but I could still feel his eyes. He didn't smile. He didn't say a word. He put his right index finger up to his lips as if to say 'shish', you know, to keep quiet, and then he walked past me without a sound."

"Did you see him leave the building?"

"I got my cigarettes and went back to the restaurant. It was real creepy. I mean, I couldn't figure out where the guy was coming from and what that thing with his finger was all about. Anyway, I went back to work. The next thing I know, I hear that Mister Gierek's body had been found in the alley and that he had jumped or fallen from one of the upper floors. Everyone assumed he committed suicide, but at that moment...*at that moment*, Dave, I knew exactly what happened. That man who he was with killed him. I don't know how, Dave, and I don't know why, but I know as sure as I'm sitting here that he did it. And I understood what the finger thing was: he was warning me to keep my mouth shut."

"That's why you quit your job and moved."

"It sure is. I was getting the hell out of there. Sure, I was making more over there than I am at this dump. But I don't want to be anywhere near that place. I don't want that guy coming after me." She finished her soda, looking at him in the hope he would understand.

"Yeah, I get it. And I understand why you would want this off the record. But why didn't you go to the cops?"

"You gotta be kidding. As if they're going to protect me! The cops were more interested in closing the case than investigating it. I wasn't going to stay around to find out either way." Claudia got up from the booth, saying she needed to get back to work. The bartender was looking over at them, obviously unhappy.

Gomes put on his coat and headed back out into the cold. He put on his wool cap and walked back to the car thinking about his discussion with Claudia.

It was now all but certain that Gierek had been murdered, probably by "Little Tony" Tavares/Da Silva. What Gomes found surprising was not that Gierek had been killed, but that Schlein evidenced no fear.

What the hell was going on here?

Gomes was so preoccupied with his thoughts, he didn't notice a man following him out of Doc's. Nor did he see the man get into his car and pull into traffic, following Gomes towards Route 95 North.

43

Gomes slept through most of Sunday from exhaustion. On Monday, after a good night's sleep, he made a fried egg sandwich, the television on in the background. He sat in his kitchen with a cup of tea, reviewing his notes. Outside there was some snow on the ground, but not enough to present any travel problems, his Volkswagen with the engine over the rear wheels would do okay as long as the snow wasn't too deep.

He put on his coat and grabbed his bag. He planned to go to Taunton first to cover a bus drivers' strike, then go back to his office. He unlocked the door and began to open it when he suddenly stopped, unsure that he had turned off the kettle, he had been thinking about having a second cup but never had it.

As he turned away from the door he heard *BOOM! BOOM!* The shotgun blasts hit the door, knocking him off his feet. He dropped to the floor as shattered glass showered him. The sound of shrieking tires pierced the air as a car took off.

Gomes crawled toward the telephone, keeping his head down. He listened carefully as he heard the car head into the distance, only then believing that it was safe to stand up. Wiping the glass off his clothes, he reached for the phone. Though shaken by the attack, he managed to prioritize four calls: to Amato, Pamela, Jacqueline and his landlord. He would call his folks later.

Amato must have driven over like a bat out of hell. The Barnstable County squad car had gotten there only minutes before the detective's arrival. Gomes was speaking with the officer when Amato rushed into the house.

"You okay, Gomes?" Amato asked, his face creased with concern. There was no joking in his voice.

"Yeah, I'm fine, Vinnie, just shaken up, to be honest."

The last time someone had fired at him he was on the Demilitarized Zone between North and South Korea. A US soldier, trying to play 'John Wayne,' had fired at a North Korean loudspeaker. This resulted in an immediate barrage of bullets that could have killed most of Gomes's unit. The exchange with the North Koreans had not lasted long, and Gomes and his buddies made sure that the soldier understood that he was never to play war again. By the time they had finished with the guy he was all shades of purple.

He knew this was different. It was personal. If Gomes had that second cup of tea and walked to his car, he would be lying on the floor, dead.

"I know you've gone over this with the officer," Amato said, looking respectfully over at Officer Almeida, who had taken Gomes' statement, "but take me through what happened."

Gomes walked Amato and Almeida through exactly what had happened. He explained about turning back to check the kettle on the stove when the shotgun blast knocked him back.

"That oversight saved your life," said Amato.

He could only describe the car as a black sedan, he only got a glimpse of it. They asked him whether he had noticed anything the night before when he had gotten home, but he hadn't seen any unexpected cars around. He had not heard anything that morning either.

When Amato went back outside to examine the tire tracks, Gomes called Pamela, who gasped when she heard what had happened. "You were almost killed, David. For *what*? For a *story*? This maniac is after you because you're getting too close. You need to speak with Jacqueline and pull out of this story. I mean it. I don't want to become a widow before I'm even married!"

"Pam, listen, I'm going to call the boss next. We'll figure something out. In the meantime, Amato is here with a whole crew."

"You better call your folks while you're at it., they need to know what's going on." He promised to contact them as soon as he'd called his boss. When Gomes reached Jacqueline, she was incredulous.

"David!" she yelled. "I told you that this was too danger-ous, you have to leave this to the police. I need you to come in here and have a discussion with me. I am going to speak with Detective Amato, you are completely unwilling to listen to me."

"Okay, Jacqueline, whatever you say. I'm going to stay home today if it's okay with you, I'm pretty shaken up." His boss told him that was a good idea and hung up.

Amato returned to the apartment. "You're thinking this was Da Silva-Shepherd, aren't you?"

"I don't know, man. Smith was killed by a silenced sniper rifle, Gierek was thrown out a window. But this thing, it was messy, know what I mean?"

"Are you telling me this has nothing to do with the story about the TJ Smith killing?" Amato was skeptical.

"Okay, it might. There's no other story that I'm working on that could piss somebody off *this* much." He told the detec-tive about his interview with Gierek's wife, his interview with Claudia Kristofferson, and his odd meeting with Jacob Schlein, who was so confident he was in no danger.

Amato took notes, shaking his head and commenting that Gomes had sure stirred up a hornet's nest. "It doesn't take a genius to see Da Silva got tired of you looking into the case. Why don't *you* see it?"

Gomes grabbed a broom and began sweeping up the broken glass. "Vinnie, this doesn't feel right. It doesn't *feel* like Da Silva."

"What the fuck do you mean, Gomes? You're doing a

story on a professional killer who appears to have killed *two* people, you open the door and get two shotgun blasts. What the hell am I missing?"

Gomes continued sweeping. "The shotgun, for one thing."

"What about the shotgun?"

"That isn't his style, Amato." He dumped the broken glass into a paper bag. "Besides, the other two murders were clean. They had the mark of a pro. This feels more like an amateur."

""What the fuck, Gomes? Are you an expert on murder now? Or the psychology of killers?"

Gomes shrugged his shoulders. "I know you're the detective and you know more about this shit than I do, but think about this for a minute, alright? We have a professional killer, a damned Air Commando who knows more ways to take me out than you do to cook pasta. He took down TJ Smith with a silenced high-powered rifle. No one saw the guy or heard a thing. You're telling me this son of a bitch would fire a double-barrel shotgun at me? It doesn't make a bit of sense, Amato, it's too clumsy."

Amato closed his notebook. "Let's say that you're right, Gomes. If it wasn't Da Silva, then who?"

Gomes went over all the people he'd contacted about the case. "Maybe it was Al Gierek's son. The guy's a fascist. He assaulted me when I was visiting his mother. The bastard was trying to provoke a fight with me and I had to teach him a lesson on race relations. Then there's the situation with Gierek."

"What 'situation' with Gierek?"

Gomes described Claudia's frightening encounter with the man coming out of the elevator who warned her to keep her mouth shut. She was too scared to tell the police.

"Did the guy fit the description of Da Silva?" Amato asked.

"Not enough information to say. Could have been him, could have been someone else."

Amato stood up to leave. "Alright, Gomes, I'm going to

have a car come by here every morning before you head off to work, give me an idea what time you're leaving in the morning. when you leave work, keep your eyes open. I'll get someone to drop by your office in the evenings when you leave work. Got it?"

"Yeah, I got it, thanks."

"And one more thing: I want you to drop this damn story. Leave it to law enforcement, you idiot! This has gone way too far for a reporter from a two-bit local paper."

"Maybe you're right. But my paper isn't a two-bit local, and even if I give up on the story, the bastard out there is *not* gonna give up on me."

44

When he got to the office the following day, Jacqueline walked him upstairs to her apartment, where they went into a dining area and Jacqueline put on some water for tea. "Well, my David, have you recovered from the assassination attempt?"

'Assassination' was a word that he always thought about in terms of other people. Martin Luther King and Bobby Kennedy had been 'assassinated.' In his case, was that the right word?

"I was pretty shaken up, Jacqueline, it was a complete surprise. I was lucky—"

"You were more than *lucky*, David. I spoke with Detective Amato. He told me the details. You could have had your head blown off. I told you to be careful, and then you went to Connecticut and New York!"

Gomes explained he had discovered important information in New Haven and New Rochelle, going over his conclusions. To her credit, Jacqueline listened while she was fixing the tea.

When Gomes finished, he put some sugar and lemon into his tea, she took honey and milk.

"David, you are off this story. It is far too dangerous. This maniac has come back to kill you and there is nothing that this paper can do to protect you."

"Jacqueline, please. I don't think the shooter was Da Silva. Not only that, I think I'm nearly at the end of the story, I just need to check out a few more things."

"What makes you think that Da Silva was not the shooter?"

"Motive and weaponry. Assuming that Da Silva was the original assassin, he was sophisticated. He shot TJ Smith with a silenced, high-powered rifle. He forced Al Gierek out a window, making it look like a suicide. I don't believe the same guy would try to get rid of me with a shotgun. Add to that, he drove off in a black car that anyone could have seen."

Jacqueline remained skeptical. Before she could object, he added, "As to motive, Da Silva has no motive to kill me."

"How can you say that, David?"

"Hear me out, boss. He knows the police and the FBI are after him. It's not that I'm feeding them information they couldn't find out. Yes, he's being slick not showing himself, but he would have no reason to come back to the Cape to take me out. He gains nothing, except more attention. Keep in mind, he did NOT kill the waitress in New Haven who saw him with Gierek."

"Fair point, but I am not convinced you are in no danger."

"I may be in some danger, but not from Da Silva." Gomes drank his tea, Jacqueline seemed to have lost her taste for it.

"Jacqueline, I have to keep working on this story. I've uncovered so much information the police missed, it's the best way to find out who really does want to do me harm."

Jacqueline took her tea cup to the sink and threw out the remainder of the tea. She turned around, an anguished expression on her face. "Monsieur Gomes, I will let you keep going, though my heart says that you should be removed from this story. I understand your determination to get to the bottom of this. But it may be very, very dangerous. And, I must tell you, if something happens, your obituary will be brief and there will be no picture!"

Gomes cracked a smile. Jacqueline's face remained deadly serious. As he stood up Jacqueline put her arms around him and held him close. Gomes was surprised by the embrace, it was warmer and more intimate than anything that he could have expected.

Gomes put his arms around Jacqueline. The smell of her perfume was intoxicating. He could feel a tear from her face fall upon him. She kissed him tenderly on the cheek, he kissed the back of her hand. "Jacqueline, your concern for me means more than you can ever imagine."

"Be very careful, *mon cher*. Pamela is not the only one who does not want to lose you."

<u>45</u>

Gomes went downstairs to his office, where he went through his notes and found the two numbers that he needed to call. First, Oscar Crane, the ground-based engineer for Lucky Legs who lived in Pittsburgh. And there was DiUbaldo in Boston.

With only Crane's home number, Gomes knew the man was unlikely to be home during the work day, but he gave it a try anyway. The phone rang about four times. Gomes was getting ready to hang up when a boy's voice said, "Hullo?"

"Good morning. My name is David Gomes from the newspaper Cape & Islands Gazette. I'm trying to reach a Mister Oscar Crane. Do I have the right number?"

"Yeah, but my dad's at work." The boy then let out a series of loud coughs.

"Well, if you could help me, is there a number to reach him at work?"

"Hold on a second, mister," said the boy. Gomes heard some sounds, and finally the boy came back. "Mister, he works at this car repair place in town. They sometimes let him take calls, but you never know. Here's the number. If you can't reach him call here after about six o'clock."

Gomes wrote the number down and thanked the boy, adding he sounded like he was under the weather. The boy thanked him, told him he had the flu, and said good-bye. Gomes thought he was remarkably polite.

Gomes dialed the number for the car repair company. On the second ring he heard a man's voice announcing

'Thompson Automotive'. Gomes asked for Oscar Crane.

"Is this emergency?" asked the voice in an accent that sounded Russian.

"No, sir. I just need a few minutes of his time."

Gomes could hear some people chatting in the background. "Listen, mister, guys here don't take calls except on their lunch hour or if it's emergency."

"If you would tell me when to call back, I can do that, no problem."

"Call back between 11:30-12:30. I will tell him to expect your call. And what is your name?"

Gomes provided his name and thanked the man before he hung up. He then dialed the number Richard DiUbaldo in East Boston. On the third ring a woman with a distinct Boston accent answered the phone. When Gomes introduced himself, Mrs. DiUbaldo, told him her husband was at work at the Bethlehem shipyard in East Boston. She did not expect him home till 4:30 at the earliest. Gomes thanked her and said he would call back later.

Gomes looked up from his phone and saw that Jacqueline had returned to her desk. She looked over at him with concern. Gomes returned the glance with a warm smile, then he got to work, he had a lot of writing to do.

At 11:45 he called Crane. The same man told Gomes to hold on for a moment. Seconds later a different voice said, "Crane, here, is this Mister Gomes?" He pronounced the name like 'goomes.'

"Yes, Mister Crane, my name is David Gomes," he said, pronouncing his name carefully. "Thank you for taking this call. I'm with the *Cape & Islands Gazette* in Hyannis, Massachusetts, on Cape Cod."

"How'd you get this number?" Crane sounded worried, though not hostile. Gomes explained he had called Crane's house and that his son had given the number. When Crane didn't say anything further, Gomes gave some background on why he was calling.

"Smith and Gierek are dead, you say?" Crane asked.

"That's right. Smith was shot and killed and I believe Gierek was thrown out of a building."

"Son of a bitch. I haven't seen or talked with those guys since, what, '46. We parted company and I came back to Pittsburgh. I wanted nothing to do with them, especially with Jansen and DiUbaldo. They can roast in hell for all I care."

"Mister Crane, I'm wondering whether you can tell me about the case of the bombardier, Antonio Tavares, who fell to his death in 1945?"

There was a moment of silence. "TT, huh? Wow, yeah. Boy, I haven't thought about him for a while. He was a great kid. Just a nice guy, full of energy. He got interested in what I was doing, thought maybe he'd become an engineer after the war. Damn, that was sad about him."

"I read the report on the accident. I noticed that you had some differences about what happened. Your story wasn't in the report, but it was referenced."

"You're damn right I had differences. When I checked the bomb rack and the bay, I couldn't find any reason that a bomb should have been stuck. Another engineer checked it, too. I asked Jansen a question and he got all pissed off. Started saying I was calling him a liar. I wasn't, I was trying to figure out what the hell had happened.

Crane asked Gomes why he was bringing up something from the past. The reporter told him that Jacob Schlein said that there was tension among the crew, did he know anything about it?"

"Schlein? He was a decent guy. Captain Jansen and DiUbaldo were thick as thieves. They could be hilarious, by the way, but they could turn around and be outright cruel. They would gang up on someone and make his life a living hell. Smith and Gierek would go along with it, but they weren't the ring-leaders, Jansen and DiUbaldo were behind everything.

"Were they cruel to Tavares? To TT?"

"Hell's bells, they didn't like TT from the beginning, especially DiUbaldo. They fucked with TT all the time, unless they were fucking with someone else."

"Why?" asked Gomes.

"Why? I'm not sure. Maybe because it was late in the war and they didn't trust a replacement who was full of energy. I don't know, for sure, but they had a name for him. They called him the 'spook.'"

"What was that about?" Gomes asked, though knowing the real answer.

"I asked Di about it and he acted as if I was a moron. The way I heard that word used was with Colored guys, but TT was Portuguese, he wasn't Colored, his skin was the same color as Di's, though if I had said that to DiUbaldo, the son of a bitch would have taken my head off."

Gomes stopped for a second, then asked his final question.

"Mister Crane, what do YOU think happened on that terrible day?"

Gomes heard voices in the background. Crane seemed to be speaking to him from a cafeteria or another eating area. "Mister Gomes, I really don't know, but if I could guess I'd say that those sick bastards in the forward part dared TT to go release the bomb. I wouldn't put anything past those sick bastards. If I never see Jansen or DiUbaldo again, it will be too soon."

"You don't have to worry about seeing Jansen, he was killed in Vietnam some years ago. It's only DiUbaldo left."

"Mister Gomes, there is a special place in hell for the likes of DiUbaldo. I don't know whether any of this helped you, but it's all that I have to offer."

Gomes thanked him and they hung up. He sat there making notes from the conversation as the full story started to come together.

46

Gomes offered to take Pamela to dinner, but she insisted he come over to her place and she would fix something. Gomes told her he would head her way after he called Richard DiUbaldo. First, he decided to call Amato and see if he'd had lunch yet.

In a diner not far from the newspaper office Gomes and Amato dug into crab cakes, mashed potatoes and stewed tomatoes. Gomes filled the detective in on Crane's story. Amato knew a little about the Cape Verdean descendants who settled in New England, but not their experience during the war.

"Dave, I was wondering how a black guy, even someone who was Portuguese, got into the Air Corps. If this DiUbaldo was calling him a spook, he must have figured out Tavares was part black, even if his skin color was no darker than his own."

"That's where I'm going with the story."

"One thing puzzles me. Some of the other guys on the crew must have known what was happening. Leave aside the engineer, he wasn't with them on the bombing runs. If someone thought the kid was black, they could have just kicked him off of the crew. Why let this go on and on? Why torment him?"

"Crane didn't think Tavares was black. He must have assumed the others thought the same thing."

◇

Gomes spent the rest of the afternoon writing up his story on the draft resistance movement and the young men (and some women) heading to Canada. There was a growing refugee population in Canada. He wondered whether any of these folks would ever be able to return to the USA, or if they would ever want to.

Seeing it was 4:45, he decided to try to reach DiUbaldo. The phone rang twice and a male voice answered. Gomes introduced himself and explained why he was calling.

"Yeah, I read about TJ being killed. That's terrible. I hadn't heard about Gierek." DiUbaldo was cranky, with a heavily accented Boston voice. "Not sure I believe that he was murdered, but who knows? What are you calling me for, Gomes?"

"Mister DiUbaldo, I'm trying to understand what happened on your plane, *Lucky Legs*. I understand there was tension between you and Antonio Tavares. I also heard about his tragic death."

"*Tension*, Gomes? TT was a smart-ass kid who was looking for glory. He wanted to win some sort of medal, no matter what it meant for the rest of us. He was always rushing off to do some sort of fuckin' heroic stunt. Yeah, I had problems with that. So what?"

"What happened on that mission when Tavares was killed?"

DiUbaldo's voice grew quiet and he spoke more precisely. "All I can tell you is this, Gomes. Captain Jansen was notified by TT that it looked like a bomb was stuck in the bomb bay. Jansen opened the bomb bay door and asked TT to try releasing the bomb. It didn't release. TT told the Captain he was gonna take a look at the situation and report back, so, we waited…and waited. No word came back, so TJ or Al, I forget who, went to take a look. They reported back that both the bomb and Tavares were gone. The kid probably decided to be a hero and got his ass killed."

"The engineer, Oscar Crane, examined the bomb bay. He

found nothing wrong with the bomb rack or the bomb bay. What do you make of that?"

"Crane was a fuckin' asshole. He was always causing trouble. The bomb was probably stuck there because the asshole didn't check the racks when he should have, so, put the blame on the Captain."

DiUbaldo was eating and drinking something, Gomes could hear the munching and the slurping. He could also hear impatience grow in DiUbaldo's voice.

"Mister DiUbaldo, I was told that you and Captain Jansen called Mister Tavares a spook. What was that about?"

DiUbaldo laughed and repeated the term "spook" a couple of times. "Yeah, we called him that. The dumb-ass would come up on you all silent and you'd turn around and there he was, like a fuckin' ghost. He was so damned quiet when he moved, it gave me the creeps, so we nicknamed him the "spook," like Casper the friendly ghost, only in this case he wasn't a friendly ghost. The war was almost over, Gomes, and this smart-assed kid was looking for glory. We just wanted to go home, and not in a box."

Gomes was about to try one more question when DiUbaldo said, "Listen, Gomes, I'm not interested in talking about this anymore. I'm sorry about TJ and about Al, too bad for them, but it doesn't involve me. I got more important things to do, don't call me again. Ever, got it?"

Gomes had the phone still up to his ear when he heard the click of the disconnection. "Bullshit," he mumbled into a dead phone. Gomes knew that "spook" meant only one damn thing.

47

Dinner with Pamela was as pleasant as always. He had picked up a bottle of wine and was sitting in the kitchen admiring Pam in her furry sweater dress, describing the precautions he was taking per instructions from Amato. Preoccupied with cooking, and still upset with his decision to pursue the DaSilva story, Pamela was not giving him much feedback. So Gomes decided to take the moment to call his Uncle Al.

Uncle Al was just finishing his dinner when Gomes called him. They chatted for a while, but Al cut to the chase and wanted to know what was going on with the story. Gomes briefed him, and then *he* cut to the chase.

"Uncle Al, the engineer on the Lucky Lady told me today that the pilot and co-pilot called Tavares a spook. The co-pilot DiUbaldo said that it had to do with the way that Tavares would seemingly appear out of nowhere, silently, like a ghost. And what sounds weird to me is, no crew member I've spoken with raises the issue of race."

Al said, "Nephew, I'd guess that it was *all* about race. They aren't being straight with you. There's no way in hell calling Tony a spook wasn't about his being Black, and you *know* that. It's like I told you: Tony wanted to fly. He wanted to be in the white man's Air Corps so he signed up as white saying he was Portuguese when he was Cape Verdean. I told him it was a seriously bad idea. That's what led to the ferocious fight that we had."

"That's just where I was going: someone figured out that Tavares wasn't white. But Uncle, if they thought he was passing, why mess with him? Why not just report him?"

"How the hell do I know? Maybe they just wanted to punish the guy."

"But uncle, why didn't the other white guys intervene against a couple of racists? Why did they ignore the situation."

"How old are you, nephew? Look at the white people of Mississippi. Or Alabama. Where were they when black men were being hung from a tree?"

"David, you've got to ask why Tony put up with the not-so-subtle racist shit. I'll tell you why: Tony wanted to fit in so much he wasn't going to let anything get in the way. My God, he *wanted* to be *white*. He saw being white as being accepted, being black, he was an outcast. A second-class citizen."

"Yeah, I get it. I hear you."

"His wife was no better and me and your aunt knew it, we just didn't want to face up to it. Nephew, Tony could not accept that he was black. To him being colored was the mark of slavery. His ancestors, ours, too, didn't come to America as slaves. They came from the Cape Verde Islands as whalers and fishermen. But they were colonized by the Portuguese so, in Tony's mind, they—*we*—were all truly Portuguese. That's why he reacted so badly when I talked with him about Tuskegee. He saw himself as having as much in common with Black Americans as he did with someone from fricking Tibet."

"Wow. This is heavy stuff, Uncle Al."

"Nephew, Tony bought into what that great writer Frantz Fanon called the 'mentality of the colonized.' He wanted to be one of *them*. One of the colonizers."

Gomes could hear in Uncle Al's voice passion, anger and sadness. Al had lost his friend Tony in more than one way. The appearance of 'Little Tony' as a murder suspect had ripped away a scab that had formed over a deep and painful wound.

"Uncle Al, had it ever occurred to you that Tavares might

have been killed by his crewmen? You know, on purpose?"

"This is the first time that *anyone* ever asked me that question. But you know what, nephew? As soon as I heard about the circumstances of Tony's death I IMMEDIATELY thought that those bastards killed him. Don't ask me why. Maybe it was that 'ESP' stuff that people talk about, I don't know, but I felt it in my bones. And I couldn't say a word to anyone, not even your aunt. Not even my own brother—your father., it would have sounded too paranoid. Too crazy. We were at war against the damn Nazis! How could anyone think that US airmen would do something like that to another airman."

"It is kind of hard to swallow," said Gomes.

"I wanted to believe that *he had been a hero*. I mean I *really* wanted to believe that my friend, Tony Tavares, had gone beyond the call of duty. And, truth be told, the entire Cape Verdean community in New Bedford wanted to believe it, too. He was OUR hero, and no one was asking how a mixed-race Cape Verdean came to be on a white man's plane."

<u>48</u>

Pamela had cooked dinner, and it was delicious, as always. It wasn't fancy, but the spaghetti sauce with anchovies was spicy, just how Gomes liked it. He told Pamela about Jacqueline's concerns, Pamela, distracted, saying little.

"You doing okay, Pam?" he asked, noting her silence.

"Sure, yes, I'm fine. Just a few things on my mind about work. Nothing important. I'm probably tired is all."

Gomes let it pass, though there was something in her voice that led him to be less than convinced. The evening passed with a cloud over them. Gomes was too tired and Pamela too distracted to try and cut through it, so Gomes kissed her good night, wishing he could fix whatever was wrong.

Pulling onto West Main Street, he smiled thinking about the contrast between summer and winter on the Cape. In July even at 10pm there would be a lot of cars on the road, especially in the Hyannis area. Tonight there was little sign of life as he headed towards Route 28.

The last two days had been an emotional whirlwind. An attempt on his life that came very close to succeeding; something seeming to go on with Pam; the emotions of his Uncle Al; it was all a lot to take in.

When he turned onto Route 28 he noticed that a car behind him also turning onto the route. He looked forward and saw one car approaching on the other side of the road, but no further signs of life. He went back to thinking about the shotgun blasts that could have killed him. Was he wrong to believe it wasn't Da Silva? Could Da Silva have concluded that he

Gomes was a real threat? In any case, what else could he do to stay alive?

Bump...

'Shit!' exclaimed Gomes, looking in his rearview mirror. "Guy must be a drunk." Gomes, shifted from third gear to fourth as he increased his speed to distance himself from the drunk driver.

The car behind him matched his speed. "What the hell?!" Gomes exclaimed. He thought the best thing was to let the guy pass, the asshole was drunk or in a rush to get home. But then a shiver of fear ran down his spine. Maybe it was the shotgun guy back to finish him off.

The car behind him hit the Volkswagen's bumper again, harder. Growing anxious, *and* pissed off, he put the pedal to the floor, the little air-cooled four cylinder raising a racket as it reached it maximum RPM.

There were no other cars on the road. Gomes kept up the speed, trying to keep his trusty VW Bug's four wheels from slipping on the wet road.

Gomes saw a red light at the next crossing. He knew that he couldn't take the chance of stopping, so he jumped the light, leaning on his horn to warn anyone that he was coming through. The pursuing car blew through the light right behind him, closing the gap.

At Five Corners he bolted left and headed toward Osterville. The pursuing car, which Gomes could still not make out clearly, made the same turn and kept up the pace. Gomes cut the apex of the curves like a race car driver, ignoring the risk of hitting oncoming traffic, but he knew the under-powered Bug could not outrun the car behind him.

Heading toward Nantucket Sound, Gomes sped past many dark houses and several with one or two lights on, not a police car or any other emergency vehicle in sight. There were few street lights to guide his way.

Bump.

This bump caused the Bug to lose traction in the rear wheels. It fish-tailed wildly, Gomes fighting to keep the nose pointed down the road. He saw the pursuing car was coming up alongside of him, maybe to let go another shotgun blast. It was a muscle car, possibly a Camaro, its V8 giving out a lusty roar.

Gomes threw his car into a sharp curve, risking a skid off the road into the nearby trees. He swerved onto the narrow shoulder, the wheels briefly riding on the snowy ground, then he was back on solid macadam, the big car losing a little ground.

The pursuing driver switched on his high beams, trying to blind Gomes. The big car hit the rear of the Bug again, Gomes fought to keep the car from spinning out of control, his heart pounding in his chest.

To his left Gomes glimpsed through trees the reflection of the Moon on the water of the Sound. He thought it didn't really matter if he survived a roll over, the maniac in the car behind him would finish him off if he survived the crash.

In a flash Gomes realized where he was. He had taken this road many times when he wanted to go for a drive. Gomes could see the dark road curving slightly to the left. If he guessed right, the pursuer would try to flank him on the brief straight-away that led to the water.

Gomes gunned the car, keeping in the right lane as the curve was fast approaching. The pursuer took advantage of the situation and shifted out of its lane, gunned the car and moved to flank Gomes. Gomes kept up the speed going into the curve. At the last second Gomes threw his car to the right onto a two-lane wooden bridge, the Bug bouncing on the uneven surface. The pursuer missed the turn, ran off the road and was swallowed in the darkness.

With windows closed and the engine screaming, Gomes could hear nothing outside, but one thing was clear: the pursuing car was gone. He kept looking into the rearview mirror but saw no car lights.

Gomes made his way back to Route 28. As he headed

toward Hyannis, he felt the fear well up inside him. His heart was pounding against his chest and he gripped the steering wheel for dear life as if hanging from a cliff.

Spotting a service station with a phone booth, he pulled into the station, though it was closed, and parked out of sight in the back beside several garbage bins. He ran to the pay phone, praying that it worked. The sound of the dial tone almost brought tears to his eyes.

He put his coins into the phone, crouched in the booth and called Amato at home. The detective answered after the first ring. Gomes wasted no time on an apology for calling so late, he told him what had happened. His teeth were chattering, from the cold, and the fear.

After hearing the name of the service station, Amato said, "Listen Gomes, you did good. I couldn't have handled it better. Now, here's what I want you to do. Go to your car, turn it on and keep the engine running and the heater on so you don't freeze. Don't leave that station until I get there. Got that?"

"Yeah, Amato. I got it. Thanks." Gomes felt the night chill pierce his body making him shiver down to his toes.

"And listen, Dave, we'll get the bastard. I promise you."

Gomes slipped back to his car and started the engine. He sat, trying to slow his breathing. He wanted to put on the radio, but he didn't want to chance missing a sound.

Several minutes later that felt like hours, he saw the flashing lights moving at high speed coming down 28 from Hyannis. The unmarked car followed by a black and white pulled into the service station. Amato got out, the second car parking by the entrance.

"Quite a night, huh?" offered Amato, after Gomes had lowered his window.

"No shit, Amato. Two attempts on my life in two days. Is that a record?"

"Probably for the Cape. Listen, I want you to ride with me and show me precisely where this all happened. Another officer will be following us. Do you think you can retrace your route and get us to where you lost this guy?"

Gomes nodded 'yes' as he turned off the engine. He walked over towards Amato's car. Amato signaled him to wait for a minute while he went to his car and got a placard out of the back seat. He told Gomes to put it in his front window. It read: "POLICE BUSINESS - DO NOT INTERFERE". It was stamped "Barnstable County Police Department." Amato and Gomes then took off down Route 28.

Gomes was able to largely reconstruct the route that he had taken in fleeing from the attacking car. When they approached the curve and the bridge, Amato slowed down and got on the radio to the officer in the other car and told him they needed to proceed with caution.

The cars pulled over to the side of the road. Amato pulled out his pistol and told Gomes to stay in the car. He got out, turned on a flashlight and proceeded to the side of the road where the pursuing car had seemed to disappear. The other officer left his car, shotgun in hand and followed Amato.

Gomes sat in the car watching the dancing beam of Amato's light as the officers walked slowly along the side of the road. They left the road and moved cautiously.

After what seemed like an eternity Gomes saw Amato approaching the car. He opened the car door and got in. Before Gomes got a chance to ask anything, Amato held up a finger to wait. He called to the station for a tow truck, providing the dispatcher with their exact location, then he turned to Gomes.

"We found a car half-submerged in the water. A black Chevrolet Camaro. But no body; no survivor. Nothing. We'll get that car out of there and look it over. My guys will search the water in the morning, but at the moment, no sign of the driver."

"You think that the guy got out?" asked Gomes.

"I don't know, but I think your good driving forced that

son of a bitch off the road. It looks like he may have hit a hole on the edge of the road and found himself in the water. If he got out, right now he's very wet and very cold. We'll search the area."

"Good, good," said Gomes.

"Sit back and relax, I've got more to do before I get you home, you cool with that?"

"Sure, thanks. As long as it's warm, I'll stay put."

Gomes soon drifted off to sleep. Amato woke him sometime later, parked in front of his apartment. Amato took his car keys, saying they would return the car after.

Gomes stumbled up the steps to his apartment. He got into his house, thinking he would write up some quick notes, but first, maybe he could lie down and just close his eyes for a quick minute before getting to work.

49

When the alarm rang the next morning, Gomes couldn't get out of bed. He left a message with the Gazette answering service that he would be running late, then he turned over and went back to sleep.

Until the phone rang.

"Gomes, wake up!" said Amato.

"I'm awake, I'm awake great leader," Gomes said, trying to joke but aching through his whole body.

"We pulled that car out of the river. It was stolen. Had Massachusetts plates on it. There was a .45 with the serial number filed down in the glove box. Even more interesting was a double-barrel shotgun in the trunk. The guy wasn't hunting deer."

Gomes was still trying to get the cobwebs out of his head. "So the two attempts on my life were from the same person."

"Yeah. It looks like this guy wanted your death to look like an accident. He had the firepower to take you out but didn't use it."

"Lucky me."

"We still don't know if he survived the crash, so be *very* careful for a while. Got it?"

"Yep, got it, Vinnie. Thanks."

Gomes lay there for a few moments wanting to go back to sleep. His body was spent but his mind was racing like the engine in his car last night, so he got up and dressed for work.

When he got to the office Jacqueline recognized

immediately that something was wrong and told him to follow her, they had to talk. They went upstairs to the sitting area in her apartment. Gomes didn't wait for a question, he spilled out what had happened the night before and how he felt at the time. Jacqueline brought them both hot tea, giving him extra sugar.

Stirring her cup, Jacqueline said, "David, you understand this is the end of your work on this story, yes? Your investigation into a murder has shifted into YOU being at the center of the story. That will not do. I have given you a lot of rope but—"

"Jacqueline, I know you think that I've been obsessed with this story, and maybe I am, but I don't think that's what's going on here."

She sipped her tea, saying nothing.

"I'm trying to be what I think a journalist should be. Someone who digs. I'm not looking for the easy story, I'm not looking to please people. I'm trying to get to the bottom of this weird set of circumstances."

"Are you looking for a Pulitzer?" Her smile was challenging, not sympathetic.

"Hell, if I got one that would be tremendous. But a Black guy from Cape Cod on a local paper is never gonna get a Pulitzer. That's not what it's about."

He stood up and paced in front of her. "This a story about race, revenge, maybe even madness. But it's a story that *my* community—you know, Cape Verdeans— needs to hear. More than anything else, *that's* motivating me. In a way, I'm doing this story for my Uncle Al."

With a sigh and a look of regret, Jacqueline said, "I understand. And I agree."

"You *agree*?" he asked, surprised and confused.

"Oui. Yes, I have been trying to protect you. I worry about you constantly. If something should happen to you I would be...well, I know that Pamela would never forgive me." Gomes nodded. "Yes, you must finish the story. Though I have fear in my heart, you must finish it."

She stood up and stepped close to him. "Is that all that you wanted to discuss?" she asked.

They looked into one another's eyes, not moving, almost not breathing. Gomes was afraid to say what he felt. Afraid of what he might do about it.

"Yeah, well, I guess I also needed to say that you mean a lot to me as well. What you think of me is of supreme importance. Thank you."

At the door, Jacqueline kissed him tenderly on the cheek. "Always," she said softly. He resisted the urge to grab her and kiss her deeply and passionately, walking slowly down the steps back to the office and the safety of other people.

50

Brrrnnng! Brrrnnng!

The ringing of his desk phone startled Gomes, who had been trying to gather his thoughts on the racial aspect of the Da Silva-Tavares case. He picked up the phone. the receptionist told him Detective Amato had called and he needed to call the detective right back.

Gomes dialed the detective's office. A female voice Gomes did not recognize told him she would patch him into Amato, who was somewhere in his car. A few minutes later Gomes heard Amato answer.

"Gomes, we think that we have him!" Amato was excited. Almost jubilant. "We got a lucky break. Someone reported a break-in in Osterville. It's a summer home not far from the bridge where your attacker went in the water. The owners only come down to the house in warm weather and the caller noticed someone in the cottage. They called us and we dispatched units to surround the house."

"What makes you think that it's my guy?"

"This wasn't a simple break-in. If this was a simple robbery they would've entered the house and left it as soon as they got enough loot. The caller, who kept us posted until some officers arrived at the scene, told us that the intruder seems to be camping out. My guess is that the guy is cold and injured. Maybe he's hoping to get some new clothes before taking off."

Amato gave Gomes the directions to the site and told him that he could meet him there. Gomes said he would head over there as soon as possible and hung up.

Gomes hurried downstairs, where he grabbed his camera, headed to his car and pulled into traffic, driving like *he* was pursuing the killer for a change.

◇

The ride to the site where the suspect was hiding was a blur to Gomes. He found himself thinking about the attempts on his life, his relationship with Pam and where that relationship may be going or not going. He also thought about Jacqueline and the 'vibes' that he picked up from her over the last few days. They had always had a good relationship, but this was different.

Gomes drove to where Amato had told him to meet. An officer was standing near the detective's car. He signaled Gomes to come with him, telling him to keep very quiet.

The house was a non-descript summer home that, in warmer weather, would have plants and flowers springing up around it. On this December day it was a bleak scenario. The house was near several other similar cottages. To the rear was a larger one that appeared to be an all-year home, no doubt the home of the caller.

Amato was standing next to one of the neighboring homes. Gomes approached him.

"We have the place surrounded," Amato told him in a low voice. He looked to his left behind a hedge leading to a driveway for the house in question. A police officer raised a bull-horn to his lips.

"THIS IS THE POLICE. THE HOUSE IS COMPLETELY SURROUNDED. OPEN THE DOOR SLOWLY, THROW OUT ANY WEAPONS YOU HAVE, AND COME OUT WITH YOUR HANDS UP. ANY ATTEMPT TO ESCAPE WILL BE MET WITH SHOOT TO KILL. YOU HAVE THIRTY SECONDS."

The officer put the megaphone down and everyone

waited, guns ready, all trained on the house. The door to the house opened slowly. "I'm coming out!" the figure yelled. He emerged, limping, his hands in the air. Under an open winter coat, he was wearing ill-fitting clothes. He looked to be a white man of average height in his late 20s, with a beard and scraggly hair.

"I don't have any weapons! My hands are up, don't shoot!"

As soon as the man had cleared the door he was surrounded, thrown on the ground and handcuffed. Gomes heard the officers read him his Miranda rights, then they lifted him up and took him to a waiting car. Within minutes the car was off. As officers entered the house, Amato breathed a sigh of relief.

"Now the hard job starts, Gomes. All we have on this guy is breaking and entering. Maybe attempted robbery. Unless we can make a connection between him and the car that followed you, we may not get much more than that."

Gomes thanked him for the head's up, took some pictures and got a few quotes from Amato. He then returned to his car and headed back to the office. As he pulled away from the scene, he realized he was emotionally and physically exhausted. He gave a thought to heading back, but decided to stop and get some food instead.

Gomes bought a sandwich and soda at a small roadside store to carry back to the office. As soon as he got there Susan wanted to hear all about the two incidents—the attempt on his life the night prior and the capture of the possible assailant. Gomes gave her a brief summary between phone calls coming in, then he headed to his desk. Jacqueline and Janice, another writer were both at their desks with two interns working on stories.

Janice looked up. "David, the boss asked me to interview you about what happened last night. Do you have a moment?"

"Sure, let's do that now, but I've got to eat, I'm spent."

Gomes told her the entire story, starting with the shotgun

attack on him Monday, then the prior night's car chase. He filled her in on the arrest of the potential assailant, suggesting she speak with Amato or the officer-in-charge of the action.

Janice asked good questions, reminding Gomes what a solid journalist she was. When she retreated to her desk to write up the story, Gomes decided not to write about this incident, but instead to continue writing about his investigation into Da Silva and the TJ Smith murder. He might include reference to the two attempts on his life in his story, but knew that Janice would do a professional job on the incident itself.

The phone on his desk rang, startling Gomes. Susan told him his mother was on the phone. He told her to put the call through.

"Mom, I was going to call..."

"*David, what's going on?*" She was anxious, almost yelling into the phone. "We have to find out from others there have been *two* attempts on your life? Your father and I are a complete mess."

After listening to his mother give him hell, he explained what happened and offered his analysis of the whole situation. His mother was certain that Da Silva was behind this, but Gomes told her he felt strongly it was someone else, not Da Silva.

Tongue-lashing over, Gomes returned to his writing, feeling guilty for having caused his parents so much anxiety. He made a silent vow to make it up to them somehow. In the afternoon after phone calls and writing he walked over to Hank's store, but Hank was not in. A friend of his was operating the store while Hank was in Boston for some sort of meeting. Frustrated, Gomes headed back to the office, missing the counsel of his good friend but satisfied the walk had cleared his head.

Gomes called Amato but had to leave a message. He sat at his desk thinking with his eyes closed.

"David, why don't you leave for the day?"

Gomes looked up into the eyes of Jacqueline.

"You have gone through a lot over the last few days. Why don't you take the rest of the day off, and tomorrow as well, we'll manage without you...though just barely," the last words offered with a smile.

"Thanks, mademoiselle. I'm going to take you up on that offer. I am really drained. And, listen, I want you to know I heard your concern about the danger I'm in." She nodded her head, looking relieved.

Gomes packed up and got ready to go when Susan announced that Amato was returning his call.

"Vinnie, thanks for calling me back. My curiosity is killing me. Any news?"

Amato chuckled. "Well, Gomes, it's sort of what I thought might happen. The guy's name is Frank Peroni. He's from Rhode Island. Pawtucket, to be specific. Claims he was here on the Cape looking for work when some stranger kidnapped him and put him in this car and started chasing another car, you, apparently, but he couldn't see, the kidnapper had him lie down in the back.

"That's crazy!"

"He claims the car had an accident and ended up in the water. The driver took off, but Peroni was hurt and got out of the car on his own. He was freezing and decided to break into this house and stay there until his clothes could dry out.

"Gomes, I've never heard such horse shit, but the interesting thing is, Peroni has a sheet. Looks like he's some low-level hood with the Providence mob, he's had a few run-ins with the law."

"What's it all about, Vinnie? Why me?"

"This guy can't be held for anything in connection with you, Gomes. His story is outlandish, but we've nothing to go on. We can hold him for breaking and entering and attempted burglary, like I told you, but he'll make bail in a day or so."

"You can't keep the guy trying to kill me in jail longer than a *day or so*?"

"I'm working on it, buddy. One thing in our favor, the Providence mob connection raises a whole lot of questions, like, is Da Silva connected with the mob? Did he just hire this thug to carry out the hit or what?"

"I still don't think Da Silva is the problem, Vinnie, but right now I'm exhausted, I need some rest."

"Why don't you crash at my place, my wife will have a home-cooked meal?"

Gomes was touched by the offer but declined. They agreed to talk the next day and hung up. He grabbed his things and headed for the car, his apartment calling him to rest. And to sleep forever.

51

When Pamela returned home from her exhibition and conference she told Gomes how much she had missed him. He admitted the same feelings of loss, but decided not to tell her about the car chase and the arrest of the mob guy in the empty summer house, knowing it would upset her.

Siting on her living room couch, Gomes sensed that something was wrong as Pamela came out of the kitchen with two beers. Christmas was fast approaching: the agreed-upon time for a discussion of their relationship. He suspected that was troubling her.

"David, what's wrong? I can tell you're troubled."

"I was going to ask you the same thing, Pam. You seem to have something on *your* mind."

She rolled the cold bottle between her palms, organizing her thoughts. "David, while I was at the conference in Amherst I received…a job offer. It's with a new magazine in New York called Positively Woman. They look at issues with a woman's eye."

"O-kay."

"They looked at my photos and they really like my work. For now, they need a good photojournalist. If everything works out, I'll take charge of the whole photography department."

Gomes was not sure how to react. That was not the news that he was expecting, he had read the situation incorrectly.

"Wow, Pam, that's…wild! I mean, that's fantastic. What did you tell them?"

Pamela took a sip of her beer and looked at him. "I told

them that I was going to talk with you and that, assuming you said yes, I would join them. So, my David, what say you?"

This was eerie. Pamela had never called him "my David." The only person to ever use that expression was Jacqueline. That threw him.

"Well, I'm not sure what to say. I wasn't expecting this, I have to put it all together."

"David, I love you very much. Probably more than you can know. But you are *never* ready to commit. I love how you encourage me to explore career options, but I don't know if we're on a journey together or we just met on the same road but are traveling to different destinations.

When David did not respond Pam added, "I know we're supposed to discuss our relationship next month, but this job offer forces me to change the schedule. And to be honest, you've done nothing to make me believe you're any closer to making a real, life-long commitment."

Gomes said, "I need to think about this." He took a sip of his beer and leaned back on the couch.

"But David, what is on *your* mind? I could see as soon as I got back that something was bothering you."

David told her about the second attempt on his life, going through the frightening details. Her mouth dropped. Tears welling up, she said, "Why didn't you tell me right away? I don't believe that we went through all of this and now you tell me!"

Gomes wiped away her tears and kissed her on the cheek. "I'm sorry, Pam. It's just, I'm still trying to put everything together."

"Was it Da Silva?"

"Doesn't look like it. The guy that they arrested was some Italian guy out of Rhode Island. Seems like a hired killer, not someone I know. The problem is they don't have enough to hold him, and more importantly, they don't know who he's working for."

"Oh, my poor David! If anything ever happened to you…" Pamela put her arms around him and held him closely. They kept talking and holding each other until Gomes realized it was 1:30 am. He told her he needed to go back to his place and he would think over everything she had said. She told him to forget about her job offer, but Gomes insisted that was not going to happen, they both needed to think through what their future might be like. They kissed and he headed back to his car with more questions to ponder. More decisions to make.

52

The holiday season grew surreal on the Monday before Christmas at the arraignment in Barnstable Court. To everyone's surprise, Peroni was represented by Oscar L'Enfant of the Providence-based law firm Manchester, MacBride, & Bridges. "MMB" was a high-powered firm that had a number of important clients alleged to be from the Providence mob. This seemed a bit out of character for a 'waspy' firm, but the Providence mob had money.

Oscar L'Enfant was a younger associate, in his late 20s. The guy looked sculptured. The shape of his face, his blond hair, manicured mustache and beard, and his impeccable clothes were the icing on the cake. Peroni getting representation from MMB meant that somebody important was paying attention to this case.

The arraignment was heard before Judge Arthur Smart, known around the court as "Judge Not-So Smart." The attorneys who faced him could never quite tell whether he had problems as a result of an undiagnosed stroke, incompetence, or laziness. In any case, attorney L'Enfant argued for a low bail on the grounds that there was nothing to suggest that Peroni had done anything other than having been at the wrong place at the wrong time. L'Enfant brought along a suit so Peroni could appear before the Judge well-dressed, not looking anything like he did when he was arrested.

The prosecution argued that the circumstances were so peculiar that the state could not and should not take the risk on bail because Peroni might flee the jurisdiction. Amato and

Gomes sat in the gallery watching this mini-play unfold. To their horror, Judge Smart granted bail for a ridiculously low amount, chastising the prosecution for not having a stronger case if they were going to argue against bail.

Peroni and L'Enfant shook hands and headed out of the courtroom in order to pay the bail and leave town. Amato looked at Gomes with concern and reassurance, indicating that the release did not mean Peroni was a danger to Gomes, it would be far too risky for him to make another attempt. Gomes was not reassured, pointing out that there could be another killer out there to replace Peroni.

Yet the arraignment of Peroni was only Act #1 in this surreal play. Later that day Gomes was sitting at his desk finishing up a story about a fishing boat that vanished without a trace off of Nantucket, when the phone rang.

"Gomes," said Amato, "hold onto your hat, you'll never believe this. I mean, you can't make this shit up."

"What are you talking about, Vinnie?"

Amato cleared his throat.

"Well, it's like this. Peroni and his fancy attorney took off and headed back to Rhode Island. An hour ago one of our cars was on Route 6 heading toward the Sagamore Bridge. They saw this car pulled over on the grass. Didn't look like an accident but they could see that a rear tire was flat, so the officer pulled over.

"When he walked over to the car to check on it—figuring that someone had abandoned it to go get help—he saw a body in the back seat. The officer assumed, wrongly, that the person was dead. It turned out that it was attorney L'Enfant. He was lying there unconscious."

"You mean that Peroni turned on his own lawyer?" asked Gomes.

"That's what I assumed at first, but when the lawyer came around, he told a crazy story: L'Enfant and Peroni were driving down Route 6 approaching the Sagamore Bridge on their way back to Providence. Peroni was laughing about his making bail. L'Enfant told him he needed to keep his nose clean for a while, he was damned lucky, another judge would never have let him out.

"L'Enfant saw a pickup truck pull up beside him on the highway. The driver had the passenger-side window down, he was yelling something and pointing toward the rear of the car. L'Enfant could not make it out but figured there must be something wrong, so he pulled over onto a grassy area. He got out of the car, taking the car keys with him, L'Enfant didn't trust Peroni, and sure enough, one of the rear tires was going flat.

"While L'Enfant was taking out the spare, the driver of the pickup walked back offering to help. L'Enfant was just thanking the good Samaritan for stopping to help, when WHACK! The lights went out and the next thing he knew, a cop is waking him up. And surprise, surprise, Peroni was long gone."

"What the hell, Amato? What do you make of this?"

"I don't know, Davey, I really don't. My guess is, someone quite powerful didn't want this guy going to trial. I don't know whether they want him out of town or whether they want him dead, but they didn't want to run the risk of a trial. But, damn, to grab him right after the arraignment! Someone must have been really worried."

There was silence for a moment on the phone line.

"Gomes, one thing I can tell you, this case is way bigger than Da Silva. Two attempts on your life and then the main suspect vanishes??? I think you need to start looking at the other stories you're doing, see whether you've stepped on someone's toes. Are you doing anything in connection with the Providence mob?"

"Nah, Amato, nothing like that. But I'll look over my stories and do some serious thinking about who I've been speaking to. I'm really going to have to watch my back!"

"You're damned right. At least until we get a bit clearer as to what's going on. I mean, the other possibility is that Da Silva is somehow tied up with the Providence mob and we misread this thing from the beginning. Maybe there really was something about TJ Smith that we missed."

"Seems too unlikely, Amato. All these connections with *Lucky Legs*, Tavares... But this situation with Peroni seems different. Maybe it's unrelated. Let me do some more checking."

Hanging up on his friend, Gomes sat back and mulled over what he had just heard.

"A penny for your thoughts."

He looked up and saw Jacqueline standing there looking almost radiant. Gomes smiled back as Jacqueline sat down at his desk. "I just had a disturbing call, Jacqueline," he said, then went on to explain what had happened to Peroni. Jacqueline became serious.

"David, I'm going to Montreal for Christmas. I should be back Tuesday or Wednesday. This might be a good time for you to leave town, at least for a while."

Gomes was not sure whether Jacqueline was inviting him to join her in Montreal. He decided against asking. "Jacqueline, you know my folks. They have plans, Pam has plans and I need to be here. But thanks for the suggestion."

Jacqueline forced a smile, though there was sadness in her eyes. And fear. She walked back to her desk. Gomes had to admit Jacqueline could be right about the danger: maybe he did need to get away for a while, not just to stay out of sight, he had too much to think over.

◇

Gomes had left his Christmas shopping until the last minute, not knowing what to get for Pam, but when he saw a beautiful gold necklace with pearls in a jewelry store window, he knew that was it. After finishing shopping on

Thursday, Christmas Eve, Gomes cooked dinner for Pamela at her house. Though not the greatest cook, he liked to fry fish supplemented with quahogs and jag, childhood favorites.

Gomes wanted to spend the evening with Pamela. They had agreed to visit with his parents on Christmas Day, on New Year's Day they would spend with Pamela's father, who lived in Boston after the death of his wife several years earlier. Pamela brought a nice bottle of wine and sat back, relaxing while Gomes cooked.

Gomes always found it difficult to do any serious talking while cooking. Coltrane's *Naima* playing in the background. He had a special love of jazz, including Freddie Hubbard and Miles Davis.

"Alright, my dear. Let me first say, 'Merry Christmas!'" said Gomes, offering a toast with the white wine that Pamela had brought. Their glasses clicked, they sipped their wine and then kissed. David went to his coat and got out the present for Pam. She smiled, told him not to move, and ran into her bedroom. When she returned she carried a wrapped gift that felt, once Gomes touched it, like a garment. They hugged and thanked each other with another round of kisses.

"David, we haven't had much time to talk. I was wondering what you think about my job offer." She looked over the rim of her glass. David was tasting the food and enjoying the wine. Satisfied, he put his fork down, surprised by her directness, he thought they would dine and chat for a while before getting serious.

"Pam, you need to take the job." He looked directly into her eyes. It was hard to describe what he saw in her face. He would later wonder whether it was disappointment. Perhaps surprise, he wasn't sure.

"I love you, Pam. You're an outstanding photographer and I don't want to stand in your way. I have little to offer you if you stay on the Cape. Look, I work for a small paper and I don't know whether it will ever grow, but you have a world to conquer, gorgeous!"

Pamela was silent. She looked at David and then at her food, which she had seemed to be enjoying until the conversation started. Gomes was trying to disentangle his own feelings. Was he being honest? Was he doing this because he did not want to be in her way? Or was he afraid to make the commitment, as Hank had been insisting for months? Both of them knew he had been ambivalent about the future of their relationship.

He realized something else was emerging within him. Though he was convinced that he didn't want to get in her way, a part of him expected that in the end she would be leaving him and the Cape for a job, or because she wanted someone more exciting. Cutting loose now felt like it would make it easier all the way around.

"Alright, then." Pamela shifted in her chair and came closer to the table. "By the way, David, this dinner is great." Pamela's smile was forced. "Do you want..." She hesitated a moment. "...do you want to try a long-distance relationship?"

Gomes had not anticipated the question. "Yes," he offered, hesitant and unsure. "Of course I'd like to try. That is, if you want to. You're going to be starting a new life and I don't want you to feel, you know, tied down."

Inside his heart was breaking but he was trying not to show it. Even with his ambivalence, the last thing he wanted was for Pam to disappear, she was so much part of his life. He didn't want to keep her from pursuing her career, and at the same time he didn't want to move with her to New York. Which raised a separate question: was he afraid that Pam was going to get in the way of his own career?

Pamela grabbed his hand. "David, let's *try*. Let's see how it develops. Hey, I might even be back here soon if the job doesn't work out!"

Pamela and Gomes smiled, though there was sadness in their eyes. They knew that she was not returning to the Cape.

When they made love later that evening they whispered many promises to one another. They conveyed their love and how much they would miss one another. They discussed how often they would visit one another and how to explain this to his parents.

They fell asleep in each other's arms, neither experiencing a comfortable sleep: they had arrived at the train station as a couple but found themselves on two trains departing the station on separate tracks.

53

Jacqueline gave everyone the Monday after Christmas off as a holiday. On Tuesday Gomes was in charge of the 'fort' while Jacqueline was in Montreal. It was quiet in Hyannis as he drove to work, the forecast called for a high of 25 degrees Fahrenheit. It was the sort of day where you just wanted to stay inside. Automobile traffic was minimal.

Alone in the car, Gomes found himself thinking about Pamela and his parents. He had put up a great front on Christmas Day, assuring his parents that everything was fine, this separation was for the best, and he and Pamela would figure out a way to stay together. Inside, however, he knew that when Pam took off in January, he had no idea if their long distance relationship would last. Uncertain what to do and how to act, he felt as if his world had been thrown into the air.

A block from his office he saw a family all bundled up carrying shopping bags. Gomes could not believe they were returning gifts at this time of the morning! He turned into the lot outside the office, just missing a man who was walking down the sidewalk crossing the driveway. Gomes parked the car, turned off the ignition and headed for the door to the building.

"Do you have a full tank of gas?"

Gomes turned and saw a white man who looked to be in his 50s, with gray hair and a gray mustache. It occurred to Gomes that this was the person who had been walking across the driveway entrance when he pulled in. The man was holding a cane and wearing a Navy pea coat, a wool cap and leather gloves. For some reason the guy was wearing sun glasses, despite the overcast skies.

"Do you have a full tank of gas?" the man asked again, this time with a full smile.

"Excuse me, sir, but I'm not sure I understand your question," responded Gomes politely and impatiently.

"Young man, the question was very straightforward. I asked 'Do you have a full tank of gas?' So, do you?"

"Well, yes, sir, I'm not sure why that would be of any interest to you. You will have to excuse me but I have to get into my office."

"Not so fast, Mister Gomes. Yes, I know your name. And I asked about gas because we have a little trip to take."

Gomes noticed that the man had moved his right hand into his pocket. His left held the cane, but Gomes could tell that the man was in no way relying on the cane for stability.

"Let's get back into your car. Please, no sudden movements. Oh, and if you're thinking of making a mad dash somewhere, I would think twice. You will be dead before you hit the ground. But, listen, Mister Gomes, it really doesn't have to get to that. Just get into the car. Please."

Gomes looked over at the building to see whether Susan or anyone else might be watching. No such luck. There was no one around. With deep fear in his stomach Gomes headed to the car. As directed by the man, he opened the passenger side first and then went to the driver's side and got in.

"Where are we going?" Gomes asked.

"You'll find out when we get there. For now, just head out to Route 6."

"Listen, mister, if I don't report in my paper will get worried. They will send people to look for me. Why should we have to go through that?"

"Mister Gomes, no one is going to be looking for you," the stranger replied. "At least not for a little while. A call was made to your office night line from Cape Foreign Cars, where you take your car for repairs. The message was from a Raymond Callas. You know Callas, he's the owner of the establishment. He was calling your office on your behalf because you were sitting in his waiting area due to a problem with your Bug. He'd been asked by you to leave a message.

"By the time your office figures out that Mister Callas didn't make the call, we will be where we need to be."

The man stopped talking as they both entered the car and he positioned himself against the car door so that he could look at Gomes. He locked the door, a .45 sitting on his lap.

"Now, Mister Gomes, a few ground rules. First, don't try to do something stupid in order to bring attention to your car for any police who might be driving by, you will be dead. More importantly, should we not arrive at our destination within the next 90 minutes, an associate of mine will take actions against a certain young woman you care for. Got it, Mister Gomes?"

Gomes nodded.

"Alright, my next ground rule. I'm not interested in talking with you during this trip. We're not going on a picnic and I'm not interested in becoming your friend. If you want to put on the radio to keep yourself company, feel free. If you have questions about directions, ask. But otherwise I don't want to discuss the weather, the Vietnam War, Christmas, the next landing on the Moon, the Temptations, or whatever. Got it?"

Gomes nodded again as they drove off.

As they approached Route 6 the man indicated that Gomes should head towards Provincetown. Gomes complied, saying nothing. Out of the corner of his eye Gomes inspected the man. He was not as old as he had first appeared. Gomes had the impression that the man may have doctored his appearance. It was not dramatic and did not look foolish, but it looked like enough was changed to confuse an observer.

There was very little traffic on Route 6. The man told

Gomes to stay slightly above the speed limit but not to go too slow or too fast. The man checked the fuel gauge and saw that there was plenty of gas in the car. He leaned back and watched Gomes.

As they entered the Orleans traffic circle the man took out a stick of gum and offered it to Gomes. Gomes accepted, the man took a piece for himself and put the rest back in his pocket. They kept driving, the man continuing to display no interest in conversation. Gomes turned the radio on just as background and to calm himself, realizing every so often how hard he was gripping the steering wheel. Here we go again, he thought, reminiscing his narrow escape from Peroni not long ago. He wondered whether he would be lucky enough to escape this time. Amato had implied that someone else— other than Peroni—might now be after him.

In his rearview mirror Gomes saw a police cruiser pull onto Route 6 from a side road. The car was fast approaching but its emergency lights were not on. Gomes decided not to attempt anything. His kidnapper seemed to have no interest in the police cruiser as it passed them. Gomes looked over at him but, due to the sunglasses that the kidnapper was wearing, it was impossible to determine whether he was awake or asleep.

They kept driving.

When they entered Wellfleet, the kidnapper stirred a bit, adjusting himself in the seat. "Right after we enter Truro we'll be making a left turn, going in the direction of Cape Cod Bay," the kidnapper said. "I'll point out where."

They continued driving, with little to look at other than many 'closed-for-the-season' motels along the route. Within a mile of entering Truro the kidnapper pointed his left hand toward a road on the left side. Gomes put on his signal and turned, while he watched a car coming from the other direction pass him. The road was heavily wooded. Gomes was heading at a 45 degree angle from Route 6 moving in the direction of the Bay. The kidnapper was paying close attention.

"Make a left at the next place that you can, it will look like a driveway but you'll see gravel."

Gomes put on his signal and made a left turn onto a small road with barely enough room for two cars to pass one another. The road went up a slight hill. Gomes noticed a small house to his right that looked vacant, followed by another house on the right with a car in the driveway but no sign of activity. The road bent slightly to the right and on the left side there was a small, grey house with a driveway.

"Turn left into the driveway and shut the car off."

Gomes did as he was instructed. He looked at the house: Gray shingles, one floor, a style common to the area, nothing noteworthy.

"Now, Mister Gomes, you will get out of the car. You don't need to lock it because there's no one else around. Don't think about yelling or running off, it would *not* be healthy."

Gomes glanced around him, saw no one. No help. He walked toward the house imagining it would be the site of his demise.

54

Gomes walked toward the nondescript house, the kidnapper close behind holding his .45 pointed at his captive's back. When they reached the front door the kidnapper took out a key and handed it to Gomes, telling him to open the door, then hand him back the key. Gomes did as he was instructed and they quickly entered the house.

Gomes looked around and saw that it was, indeed, a summer home. The furniture was covered and the house, though a bit warmer than outside, was not built for cold weather. Gomes walked forward, hearing a clanging sound that he could not make out. The kidnapper pointed the .45 toward a door and told Gomes to open it.

The door opened to stairs going down to a cellar. Gomes heard the clanging sound from below: a sound like chains. He walked down the stairs into a cellar with a single naked bulb illuminating the space. Two small windows near the ceiling let in a cold, dim light. A foul smell filled the air.

Gomes looked around as the kidnapper walked down the stairs behind him. Standing in front of him were two men, both in chains connected to a pipe in the ceiling. The connection allowed them to walk up and down and use a covered bucket for a toilet. Gomes noticed some food and sodas on a crude table. There were two cots and two chairs, along with a small space heater. The chains did not extend very far, so it was impossible for the captives to get to the stairs. Gomes realized if the men cried out for help, no one would hear them, the surrounding homes were closed for the winter.

The two disheveled men stared at Gomes and the kidnapper. Gomes immediately recognized the face of Peroni, the would-be assassin who had attempted to snuff out Gomes's life and then disappeared on Route 6. The other face Gomes did not recognize.

"Gentleman, allow me to do the introductions," said the kidnapper as if he were opening a meeting. He took off his gloves and opened his coat, the picture of politeness and outwardly friendly.

"This, as you know," the kidnapper said looking at the two men in chains, "is Mister David Gomes of the Cape and Islands Gazette. As to our guests in chains, standing to your left, Mister Gomes, is a gentleman you already know, Mister Frank Peroni of Pawtucket, Rhode Island. A hired killer and thug, he joins us in our summer home.

"To your right is a gentleman whose acquaintance I do not believe you have made, though you may have spoken with him. Meet Mister Richard DiUbaldo from East Boston, Massachusetts."

It was clear that fear gripped Peroni. DiUbaldo had the appearance of an angry cat in a zoo. He was almost snarling. From the bruises on their faces, both men looked as if they had gone several rounds in a boxing match.

"No greetings?" the kidnapper asked the two in chains. "Well then allow me to introduce myself. As you may now have guessed, Mister Gomes, I am Antonio Da Silva, the individual about whom you have been most curious."

There was an eloquence and elegance in Da Silva's speech. His style of speaking reminded Gomes of the Mexican-born actor Ricardo Montalban. Gomes could not figure out whether Da Silva was playing a game, a role, or whether he actually spoke in that manner.

"Gentleman, the silence is deafening. I expected conversations, or at least some pleas to be offered," Da Silva said with a smirk on his face.   Peroni and DiUbaldo said nothing.

"Gentleman, please be seated." Da Silva walked over to a wall, where he brought back two folding chairs. He handed one to Gomes and pointed to it with his .45, indicating that he sit down. Da Silva opened his chair and sat, all the while keeping the .45 visible.

Apparently remembering something, Da Silva stood up, walked over to a corner of the room and brought back a tape recorder. He set it down on a table in the middle of the room and turned it on.

"Gentleman, let's not be shy. Mister Gomes is visiting with us in order to hear your stories. I think, Mister DiUbaldo, that he will be most interested in yours, but we will start with you, Mister Peroni. Please tell us why you had a reason to kill Mister Gomes. Don't be bashful."

Peroni was looking nervous, he seemed to be having trouble breathing. Da Silva, on the other hand remained calm and patient.

"Ah, well, I'm not sure where to begin. Ah, well, I guess I was paid to whack Gomes." Peroni kept looking at Da Silva who, having removed his sunglasses, just stared at the tongue-tied man.

"Who paid you to kill Mister Gomes?" Da Silva asked, still calm.

"Well...ah...well, I was called by this friend. Well, he's not exactly a friend, but someone I know. This guy tells me that someone has a job for me and asks me whether I'm interested. He tells me that it's a sort of freelance job, you know, it's not part of the organization but a way for me to make a few bucks. So, I say, yeah, sure. So my friend, he puts together this meeting with this guy here, Richie DiUbaldo. Richie gives me the instructions, half of the money and, well, I went to take care of it."

Da Silva turned towards Gomes. "Have you any questions, Mister Gomes?"

Gomes felt as if he were in some sort of play, or maybe a

dream, there was something so unreal about this situation. He also felt scared to death. Gomes wasn't sure how he was supposed to react to this. Was Da Silva testing him? Did he plan to kill *all* of them?

"Uh, Mister Peroni," said Gomes, "then this was not a mob hit?"

Peroni shook his head. "No fuckin' way. Yeah, Richie knows some of the made guys in Providence, and I assume that's how he found out about me, but, nah, this was a private operation. Nothing personal, Mister Gomes. I have no idea who you are. This was a chunk of money that I needed, I have a lot of debts to pay off, if you know what I mean?"

Gomes could not believe the way that Peroni was talking. It was as if he were talking about buying a car or refrigerator.

"Alright, then," Da Silva said, shifting his position and facing DiUbaldo. "We now come to a major player in this drama. Mister DiUbaldo, most recently of East Boston. Former co-pilot in a B-24 bomber called Lucky Legs, which is where he met my late father, Antonio Tavares. Mister DiUbaldo, please tell us your contribution to this tragedy."

DiUbaldo looked briefly at Da Silva, then turned his head and spit on the floor. He said nothing. Da Silva sat silently in his chair for a moment, looking toward the stairs. He stood up and stretched, finally walking over to DiUbaldo. The punch that he landed on DiUbaldo was swift and silent. DiUbaldo's yell and grunt were anything but silent.

"Mister DiUbaldo, I told you we are using someone else's home for our little conference. You are to respect their property and my time. So, let's try it again. What's your contribution?"

DiUbaldo looked at both Da Silva and Gomes, but said nothing.

"You know, Mister Gomes," Da Silva said, "I was trying to decide whether there were effective measures that I could take to encourage Mister DiUbaldo to tell us his story. The problem with those measures—what is sometimes called less than politely, torture—is that people end up telling you what you want to hear rather than the truth.

"Fortunately, Mister Gomes, I know the story through other sources. So if you will permit me, I will tell you a tale that as yet has no ending. A tale that is as complicated as it is sad."

Gomes looked from Da Silva to DiUbaldo with amazement. Realizing that Da Silva was going to unravel the mystery of TJ Smith's murder and the death of "TT" Tavares at the end of World War II, the stories he had been pursuing for so long, he nodded to Da Silva to continue.

"In late 1944, a young, energetic and naïve bombardier was assigned to a B-24 called Lucky Legs. The plane was based in Italy. This young man, Antonio Tavares, who soon gained the nickname 'TT', was anxious to prove himself.

"Well, TT tried everything that he could to fit in, but the pilot and co-pilot of this plane could not stand him. At first they were not sure why they hated TT so much. But eventually, through the help of Mr. DiUbaldo, they came to the conclusion that TT, despite claiming to be Portuguese, was not white at all but was, what did you call him, Mr. DiUbaldo? A 'dirty nigger with a Portagee name'? A 'spook?'"

DiUbaldo looked at the floor, staying silent, though Gomes could tell the man was captivated, despite himself.

"Well, Mister DiUbaldo, you were right that TT was not white. He was Cape Verdean. But he so much wanted to be part of the Air Corps that he was prepared to pretend that he was white. I never knew him, but from what I've heard he may even have believed it. Who knows?"

Da Silva looked at Gomes. "Captain Jansen and Lientenant DiUbaldo made my father's life a living hell. Mister DiUbaldo, please tell Mister Gomes how you determined that TT was a 'nigger', as you called him."

DiUbaldo said nothing, his look an expression of nervousness and contempt. Da Silva sat quietly, screwing something onto his .45 and looking over at his captive. Gomes saw it was a silencer. He looked at Da Silva's hands, noticing a black onyx ring set in gold with an unusual design. Da Silva seemed to be looking absent mindedly at the ring and the silencer. DiUbaldo remained silent. Gomes also noticed that Da Silva had switched off the 'safety' on the .45 as he stood up. He walked over to DiUbaldo.

As Da Silva walked towards him, DiUbaldo seemed to freeze up. The perspiration on his face even stopped mid-drop.

What happened next seemed to occur at light speed. Suddenly Da Silva turned towards Peroni, pointed the gun at his head and pulled the trigger. With the muffled report and the force of the bullet, Peroni was knocked off his chair and fell to the floor, dead.

"Well now, Mister DiUbaldo, one less hired killer on the loose. I hope I've made it clear that I have limited patience. I cared little for Mister Peroni and, as I'm sure you can guess, I despise you. So, let's put 1 + 1 together and see where that lands us. If I was willing to put a bullet through Mister Peroni's head, what stops me from doing the same to you?"

55

DiUbaldo tried acting tough but was clearly frightened by what was unfolding. He coughed for a second, perspiration running down his face.

Da Silva said, "So, let's try this again: *what was it that led you to conclude that Antonio Tavares was not white?*"

DiUbaldo looked up. In a low growl he said, "Ah...umh... the picture. He had this picture that we stumbled across. It was in his locker. It was a picture of him with these Colored folks. It looked like a family reunion or something, but we could tell that it was *his* family. We could see the resemblance even if the complexions were different."

"Ah," replied Da Silva, "so, on the basis of that photo you decided to persecute Tavares?"

"Well, yeah, we were messin' with him. We wanted him out of the unit. It was a white man's Air Corps, there was no place for someone like him. But he wouldn't get it! No matter how bad it was, he stayed around. No matter how much we made it clear that we wanted him out, he wouldn't budge. I wouldn't call it 'persecutin'' him. We just wanted the...well, we wanted him out."

Da Silva had placed the gun down, out of reach of both DiUbaldo and Gomes. He sat there looking at DiUbaldo, who said, "How'd you find out any of this shit, anyway?"

Gomes found it amazing that given these circumstances DiUbaldo still came across egotistical and demanding.

Da Silva turned towards Gomes. "Mister Gomes, let me tell you another story. When I was in the 'Nam some years ago, I was hanging out with a friend. His name is not important. We were on leave in Saigon and he had this gorgeous Vietnamese hooker who would hang out with him. Every time that he was on leave he would see her, and I think—truth be told—that he fell in love with her.

"One day this lady friend of mine and I were out with the two of them. We were quite high on this excellent grass." In telling the story, Da Silva seemed to go off into another world. He looked down at the floor, and occasionally at Gomes, not at DiUbaldo. He completely ignored the body of Peroni, whose blood was spilling onto the rug beneath him.

"My friend's lady, who was very high, told us this story about one of her clients. My friend didn't really like hearing about her clients. That's when I could tell he was truly in love with her. I could never tell whether the feeling was mutual.

"In any case, she told us about how she and this US Air Force guy had been fucking and he drifted off to sleep. She got cleaned up and dressed and was getting ready to leave the hotel room they were using, I don't know, somewhere in Saigon. Just as she got to the door she heard this guy yell out. Well, she had no idea what happened, so she ran back to the bed to check on him.

"The guy was half asleep, but basically coming back to consciousness. He told her that he'd had a nightmare. In this nightmare a guy he had killed was coming back to life and coming after him. He chuckled because he said that it was so ridiculous."

Da Silva took a sip of some soda and sat there for a moment composing himself. "This lady was shocked at what she heard next. This Air Force guy told her that he had thrown a *'nigger'* out of a plane during World War II. He went on and on about this 'nigger' infiltrating the white man's army and that he had to be taught a lesson. He seemed to think that it was hilarious. And of course, he'd gotten away with it.

"So, knowing that my father had fallen out of a plane, I

wanted to find out more. I asked a few questions and found out that the guy was a Colonel Jansen in the Military Air Transport Service based at Tan Son Nhut airbase. Well, my curiosity was killing me so I did my best to get to know the guy. It turned out that he liked good grass and he loved to play poker. I figured out a way to get close to him until we were buddies. Really tight. I supplied him with the best grass, plus a little opium. One day when he was really high I got him to tell me the whole story. I forced myself to laugh as he told me how he had hated this 'nigger.' How he had conspired to have this 'nigger' knocked unconscious and thrown out of the plane, and how his co-pilot, our Mister DiUbaldo, had been the person to carry out the dirty deed. Of course, Jansen assumed I was white."

DiUbaldo offered no explanation or response, he just looked at Da Silva, who at that moment was looking directly at DiUbaldo.

"I told Jansen about a place where he could get the best grass and the best women. We went to this cheap motel in Saigon. I locked him up and started giving him heroin. I made sure that the bastard was good and high and I kept him there, with help from a Vietnamese friend of mine. We kept him on the heroin for days until he was crying if he didn't get it. My friend and I would take turns visiting the bastard and shooting him up. The bastard was pathetic. By the time we were finished with him he was begging us for more, telling me anything that I wanted to hear. He told me more about the murder of my father. He told me *everything*. So, I decided we would play a bit of Russian roulette.

"He lost."

Da Silva looked down at the .45 on the table. Gomes wondered if it was the same gun he'd used in Viet Nam.

"The Air Force was looking for Jansen, of course. I mean, he was gone for two weeks with no explanation and not being on leave. They had no idea where he was. We finally let word leak out that Jansen had been operating with some Vietnamese gangs and gotten killed. We directed the MPs to the location where they found Jansen's body. He was completely discredited and his reputation ruined."

Da Silva picked up the gun and gave it a little loving stroke. "At that moment I decided that step #1 had been accomplished."

Da Silva looked at Gomes, saying no more.

DiUbaldo said, "Da Silva, Jansen didn't know what the fuck he was saying, he was high as kite. Yeah, we both hated Tavares, but that's not the same thing as killing the son of a bitch!" DiUbldo said this without thinking and then looked embarrassed.

Da Silva turned toward Gomes. "What do you think?"

Gomes cleared his throat, giving himself a chance to think. His mouth was dry and his throat felt like he was choking. "I think that DiUbaldo should be investigated and taken in for a trial. If what you say is correct, then he needs to be held accountable."

Da Silva nodded his head, apparently agreeing with Gomes. Gomes relaxed a little, feeling he might be on the verge of a breakthrough. He doubted that he could get Da Silva to surrender, but maybe there would be one less killing today.

"Well said, Mister Gomes!" Da Silva's words and approach were reassuring. "That is what I would expect a man of journalism would say. Let the courts render their verdict on Mister DiUbaldo. Let justice prevail, right?"

Gomes nodded his head, though it was clear Da Silva was not interested in turning his captive over to the police.

"My friend, you have more confidence in the system than I do. Let me tell you what would happen if I turned him over. There would be a superficial investigation, DiUbaldo would insist that he was kidnapped by a crazy black man, the Air Force would look at the report and conclude that the son of this Air Corps hero was distraught over the death of his father and needed someone to blame. Then they would close the book and continue looking for me. Isn't that right, Mister DiUbaldo?"

DiUbaldo said nothing, he just stared at the floor.

Looking at Da Silva's warm, smiling face, Gomes realized that he was not dealing with a madman, but with a man obsessed with revenge. The outrage and sorrow had eaten away the man's sense of right and wrong, replacing it with the justification for revenge. "Mister Da Silva, there's something I don't quite understand."

"And what pray tell is that, Mister Journalist? I thought you would have the whole thing figured out by now."

"Sorry, I'm not that smart. Why were TJ Smith and Al Gierek killed? They didn't have anything to do with murdering your father, did they?"

Da Silva aimed the .45 up to the ceiling. He seemed to be staring at the opening of the barrel. Was the darkness inside the gun a symbol for him? An answer? A salvation?

Da Silva's look was rueful. Almost religious. "Smith and Gierek were involved, their white hands weren't clean. The masterminds were Jansen and our friend here, but the four of them worked out the plan and helped to carry it out. DiUbaldo knocked my father out while Smith and Gierek pulled his body into the bomb bay. Then it was 'Tavares away!'"

Da Silva's face was tortured, torn between joy and infinite sorrow. He sat with his head slightly turned up to the ceiling. Or was it heaven, Gomes couldn't be sure.

"But Mister Da Silva, you're saying that Smith and Gierek were involved in a racist killing, but when you look at the lives of these two guys after the War— I mean Smith and Gierek, not Jansen and DiUbaldo—they seemed like solid citizens. I know you tried to smear their reputations, I looked into the phony bank account, that was you, hands down."

Da Silva shrugged, not denying his role.

"I mean, when you cut through the bullshit, Smith was—at least according to everyone I spoke with—a thoroughly decent guy. What you're telling me doesn't add up!"

Da Silva now had a look of disgust. Of loathing. He turned directly to face Gomes. "You know, there's something funny about Americans. I mean, white Americans. They can commit the most terrible crimes and think they can then go on with their lives. Or maybe they feel they can make up for the crimes by being a better person. But they NEVER want to admit to the crime. *They never want to answer for the real damage.*

"So in the case of Smith and Gierek, yeah, from what I can tell they went on to lead pretty good lives. They treated their neighbors well. Probably were kind to stray dogs and cats. But when they had a chance to admit to the crime that they committed, they kept their dirty mouths shut."

"How do you know?" said Gomes. "How do you know they never admitted their guilt? To somebody?"

"Because I warned them!" Da Silva replied, his voice an animal growl. "I warned them both through letters that I KNOW that they received. I gave them enough information that they knew they weren't written by some nut. I told them they needed to come clean about the murder of Antonio Tavares. I gave them *deadlines*. I told them what they needed to *say*. They did not do *ANYTHING!* DiUbaldo received the same letter."

"So, what happened with Al Gierek? I mean, his wife said he didn't even like rum!" Da Silva let out a laugh. Gomes forced a smile, trying to form an emotional bond between them. DiUbaldo didn't find any of it funny.

"Yes, I discovered that fact after I grabbed Mister Gierek. Maybe I should have gotten a bottle of Jack Daniels. In any case, I put a gun to his head and told him that he either drank the rum or he ate a bullet. The choice was not difficult. He drank and we talked. He accepted his fate, though he hoped that all that I wanted was a confession and that I would let him go. But you see, it was too late. A confession under those circumstances is meaningless, it can easily be recanted."

Gomes said, "Mister DiUbaldo, did Smith and Gierek pull this whole thing off with you?"

DiUbaldo shook his head. "There was nothing that happened except TT had an accident!" DiUbaldo said. He tried to sound sincere, but his eyes betrayed him.

"Tch, tch, tch. So many lies." Da Silva looked at Peroni's body. "Shame to stain such a lovely rug. I don't think the blood will ever wash off." He looked hard at DiUbaldo to see if the man picked up the meaning of his word, then turned to Gomes.

"Mister Gomes, you're going to help me with a little clean up. Please, help me load Mister Peroni's body into that rug."

Putting the gun in his belt, Da Silva ordered Gomes to wrap the rug around Peroni's body. They carried the body up the stairs and out into the overcast wintery day. They walked toward the rear of the house, where there was a sharp drop off into a wooded, marsh-like area. Da Silva signaled that they would throw the body over the side at the count of three. With the body thrown into the marsh, Da Silva pointed toward the house, the metal gun glinting in the soft moonlight, and they walked toward the house.

Gomes asked, "Are we going to be throwing DiUbaldo's body over the side next? And mine?"

Da Silva had a peculiar smile on his face. "You will walk away from this, my friend…if you make the right choice."

As they approached the door Gomes was struck by the silence. He could hear no cars, they were too far from Route 6. No one was driving by and there was no one in sight, only the sound of a lonely wind blowing through the trees. It was a haunting sound that seemed to foreshadow only death.

Back inside the house they headed downstairs, Gomes ahead of Da Silva, each taking their original seats. Da Silva picked up a can of soda and took a few sips. Gomes did like-wise. He watched as Da Silva took a white cooking timer from his jacket pocket. He placed it on the cement floor. Gomes wondered what new mind game the man was setting up. He turned toward DiUbaldo, who was looking scared. Gomes thought the tough guy was about to cry.

"How did he catch you? I thought you were supposed to have police protection?"

DiUbaldo shook his head. "Protection! What a joke. I was going crazy just going to work and heading home. I needed to get out of the house so I snuck out one evening and went for a drink. I was with some friends. This guy came over and started mentioning the names of some friends of mine. I didn't know who the fuck he was, but he paid for the drinks, so what the hell.

"He sat with me and a couple of guys and we all joked around, then he got up and left. I started feeling weird. I left the bar to go home, and the last thing I remember was walking down the street. Next thing I knew I was in a dark, cramped space. It was the trunk of the bastard's car. After a long ride, bumping around, we ended up here. Yeah, I know, if I'd stayed in the house we wouldn't be having this discussion now."

They looked down at the blood stain that had seeped through the rug.

"I suspect Da Silva would have found a way to get hold of you anyway. This man is a professional and he's more than determined." DiUbaldo grunted something unintelligible.

Da Silva said, "Mister DiUbaldo, do you have anything more that you would like to add? Anything that you think that we should know about your case that might explain your actions in 1945?"

DiUbaldo looked up. "Listen, Da Silva, I'm not on trial. *You* will be when the cops catch up with you. There was an investigation of Tavares's death and there was no fault found. You keep insisting that he was murdered. You let me go and we'll forget about this. You can just drop me off on Route 6 and I'll get back to Boston. We don't have to go any further with this shit."

Da Silva looked as if he was considering the proposition, but Gomes knew the man had his mind made up.

"Let me give you an alternative plan." Da Silva looked at his watch, then he rotated the dial on the cooking timer. "In exactly fifteen minutes a bomb will go off in this basement. The basement will be destroyed, of course, the house will collapse, and good night sweet Prince!"

DiUbaldo's mouth dropped. His eyes seemed to grow out of his head.

"Now, my dear journalist friend, I've set the timer. You have exactly fifteen minutes and no more to speak with our guilty party. You can try to help him to escape, or you can try to find the bomb. You can do whatever you like in that time. When the buzzer goes off..." In the silence that followed Gomes heard the little device go *tick, tick, tick.*

"When you do leave the house, I would not recommend standing too close to the building, the blast will be felt for a hundred yards beyond the walls."

Da Silva gave them a snappy salute, mocking the military code his father had followed. Gomes and DiUbaldo were speechless.

"What the fuck are you talking about Da Silva? You can't just leave me here to be blown up!!! I tell you, I didn't do anything. Are you nuts??? Let me outta here!"

"Mister Da Silva, please," Gomes said, "I realize this guy is a bastard, but this isn't the way to handle it."

"Gentlemen, please. Twenty-five years ago you, *Mister* DiUbaldo made the life of an innocent guy miserable and, ultimately, you killed him. The evidence is clear. So, you'll have fifteen minutes to reflect on your life, a much more generous amount of time than you gave my father."

DaSilva looked at Gomes, dead serious. "I hope you appreciate the irony here. I am blowing DiUbaldo up. *Up*, get it? Like up in the air. In the great blue sky."

Da Silva turned and walked up the stairs, taking the tape recorder with him. DiUbaldo began to come apart. Sweating like a pig, he yelled after Da Silva, "Alright, Da Silva, alright! You want a confession? I'll give you a fuckin' confession! Just get me the fuck out of here! *Yes*, we killed TT! *Yes*, he snuck into the white man's army and had no business on that plane. He couldn't take a hint to leave. Okay, we got rid of him. He never knew what happened to him. The four of us couldn't stand the idea of a nn—, a colored guy in the unit. We did all that we could to get him out but he wouldn't leave. He stood firm for whatever fuckin' reason.

"Da Silva, you still there? That's what you wanted to hear, right? I confessed! I've told you what only three other men knew. The other guys on the plane could only guess what happened but none of them really knew. Now GET ME THE FUCK OUT OF HERE, DA SILVA!!!!"

Gomes and DiUbaldo heard DaSilva's footsteps walking away. A door opened and closed, then, silence.

"Do something, mother-fucker!" DiUbaldo yelled at Gomes. "Get me the fuck out of here! Come on, do something!!!"

Gomes stood still for a moment. He realized he was being insulted by a racist who was about to be blown up. Maybe the best thing would be to clear out. He couldn't believe that DiUbaldo, facing certain death, would continue to insult him. But Gomes, was a black man, and apparently that was all that DiUbaldo saw.

The ticking of the timer focused Gomes' attention. He looked around for some tools to break the chain. The killer had planned well, there was nothing resembling a tool anywhere in sight. He ran upstairs, yelling back at DiUbaldo that he was looking for some tools. He dashed into the kitchen but could not find anything that could put a dent into the chain.

He ran outside and saw a tool shed. Though locked, it was easy for him to get it open. He rummaged through the clutter until he found a hammer and a pickaxe. Grabbing them, he ran back to the house and down the stairs.

Gomes looked at the timer, saw that he had only seven minutes left. He used the hammer to whack at the chain, but with no luck, the links were thick and strong. He continued driving the hammer down on the chair, the ticking of the timer filling the silence between the blows.

Throwing the hammer away, Gomes reached for the pickaxe. "Lean your head back," he said. With DiUbaldo leaning back, Gomes stretched the chain out over the cement floor. He lifted the pickaxe and sent it down with a crash onto the chain. The metal links were unbroken. Another blow, with the same results.

"Harder, asshole, hit it harder!" screamed DiUbaldo.

Suddenly the timer went off. DiUbaldo screamed to Gomes not to leave him there. Gomes held the pickaxe in his hand, considering whether to run and save himself or stay and try again. DiUbaldo's face was contorted with fear. The new silence was deafening.

Gomes raised the axe and hit the chain with a furious blow. With a click the chain snapped. Gomes grabbed DiUbaldo and pushed him towards the stairs, yelling at him to run. The chain rattled behind him as DiUbaldo clambered up the steps.

Reaching the first floor, Gomes threw the door open. They spilled out onto the yard with the man in chains tumbling behind him.

"There's a ditch!" yelled Gomes. He pushed DiUbaldo to the other side of the driveway where there was a slight depression. They jumped down and covered their heads with their arms. Gomes shut his eyes, as if that would lessen the force of the explosion. He waited.

And waited.

It was way past ten minutes. He wondered if Da Silva had dialed in a few extra minutes.

"What the fuck?" DiUbaldo was muttering. "What the fuck is going on?"

<u>56</u>

As they lay in the ditch waiting for the explosion, DiUbaldo said, "Hey Gomes, how come you didn't run off and leave me?"

Gomes turned his head to face the man. "It wouldn't have been right."

"Who woulda believed it, a fricking black boy scout saved my ass."

After waiting another ten minutes, Gomes and DiUbaldo cautiously raised their heads and looked at the building. Twenty minutes had passed with no explosion.

"What the fuck is going on?" asked DiUbaldo, his hands still wrapped in chains.

"I'm not sure. Maybe the detonator got screwed up. I don't know."

There were no sounds other than the wind blowing through the trees. The two men stood up. Gomes walked to his car and opened the passenger door. "Get in, I'm taking you to the—"

BOOM!

The explosion blew out the windows of the house, knocking Gomes and DiUbaldo off their feet. Wooden debris rained down on them as smoke rose up from the house, now ablaze.

Brushing the debris out of his hair, Gomes stood up and pulled DiUbaldo to his feet. Leading the man to the car, Gomes walked around to the driver's side and opened the door. On the seat he found the tape recorder with a piece of paper taped to it. He grabbed the paper and read it standing beside the car, then he handed the paper to DiUbaldo.

"Dear Mr. Gomes: If you are reading this letter you have survived my little fireworks display. Congratulation. You may take the tape recorder to the police and tell them what you heard and offer up your own conclusions. We shall see what the forces of law and order do. If you were unable to save that loathsome creature DiUbaldo, c'est la vie. If you have freed him, make it clear to DiUbaldo that I will never be far away from him. The terror he offered my father will be visited upon him. If the authorities let DiUbaldo go free, I will come for him. He will not know when it will happen or where, but you can tell him that when it happens he will feel pain before he dies. It will not be a quick end, as opposed to what happened with his friend, Mr. Peroni. DiUbaldo will squirm and beg for mercy while he awaits his end. Sorry I cannot hang around but, as you can imagine I need to get off the Cape. I hope to read your story about this case."

DiUbaldo exploded. "That fuckin' nigger! They're all the same. This *ass*-hole. Who the fuck does he think that he is?"

"Cut the 'nigger' stuff, DiUbaldo. This 'nigger' freed you from chains when you thought that you were going to have your ass blown up. Remember?"

"This is all your fault, Gomes. You couldn't stop tracking down the story. You kept pushing. You people are always trying to prove something. Are you trying to prove that you can write or something?"

"I told you to cool out, DiUbaldo. Let's get to the police."

"Don't tell me to cool out, you fuckin' coon, you're no better than—"

Crack! Gomes landed his fist dead center on DiUbaldo's nose, followed by another fist in the stomach. The man doubled over and fell back into the depression on the side of the driveway. Gomes realized he enjoyed the double shot immensely. With a smile on his face he got into the driver's side, put his seatbelt on, placed the key in the ignition, then sat there quietly.

A moment later Gomes heard the sound of the chains. He saw DiUbaldo approach the car, open the door and settle into the seat without a word. Gomes turned the ignition. The little opposed-four engine rattled into life. Backing out of the driveway, Gomes saw that the car that he had glimpsed when he originally drove in was gone. He wondered about that. DiUbaldo sat silently, staring like a stone at nothing.

They turned onto Route 6, heading back to Hyannis, Gomes searching for a payphone. Within a mile they came across a gas station with a phone booth. Gomes barely looked at DiUbaldo as he got out of the car and went to the phone booth. A young white attendant in the station stepped out and looked at the car. When he saw the passenger in chains he retreated back inside the station.

Gomes took coins out of his pocket and called Amato's line. A woman answering told him Amato was out. Before she could hang up, Gomes explained to her what had happened and where they were. The voice on the other end told him to remain at the gas station until a police cruiser showed up. Gomes hung up, walked back to the Bug and got in, while the station attendant poked his head out to observe the situation.

Gomes turned the car back on and pumped up the heater. He and DiUbaldo sat in silence. Ten minutes later Gomes heard the wail of a police car, then saw the red and white flashing lights approaching, Gomes flashed his headlights twice.

As the cruiser came to a stop, the officer got out and stood behind the open door. Gomes got out of his car and approached the cruiser. "Officer, my name is David Gomes. I'm the person who called Detective Amato's office about this incident—"

The officer pulled his gun from the holster. "Stop where you are and raise your hands! HANDS! I WANNA SEE HANDS!'

Gomes froze in place.

"What's going on with that man in the car?"

The station attendant poked his head out, crying, "Officer, I'm the guy who called about this car driving up looking suspicious!"

The officer cautiously moved closer to the Volkswagen, looking at DiUbaldo.

"Officer, that man is Richard DiUbaldo. He paid for someone named Peroni to kill me with a shotgun. He was kidnapped by a man you are searching for, Antonio Da Silva."

The officer signaled for DiUbaldo to get out. The man stumbled out, the chains clanking as he stepped away from the car.

"What the fuck is this?" said the officer.

"Officer, this nigger here beat me up and held me in his car."

"That's bullshit!" said Gomes. "I'm a reporter with the Cape & Islands Gazette. I was kidnapped earlier this morning by Da Silva. I helped Mister DiUbaldo escape. If it wasn't for me, he'd be dead by now in an explosion that—"

"Explosion? What do you know about the house fire the other side of Route Six?"

Gomes opened his mouth to try to explain, but before he could get a word out the officer turned him around, locked handcuffs on him and led him to the back of the police car.

"Never mind, I'm taking you to the station, we'll sort this crap out there." Putting DiUbaldo beside Gomes, the officer pulled out, lights still flashing, and drove to the station.

To Gomes' great relief, Detective Amato was waiting for them when the cruiser pulled into the police station. After a short conversation with the arresting officer, Amato ordered Gomes released. They led DiUbaldo to a cell.

"Hey!" cried the suspect, "what about these fricking chains?"

Amato winked at the junior officer. "Guess we better try and find a file, he can start working on one of the links."

◇

After Gomes finished giving his written statement to the police, he and Amato stopped at an all-night diner on the way back to David's Volkswagen. Over steaming bowls of soup and coffee, they reviewed what had happened. Gomes confirmed that it was Peroni who tried to kill him with the shotgun blast and run him off the road. Amato agreed that Da Silva must have made himself up to look like Smith when he opened the fake bank account and deposited the money. Gomes marveled at how the man had planted the stolen gun under Smith's desk.

"The sheer tenacity of this guy is incredible," Gomes said. "I mean, Da Silva, Tavares, Shepherd, whatever you call him: he didn't just plan to kill Smith, he wanted to kill his reputation. He wanted to ruin his fricking family!"

Amato agreed, saying, "Revenge. It's a powerful motive. Especially when it's mixed with madness, and this man is not sane."

"No, Vinnie, he's not insane, he's filled with an explosive anger like I've never seen before."

Driving Gomes to the lonely gas station, Amato asked if David was awake enough to drive home. Gomes assured him he would drive with the windows down and the music blaring, then he was going to sleep for a night and a day.

57

David Gomes sat back at the dining room table in his parent's house after completing the story. His father was speechless, his mother, anxious for her son's safety. Parents. Pamela threw her arms around him, kissing the top of his head and saying how relieved she was he wasn't hurt.

Or dead.

"How'd you convince the cops that you weren't involved with any of the crime?" asked Jack.

"The officer who arrested me sure didn't listen to anything I said. On the radio he reported that he had some 'white guy' held in chains by a 'colored guy.' Yeah, that's what he said, and I didn't know where Amato was or if he was even on duty. It wasn't 'til we got to the station and thank god Amato was there to sort it all out."

"Did they ever get the chains off him?" asked Helena.

"The police had heavy duty bolt cutters that took care of the chains. By then the fire at the house had been put out. The police recovered Peroni's body after I told them how we had dumped it behind the house. I told them where the tape recorder was, too."

"Amazing," said Jack. "You couldn't make a story like this up."

"No, you couldn't," said Pamela. "It will make good reading in the paper, that's for sure." She put his hand in hers, letting him know she was proud of what he had done, and of what he would write.

His mother asked, "Are you in any danger now, David,

this mad killer could be anywhere."

"It's complicated, Mom. DiUbaldo is being held for questioning but Amato says that he'll probably be released. Before you say anything, he'll claim he was forced to make the confession that I heard, but DiUbaldo would be crazy to try and harm me. As for Da Silva, I was never his target."

Jack rose from the table and walked into the kitchen to wash the dishes. Helena could tell her husband was anxious about this whole thing but didn't like to express his emotion in front of others. She remained at the table while they chatted. The discussion was briefly halted when Amato called to check in on David and to tell him that he was needed for additional questioning in the morning.

David excused himself and went into the study to call Jacqueline. She was home and glad to hear from Gomes. He explained that he wanted her to know that he was fine and would check in with her the following day when he got to the office. In a soft whisper of a voice, Jacqueline told him to take care of himself. "You must be most careful, my David. Please be most careful."

Gomes promised he would watch his back and said goodnight, then returned to the dining room table.

"Do you think this mad man will kill DiUbaldo in the end?" Helena asked.

"Mom, maybe he will. I think that in his tortured mind, Da Silva believes the only way to get justice for his father's murder is to do it himself. The government trained him to be a killer, so he put his skill to good use, as least, in his mind."

Jack walked back into dining room and seated himself. "Son, Big Tony fooled himself into believing that he was something or someone else. That's what your uncle and aunt were trying to tell you. After all of these years my brother Al is still broken up by the fight he had with Tony before they both enlisted. Al couldn't quite say it, but I can: Tony hated the fact that there was black blood—African blood—running through his veins. He was not going to let that blood get in his way, given that he was so light and had married light.

"He was playing a dangerous game," said Gomes.

"Indeed he was. You know what's truly pathetic, son? I would bet that Tony had no idea what was behind the hatred that the pilot and co-pilot held for him. I don't think that it ever crossed his mind that they hated him so deeply because he was black."

"What a waste of a life," said Helena.

"That's just what Uncle Al said to me, Mom," David responded.

Jack sat back and took a sip of whisky he'd brought out to the table. He offered some to everyone and they toasted David's escape from death. After the toast David thought he saw tears in his father's eyes, but Jack turned his face away, hiding his eyes.

58

The early weeks of 1971 blew by like a hurricane. It started with the story about the kidnapping of Gomes and DiUbaldo, and their escape. Gomes's phone rang off the hook all day long. The paper announced they would soon be publishing a longer examination on the entire case.

One morning at work, Gomes received a call from Margie Smith. "Good morning, Missus Smith! I was planning on calling you."

"Mister Gomes, I read about what happened to you and was horrified. Are you alright?"

"Yes, absolutely. That whole week was scary as hell, but I'm fine. Listen, Missus Smith, there are some matters about this case that I wanted to discuss with you before I publish my complete story. Do you have time for me to drop by later today?"

"Certainly. It sounds a bit ominous. I should be home after 5:30 if you want to drop by?"

"Thanks, 5:30 is fine. There are some complications in the whole story that I want you to know about. I'll see you this evening!"

Gomes knew that he would have to prepare himself for a difficult discussion. What's more, he had another challenging discussion to face, as if being the target of an assassin wasn't enough. Was this how his career as a journalist was going to go?

He decided to visit Hank, though it was even money the store would be open, when the business was slow Hank liked to take January off and go to Florida.

To his delight, the store was open. Gomes walked in as Hank was finishing up with a customer. His friend looked up from the cash register and grimaced when he saw Gomes, wondering what was up.

The bell on the door chimed as the customers made his leave.

"How is January treating you, David?" asked Hank.

"Busier than ever, with my story and all. But I can live with that. I have to visit Missus Smith this evening, I want to tell her what really happened to her husband before the story goes to press. Then I have to have what will be an unpleasant conversation with Susana Da Silva."

Hank had a strange look on his face. Was it despair? Disgust? Gomes couldn't tell.

"You're going to tell them their husbands weren't the men they thought they knew," said Hank. "That's a hard road to go down."

"Yeah, I'm not looking forward to it. I just came by to thank you for digging up that information about the Lucky Legs. I couldn't have done this without your help. You didn't get into any trouble, did you?"

Hank laughed a hearty laugh. "Not at all, David. There are a few people in the Air Force at the moment who are trying to figure out how you put everything together, but neither you nor I have anything to worry about. We both did what we needed to do."

"Hank, very little about this seemed to surprise you."

"I was surprised, but as soon as you confirmed that Tavares was black and that he flew in that B-24 I knew there was a big problem. There have been stories for years about black soldiers who passed for white. I'm not sure how many got thrown out of planes, but that's something else."

A weary, somber look on his face, Hank added, "David, when you speak with these widows be prepared to not be thanked. You are challenging almost everything that they believed to have been the truth."

As Gomes got ready to leave, Hank said, "One more thing, David. You know, with you and Pam…"

Gomes held up his hand to have Hank pause. "Hank, listen. You've been a good friend to both me and Pam. I am at peace with the situation. Pam needs to move on. It's not about whether we love each other or not,we both do, but she has to move on."

Hank looked down at the floor—something he rarely did—and then looked up at Gomes.

"David, this is the last that I'm going to say on the matter. You and Pam were meant to be with one another. I believe that she needs to pursue this dream and I know that she'll be great, but, distance does not make the heart grow fonder, my friend, it tears the heart in two."

The two friends shook hands and smiled at one another, but they were sad smiles. Smiles of caring but not happiness.

◇

At 5pm, Gomes picked up the phone and called Susana Da Silva. Not knowing if she would be home, he was praying that Bruno did not answer the phone. He counted six rings. As he was about to give up, Susana Da Silva's voice came on the line.

"Missus Da Silva, this is David Gomes, the reporter. I hope that you're well. Do you have a few minutes?"

"Yes, Mister Gomes, I got home about an hour ago and my husband is not home yet so I have some time to talk. I wondered when you were going to call. I heard that you… met my son."

Susana's voice shifted to a combination of nervousness and defensiveness, though she never lost her politeness.

Gomes explained to her in detail what had happened. She was silent, though occasionally she asked a question. He told the story through his escape and the encounter with Officer

Hudson. When he completed the story, there was silence. In the background Gomes heard the occasional sound of cars driving by.

"Well, Mister Gomes, you're telling me that my husband was NOT a war hero and you're also telling me that my son has murdered at least four different people, and almost killed you. That's enough to make this day, I would say." Susana's voice was laced with tremendous anger and irony, though she uttered a bizarre chuckling sound

"I wanted you to hear this from me before it came out in print, Missus Da Silva.

"So, I guess that now I become the joke around town. The 'hero of New Bedford' has just become another unfortunate *krioulo* who, in this case, was thrown out of a plane. And you want me to be *proud* of you for uncovering that? They named a street after Tony. They named a library after Tony. And now we have to tell everyone that he wasn't a hero after all but just a murder victim? Another *colored* murder victim?"

Gomes heard a voice in the background. Susana stepped away from the phone and was talking. Gomes thought that he recognized Bruno's voice. A few moments later the phone was picked up. It was Bruno.

"So, Gomes, you found out that Tavares was murdered? After all of this it turns out that he was no fuckin' hero, huh? After all the shit that that little squirt put me through about his father-the-hero, it turns out that he was just in the wrong place at the wrong time. Well, ain't that the living end?!"

There was more noise, muffled voices. Then, Susana back on the line. "Thank you, Mister Gomes. I'm sorry that you were hurt in this. I'm not sure you did anyone much good in this investigation. You've certainly thrown my life up in the air. Tell your uncle and aunt that I said hello. Good night, Mister Gomes. I don't ever want to hear from you again."

The phone line went dead. Gomes sat there holding the phone in his ear.

59

After his unpleasant phone conversation with Susanna Da Silva, Gomes looked at his watch and decided to head to the Smith's. But first he sat with Jacqueline and described the phone call with Susana Da Silva.

"You told her that her husband had been murdered and she was worried about his no longer being a hero?" she asked, incredulous.

"That's the way it looks. I think that Susana Da Silva spent the last twenty-five years caught up in a myth, being a professional widow. I don't know. I certainly feel for her, but damn, what a reaction."

He told Jacqueline he wished he didn't have to pay a visit to Margie Smith, knowing it would be an even harder visit, but he felt an obligation to the widow. And to himself.

When he arrived at the Smith residence the lights were on outside so he assumed that Margie was home. He drove into the driveway and then walked up to the front door. Before he could ring the bell, the door opened and Margie Smith stood there to let Gomes inside. He smiled and walked in out of the cold.

"Thank you, Missus Smith. I really appreciate your taking the time to meet with me," he said, taking off his coat, gloves and hat.

"No problem, Mister Gomes. Please, have a seat. Would you like some tea or coffee? And remember, its 'Margie'. Each time you call me Missus Smith I feel like an old woman," she offered with a smile.

"Tea would be great. Margie."

Margie pointed towards the living room for Gomes to seat himself while she went into the kitchen. A few minutes later she came out with two cups of hot tea, lemon and sugar.

They chatted for a moment about the cold, about a recent snow and how lucky the Cape was compared with Boston when it came to snowfall, all while they fixed their tea. Gomes took a few sips, put the tea cup down, and then sat forward on the couch.

"Margie, this is going to be difficult, so let me start at the beginning. If it's okay with you, let me finish the story and then you can ask me *any* questions you happen to have. Okay?"

"Do I need to get something stronger than tea, David?"

Gomes saw a rivulet of fear in the woman's eyes. When she nodded her head for David to start speaking, he began his story. As the tale unfolded he could see by the way she gripped the tea cup that it tearing at her. When he was finished he picked up the now lukewarm tea for a few sips. Margie finally put her cup down on the table, visibly shaken.

"Mister Gomes," she started, slowly, "the man that you described…the TJ Smith that *you* described…I *never* knew such a man. I would never have married such a man. I would never have had his children. None of this can possibly be true! When me and my kids came to visit you, it was with the aim of clearing TJ's name. Well, you have apparently proven beyond a doubt that TJ was NOT corrupt, but now you are insisting that he was a racist murderer. And you're going *public* with this?"

Shaking her head in anger and sorrow, Margie stood up and left the room. Gomes sat there silently finishing his tea and awaiting her return. She returned and sat there just looking at Gomes.

"Margie, when you and your children came to see me, I told you then that I could *not* make any promises. That

I didn't know what I would uncover. I believe that your husband in his own way tried to make up for what he did... what he participated in during the War, but at the same time he could not accept responsibility."

"But why do you believe this murderer, David? Why don't you look at the life of TJ Smith and understand that this could NOT have been my husband?"

Gomes sat silently for a few moments, looking at the floor. He breathed in slowly and looked up. "Because, Margie, and I'm sorry to say this, it all adds up. The information that Da Silva got from Jansen, the way that DiUbaldo was acting, including that last minute confession, and what you and your children told me about the final months for both TJ and Mister Gierek: it all adds up. I think that your husband was nervous for a long time but then came to believe that nothing would happen to him."

"No, David, I think that he might have known that something *would* happen to him," she said, surprising Gomes.

At that point Margie would not make any eye contact with Gomes. The ensuing silence told him it was time to leave. He stood to excuse himself, Margie remained seated mumbling something Gomes could not decipher. He thanked her and headed to his car. Margie remained in her seat, silent, not acknowledging his exit.

Instead of heading home, Gomes returned to his office, not bothering to pick up any food. He parked the car in the small lot and then went around back to the entryway for Jacqueline's apartment. The outside light was on. He rang the bell.

Jacqueline opened the door and looked surprised, though Gomes thought that she expected he would drop in after the Margie Smith exchange.

He walked upstairs, followed by Jacqueline. She was dressed casually, and Gomes could smell the scent of food cooking.

"Before you say anything, I am preparing dinner and

I have enough for two. It's nothing special, just some fish, potatoes and salad. I also have some very good French wine to accompany it."

Smiling, Gomes acknowledged he was quite hungry and could not turn down such an offer. Jacqueline pointed toward the dining area. She brought out a place-setting, followed by the food and wine.

They sat eating and talking about his two conversations. Jacqueline mainly listened. Gomes had difficulty getting his mind around how two murderers—Smith and Gierek—had behaved so differently after the War.

Jacqueline picked up her wine glass, took a sip and sat back against her chair, looking over at Gomes. "My David, let me tell you a story. When I was in my early teen years, a Frenchman named Paul Portier moved to Montreal. He was originally from Cherbourg, on the coast of France, or at least that is what he told us. Portier was a teacher. A great teacher. I took a class from him in high school. He said that he had left France after the War to start over. Portier was funny, and he had a very nice singing voice. He directed our school choir.

"One day Portier disappeared. A story came out identifying Portier as having been part of the Milice Francaise during World War Two. Are you familiar with the Milice Francaise, David?"

"No, I can't say that I am."

"The Milice were a secret paramilitary arm of the collaborationist Vichy regime in France during the war. They carried out many, many atrocities, working with the Gestapo and the SS. They worked against the Resistance. They were terrible."

"How tragic," said Gomes, beginning to lose his appetite.

"Bien, Monsieur Portier had allegedly been a member of the Milice. He supposedly escaped France and changed his identity, ending up in Montreal. No one would ever have guessed that he had been a collaborator who, as it turned out, was responsible for many deaths. It was only by accident that someone identified him and an investigation ensued, leading to his arrest.

"David, I don't know whether Monsieur Portier became a different person after the War or if it was all a charade. But I do know that when they say that 'actions speak louder than words,' well, my David, that is not entirely true. Actions today can contradict a behavior from yesterday and you are left wondering, who was the real TJ Smith. I would guess that TJ Smith was both murderer and upstanding citizen."

Gomes stood up and started cleaning off the table, lost in thought. Jacqueline said nothing but joined him in cleaning up. Gomes went to the sink and started to wash the dishes. He chatted with Jacqueline about other matters, particularly focused on the paper. When he completed the dishes he turned to her.

"Did I open Pandora's box, Jaqueline?"

"No, David. It was opened the moment that Da Silva discovered the truth about the murder of his father. With that terrible truth, plus his military training, it was only a matter of time before he took matters into his own hands.

"You are not responsible for the deaths. You are responsible for the revelation of a story. I hope that such a story will serve as the same lesson that the arrest and extradition of Portier did for so many."

"You are very wise, boss," he offered with a sad smile.

She kissed him tenderly on the cheek. The smell of her perfume was intoxicating.

"I probably should head home, Jacqueline."

She stood still a moment, waiting to see if he would take the first step to the door. With heavy feet Gomes made his way down the stairs and out the door without looking back. He knew that if he turned and saw her, he would go back inside and stay the night.

The sound of the lock being turned brought the temptation to an end.

60

When the full story broke about Tony Da Silva, the murder of Antonio Tavares and the role of Richie DiUbaldo, Gomes was the center of attention. His series on the case had people riveted. With circulation for the *C&IG* shooting up, Gomes was constantly getting calls from various New England news outlets.

DiUbaldo had been released for lack of evidence in the attempted murder of Gomes, though he was badly shaken by the whole episode. He kept talking about how "niggers" were always out to get him. Amato thought that he might be on the verge of losing his mind. The Air Force issued a statement to the effect that they would reopen the case of Antonio Tavares, but no one believed that the truth would be uncovered, though it sounded good at the time.

Positively Woman had pressured Pamela to move to New York sooner rather than later. They wanted her to start working in January. A friend in Manhattan found her a small comfortable apartment on West 85th Street close to Broadway. Pamela agreed to move the first week in February and start working right away.

Gomes spent most of his free time with Pamela, helping her prepare for the move. He offered to drive a rental truck to move her things to the new apartment. The day tore at his heart, and when Gomes left Pamela the next morning to return to the Cape, he felt a wound that promised to never heal. He was afraid their different career tracks would sever the ties of love forever.

After returning to the Cape Gomes found himself settling into a new life. He and Pamela had promised to try and see each other every 4-6 weeks. They would alternate in traveling. This plan worked for two months. After that, trips started being cancelled. Pamela was overwhelmed with her new job. She was excited to be working in New York, and Gomes could tell she was doing great things for the magazine. But the net impact was she was always low on time—and admittedly—low on emotional energy for Gomes.

Gomes was going through something different. His writing on the Tavares/Da Silva case had thrust him into the limelight more than at any point in his life. Then something happened for which he was unprepared. He would later describe it as akin to a sugar crash, when you have consumed a great deal of sugar and seem to have a lot of energy only to lose it all and find yourself tired and depressed. This is what happened to Gomes when the interest in 'the man who fell from the sky' dried up and the calls stopped coming.

His disappointment was compounded by a bitter fact: there was still no trace of the mysterious Antonio Da Silva.

61

March 2004

Every time David Gomes looked around his townhouse on Boston's Rutland Square he felt a ripple of joy. Years before he'd been lucky enough to purchase an abandoned townhouse in what eventually became the gentrifying South End. It was a beautiful home, with plenty of space for him and his wife and daughter. He loved to sit in his office at the back of the first floor, where it was quiet and peaceful, and work on his third book. Now that he was semi-retired from the Boston newspaper he'd joined after the Cape & Islands Gazette folded, there was time enough to reflect and to write.

The morning routine was straightforward. Gomes always arose first, dressed and fixed breakfast. Pamela, who often stayed up late preparing for her university teaching or working on her photography, arose later. Their daughter Zahira, a stellar student, decided to stay in the Boston area and had graduated from MIT. Though she no longer lived at home, Zahira remained close with her parents. Gomes was so proud of his daughter, the Black mathematician. He would always say to Zahira, "To hell with math phobias, just work the problem."

On this early Spring morning Gomes was surprised when Pamela came to his office to say there was a man from the military there to see him. The business card she held out to him read: Major Marcel Silveira, _Forcas Armadas Cabo Verdeanas_ – Cape Verdean Armed Forces. She handed Gomes the card, kissed him and excused herself, heading back to her work.

Rising from his chair quickly, despite a stab of low back pain from an old injury, he stepped to the living room to see what was going on. He saw a man in a crisply tailored suit sitting on the sofa. "Good morning, I'm David Gomes."

As he shook hands with the man, he was surprised to find the face strangely familiar, though he couldn't place him. He knew that face, but from where?

"Mister Gomes, allow me to introduce myself. I am Major Marcel Silveira from the *Forcas Armadas Cabo Verdeanas* — the Cape Verdean Armed Forces. I am here with a delegation from my country. Thank you for taking the time to meet with me."

"Certainly, Major Silveira, though I'm not sure how I can help a member of the Cape Verdean military."

Taking a seat, Gomes found the whole situation curious and unsettling. Something about this encounter gave him a feeling of anxiety. Even, of danger.

"Mister Gomes, this is not an official matter, though I believe it has some importance. By the way, is there anywhere nearby where I might find something to eat and some good coffee? I had an early meeting where I thought breakfast would be provided but they had only bad coffee and a Danish." Silveira had the look of someone who desperately needed a cup of strong coffee.

"We have bagels and a very good coffee right here, I'll put on a pot." His guest followed Gomes to the kitchen, a large sunny room with a central island where Silveira took a seat.

As he waited for the water to boil, Major Silveira mentioned having been in Boston years ago and how much had changed. Gomes was impressed with his command of English and wondered if he had lived in the States at some time.

Gomes set out a pot of heavy cream, which brought a

smile to Silveira's lips. "Ah, true cream. I find the milk that is served with coffee to be thin and without flavor, don't you?"

"I suppose people get used to it after a while." Gomes put out a tray with bagels and cream cheese and two mugs. "Well, Major Silveira, what can I do for you?"

"To begin, you should know that I am on a mission for a friend." He spread cream cheese thickly on his bagel and took a first bite. Silveira took his time, enjoying the flavor while his host poured the coffee.

Studying the man's face, Gomes realized it held a strong resemblance to one of his mother's younger brothers. Similar complexion, hair, cheekbones, eyes...it was remarkable. With that recognition Gomes became more comfortable.

"Mister Gomes, a Mister Antonio Da Silva asked me to convey a message to you when he heard that I was traveling to the United States." The Major waited patiently for his companion's reaction.

"Antonio Da Silva? You must be kidding? THE Antonio Da Silva? How do you know Da Silva?"

Silveira savored the fresh coffee with a smile. "Antonio Da Silva is a ranking member of our military, Mister Gomes. You would probably not recognize him."

"But how did he get to Cape Verde? How did any of this happen? The last time I saw him, some thirty years ago..."

"The last time you saw him was in a house in Truro when you and a Mister DiUbaldo believed you were about to be blown up. Yes, I know the story. By the way, Da Silva wanted you to know that you did a truly professional job in the news stories about his father and the crew of their plane."

Gomes was stunned that Silveira was so familiar with the events from long ago. Silveira calmly continued eating. And talking.

"Da Silva made his way to Boston, where he remained in hiding and watched DiUbaldo. DiUbaldo knew that he was being watched, but he could not prove it. Every time that he reported it to the police, they could find nothing. Eventually they started to treat him as a nut. DiUbaldo was eventually confined to a mental hospital, where he remains incoherent and irrational."

"Yes, I heard about his condition," said Gomes. "The bastard apparently kept yelling about being followed. But you still haven't told me how Da Silva ended up in Cape Verde."

"Da Silva realized he had no future in Boston, or even the USA. He was a wanted man, and while he stayed ahead of the police, it was likely they would eventually catch him.

"He became acquainted with some Panthers who were talking about the national liberation war against Portugal going on in Guinea-Bissau and Cape Verde. He was a good soldier, so he decided he would join the fight. He made his way to Algeria with a couple of the Panthers, and from Algeria they reached Guinea-Conakry. After that he and his comrades made their way to a PAIGC base near the border of Guinea-Bissau and joined the resistance."

"What an amazing journey," said Gomes.

"He is a most resourceful man, as you know. At first, the military leaders accused Da Silva of being a spy for NATO and the Portuguese. He was imprisoned and set to be shot, but a Cuban doctor who was on site suggested that the PAIGC forces not be so fast to execute, and they spared Da Silva's life."

"They released him?"

"No. Da Silva remained in a terrible jail, until one day he was awakened by explosions. The camp's location had been betrayed to the Portuguese, ironically by some of the people who had accused him of being an agent! Portuguese jets hit the camp, followed by helicopters bringing in troops. Da Silva took up a machine gun from a fallen fighter and brought down one of the helicopters. The attack was successfully repulsed. After that, he moved rapidly up in rank in the PAIGC military. When Cape Verde and Guinea-Bissau split,

Da Silva relocated to Cape Verde and continued his career with the Cape Verdean armed forces."

As Silveira picked up the last of his bagel, Gomes noted the ring on the man's hand. It was striking, and unusual.

"Does the Cape Verdean government know that Da Silva is a wanted man in the US?"

"A small number of people do. But he has reinvented himself." Silveira drained the last of his coffee and placed his napkin on the plate. "Mister Gomes, Da Silva wanted you to know how much he appreciated what you did. You put your life on the line for a truth. He is deeply, deeply grateful."

Gomes looked at his watch, then at Silveira. "I appreciate that, Major. I'm sorry, but I have to get back to work, I have a conference call shortly. I hope you understand."

"Of course. I appreciate this time with you. I also have meetings to attend to."

Escorting Silveira to the front door, Gomes placed his hand on the door knob but did not turn it. "Why did you return?"

"I told you that I am here as part of a delegation—"

"No, why did YOU return...Antonio?" Gomes let the man's real name hang in the air between them for a long minute. "There is a price on your head. Why would you take the chance?"

"When did you figure it out?"

"When you first came in I saw that you look like one of my mother's brothers, who is Cape Verdean and Portuguese, but I wrote it off. But then I saw your ring, and I remembered it from the house in Truro. Then I saw in you the face of a younger man, thinner, with more hair, and I knew it was you."

"Ah, my ring! A present from my mother so many years ago that I have always cherished. I simply couldn't let it go."

"But why did you come back? Not to finally kill DiUbaldo?"

"No, there is no need, you said it yourself, the man remains in a mental hospital. He rants and wails and fears going to sleep, for he knows sleep will bring nightmares." With a hand on Gomes' shoulder, Silveira added, "Perhaps in the end, justice was served."

"Yes, I suppose it was." Gomes turned the knob and opened the door.

"I returned to the States, Mister Gomes, to visit my mother's gravesite. It was a great sadness that I could not attend her funeral. What son could refuse such a task?"

"Of course, you had to go. I attended a funeral myself just last week." Gomes fought to keep the tears from welling up in his eyes. "For Hank Matthews. A dear friend from the Cape." Taking a minute to compose himself, Gomes went on: "You won't be arrested? I mean, coming back to the States?"

"There is no risk, I am covered by diplomatic immunity. Besides, I have a different identity and I'm not planning on creating any problems. I corresponded with my mother over the years. She even came to Cape Verde and we saw each other for the first time in too many years. When I decided to fulfill my commitment to her, I thought to visit you as well."

"And that story that you told, it's true?" Gomes asked.

"Yes, all true." Silveira stepped out onto the front steps. He looked back into the townhouse. "You have done well for yourself, Mister Gomes. I lost track of you when I left the country. You've been with your wife, Pamela, since I first met you? That's quite something."

"Pam and I broke up in early '71 after she moved to New York City. It felt like our careers, maybe even our lives, were moving us in different directions. Truth be told, I wasn't ready to really commit. I was an ass."

Silveira nodded his head supportively, with a slight smile. Gomes stopped for a moment, looking away, thinking about the time that he had lost, but also thinking about how he and Pamela had grown, together and separately.

"A few years later I was at a conference in New York. We

hadn't talked for quite a while. It was never hostile, we'd just gone in different directions. Well, there we were at this conference. I saw her from a distance talking to someone. I walked up behind her and said, 'How's New York treating you?' She turned around and gave me this wonderful smile. And hug. We rediscovered each other. It was a new relationship, not recycled. Something different. Something fresh. I realized that we were soulmates and, truth be told, we never stopped talking from that point on." Gomes smiled, more to himself than to Silveira.

"You are fortunate, Mister Gomes, to have found someone like that. For me, I think that I have too many demons."

"Was it worth it, Major? Was it worth it to have killed those men and gone on the run, losing contact with your family?"

"Worth it? I did what I had to do, Mister Gomes. The better question is whether I found peace carrying out those… operations. The answer to that is 'no.' A certain satisfaction, perhaps, but no peace."

As Silveira walked down the steps to the street, Gomes called after him: "Major, how do you know I'm not going to call the police on you?"

Silveira stopped, turned and looked up at Gomes. With a half salute, he said, "Because that's not who you are."

Gomes wished Major Silveira a safe journey and a peaceful repose. He watched the man cross the street and disappear around a corner.

Standing on his front porch, Gomes looked into the sky and mumbled to himself, "You can't make something like this up." He turned to gaze at the forsythia in bloom and the first daffodils of Spring. Pam came out onto the porch and put her arms around him.

"What was that about, David?" she asked, looking at him curiously.

Gomes stood for a moment searching for words. "I guess the best way to describe it was 'reconnecting.'"

"An old friend come to visit?"

He kissed her gently. Tenderly. "I guess, yeah, you could say that. Some kind of old friend."

Acknowledgements

The Man Who Fell from the Sky began when I met the Daluz family in Hyannis, Massachusetts in the early 1960s. I was a young New Yorker who came across a Black family that had a different and unusual last name — a name with which I was unfamiliar. Through the Daluz family I met other Blacks on Cape Cod who also had "strange" names. I thought little about it at the time until I noticed that they and others periodically referred to themselves as Portuguese. I did not know what to make of that and chalked it up to a difference between New Yorkers and rural folk.

Through the Daluz family and many of their friends— some of whom became my friends — I came to learn about and appreciate the Cape Verdean community. A proud and fascinating community, they have frequently been ignored and collapsed into the larger African American community without recognizing their distinctiveness.

Thus, this book begins by paying tribute to Cape Verdean Americans, the first post-1492 African population to come to the United States voluntarily.

I wish to thank the late Joseph Daluz, Sr. and his family, whose pride in his Cape Verdean heritage knew few bounds.

I also wish to thank Sean Gonsalves, whose work as a writer and journalist created an image that influenced my thinking about David Gomes.

Denise Perry was indispensable in the construction of this story and gave me periodic reality checks on the Cape Verdean experience. Denise was generous with her time in reviewing early drafts.

The late Jack Custodio, an icon within the New Bedford Cape Verdean population, offered me a framework decades ago in order to understand the Cape Verdean experience in the USA.

The mystery writer Walter Mosley served as an inspiration, demonstrating time and again the ability of the mystery genre to raise profound political issues.

I want to thank activist and actor Danny Glover, who consistently encouraged the creative side of me.

My publisher, Tim Sheard, believed both in me and this story, and was willing to take a risk...and also do a lot of editing.

My mother and sister were tremendously supportive.

Thanks to my cousin, Robert (Bob) Hayden, Jr., an important historian who has focused on African Americans and Cape Verdean Americans as part of his research.

Finally, a special thanks to my cousin, Peter Agard, my wife, Candice Cason, my daughter, Yasmin Fletcher, and my good friend Jeff Crosby. The four of them read the first draft and gave me the thumbs up and encouragement to go forward.

—Bill Fletcher, Jr.

About the Author

Bill Fletcher Jr., the author of *They're Bankrupting Us!* (Beacon Press, 2012), and co-author (with Dr. Fernando Gapasin) of *Solidarity Divided* (UC Press, 2009) is a long-time racial-justice, labor, and international activist, scholar, and author. He has been involved in the labor movement for decades, and is a widely known speaker and writer in print and on radio, television, and the Web. He has served in senior staff positions with many prominent union and labor organizations, including the Service Employees International Union, national AFL-CIO and the American Federation of Government Employees. He is also the former president of TransAfrica Forum

Photo courtesy of Charles Brave

TITLES FROM HARD BALL PRESS

A Great Vision: A Militant Family's Journey Through the Twentieth Century, Richard March

Caring: 1199 Nursing Home Workers Tell Their Story, Tim Sheard, ed.

Fight For Your Long Day, Classroom Edition, by Alex Kudera

I Still Can't Fly: Confessions of a Lifelong Troublemaker, Kevin John Carroll (Winter 2018-19)

Love Dies – A Thriller, Timothy Sheard

The Man Who Fell From the Sky – Bill Fletcher Jr.

Murder of a Post Office Manager – A Legal Thriller, Paul Felton

New York Hustle: Pool Rooms, School Rooms and Street Corner, A Memoir, Stan Maron

Passion's Pride: Return to the Dawning – Cathie Wright- Lewis

The Secrets of the Snow –Poetry, Hiva Panahi

Sixteen Tons – A Novel, Kevin Corley

Throw Out the Water – Sequel to Sixteen Tons, Kevin Corley

We Are One: Stories of Work, Life & Love – Elizabeth Gottieb, ed.

What Did You Learn at Work Today? The Forbidden Lessons of Labor Education, Helena Worthen

With Our Loving Hands: 1199 Nursing Home Workers Tell Their Story, Timothy Sheard, ed.

Winning Richmond: How a Progressive Alliance Won City Hall – Gayle McLaughlin

Woman Missing – A Mill Town Mystery, Linda Nordquist

The Lenny Moss Mysteries – Timothy Sheard

This Won't Hurt A Bit

Some Cuts Never Heal

A Race Against Death

No Place To Be Sick

Slim To None

A Bitter Pill

Someone Has To Die

CHILDREN'S BOOKS from HARD BALL PRESS

Joelito's Big Decision, La gran Decisión de Joelito:
Ann Berlak (Author), Daniel Camacho (Illustrator),
José Antonio Galloso (Translator)
Manny and the Mango Tree, Many y el Árbol de Mango:
Alí R. and Valerie Bustamante (Authors), Monica Lunot-Kuker (Illustrator). Mauricio Niebla (Translator)
The Cabbage That Came Back, El Repollo que Volvió
Stephen Pearl & Rafael Pearl (Authors), Rafael Pearl (Illustrator), Sara Pearl (Translator)
Hats Off For Gabbie, ¡Aplausos para Gaby!:
Marivir Montebon (Author), Yana Murashko (Illustrator),
Mauricio Niebla (Translator)
Margarito's Forest/El Bosque de Don Margarito:
Andy Carter (Author), Alison Havens (Illustrator), Sergio
Villatoro (Graphic Design),
Artwork contributions by the children of the Saq Ja' elementary school
K'iche tranlations by Eduardo Elas and Manuel Hernandez
Translated by Omar Mejia
Jimmy's Carwash Adventure, La Aventura de Jaime en el Autolavado:
Victor Narro (Author), Yana Murashko (Illustrator), Madelin
Arroyo (Translator)
Good Guy Jake/Buen Chico Jake,
Mark Torres (author), Yana Murashko (illustrator), Madelin
Arroyo (translator)
Polar Bear Pete's Ice Is Melting!
Timothy Sheard (author), Kayla Fils-Amie (illustrator),
Madelin Arroyo (translator)

HOW TO ORDER BOOKS:

Order books from www.hardballpress.com, Amazon.com,
or independent booksellers everywhere.

Receive a 20% discount for orders of 10 or more, a 40% discount for orders of 50 or more when ordering from www.hardballpress.com.